Denali
National Park • Alaska
Guide to Hiking, Photography and Camping

Third Edition

Ike Waits

Wild Rose Guidebooks
Anchorage, Alaska

Denali National Park, Alaska:
Guide to Hiking, Photography and Camping

Third Edition © 2010 Ike Waits
All rights are reserved.

ISBN 978-0-9677327-2-5
Printed in U.S.A.

Wild Rose Guidebooks
P.O. Box 100200
Anchorage, Alaska 99510-0200
Phone: 907-274-0471
Cell: 602-616-2545
www.denaliguidebook.com
ikewaits@denaliguidebook.com

Design: Greatland Graphics
Cartography: Highland Graphics

Part of this book was first published as the *Denali Guidebook to Hiking, Camping, and Photography in Denali National Park, Alaska* (Ike Waits, 2001). Other parts were previously included in *15 Hikes in Denali National Park* by Don Croner published by TransAlaska Publishing Company, Anchorage, Alaska, 1989.

No portion of this guide may be reproduced, stored or presented in any form or means without permission in writing from the publisher except for brief quotations incorporated in reviews or articles referencing this publication.

All photos by Ike Waits unless otherwise noted.

Front cover: Mount McKinley as seen from near Wonder Lake Campground
Title page: Bull caribou
Back cover: View of Mount McKinley from near Wonder Lake (Hike 56). Also shown, moose.

Page 2: author photo by Neil Moomey.

Acknowledgements

Many Denali shuttle bus drivers have been informative and helpful. Most of the bus drivers I met have been driving in the park for more than 10 years, some as long as 25 years. They know the park well and provide helpful information. A special thanks goes to several bus drivers who have helped me solve lost equipment problems. These drivers include Dick Merrill, "Irish" Lee, Cindy, and Lee Lipscomb. My apologies to those whose last names I do not remember. I look forward to my rides on the shuttle and camper buses.

A special thanks goes to friends who accompanied me on some of these hikes and patiently tolerated my requests to "stop" or to "stand over there" so I could photograph them. Their enjoyment of Denali and companionship kept me inspired to continue this effort even on stormy days.

My mother, Mary Waits, says "A trip to Alaska is not complete without going to Denali." During the past 10+ years, her enjoyment of our picnics and walks in the tundra encouraged me to include hikes that would inspire others to get off the bus for at least a few hours.

About the author

I first hiked in Denali National Park while working summer jobs there in 1967 and 1968. I worked throughout Alaska in community development career and am now pursuing photography and writing fulltime. I decided to produce this book to encourage more people to get off the bus and explore Denali.

The Naming of Mount McKinley

In 1896, a Princeton-educated prospector William A. Dickey "named" Mount McKinley. According to one account, Dickey was prospecting for gold on the southern slopes of the Alaska Range when he came across two fellow prospectors who were rabid champions of the "silver standard" monetary system. After many weary days of listening to their arguments Dickey finally got fed up and, in retaliation, named the highest mountain in sight after William McKinley of Ohio, who was running for president as the "gold standard" candidate.

Dickey later wrote a letter to the *New York Sun* in which he referred to the mountain as Mount McKinley, and the name stuck. Mount McKinley is still its official name, although many Alaskans prefer to call it by its native name, "Denali." The name of the park was changed from Mount McKinley to Denali in 1980, but numerous attempts to officially change the name of the mountain have failed.

—Don Croner

Photo A. **Enjoying a clear view of Mount McKinley near Eielson Visitor Center.**

Contents

Acknowledgements 2
Naming of Mount McKinley 3

Introduction
    Philosophy and purpose 9
    Safety is your responsibility 9

Chapter 1: Trip Planning and Logistics
    Selecting the time for your visit 11
    Transportation to the park 12
    Lodging and campgrounds near the park 12
    Hike locations and campground map 13
    Denali shuttle bus is your car in the park 14
    Savage River shuttle bus 16
    Camper bus 16
    Campgrounds 16
    Bicycling 17
    Backountry camping permits, showers 18

Chapter 2: Photographing in Denali
    Using the bus as your vehicle 19
    Photographing wildlife from the bus 20
    Opportunities to photograph from your vehicle 21
    Lighting 22
    Photographing Mount McKinley 23
    Photographing the Wonder Lake area 24
    Flower and foliage photography 25
    Wildlife photography times and locations 25
    Required minimum distances from animals 25
    Mammal photography 26
    Bird photography 28

Chapter 3: Hiking Environment and Preparation
    Denali—a great place to hike without trails 31
    Help keep Denali trailless 32
    Guided hikes 32
    Hard to get lost 32
    Finding where to start 33

Trailless hiking pointers 34
Stream crossings 35
Hiking with bears 36
Hiking with mosquitoes 37
Books and maps to use with this book 37
Other books to enhance your Denali experience 38
Preparing to hike 38
Other hiking precautions 38
Daypack checklist 39
Emergency help 39

Chapter 4: Denali National Park Hike Descriptions

Hiking times and difficulty ratings 41
Selecting a hike 43
Denali National Park Entrance Area Map 44
Hike 1: Horseshoe Lake 45
Hike 2: Mount Healy Overlook Trail 46
    Vegetation and Animals Along Mount Healy Overlook Trail ... 47
Hike 3: Triple Lakes 48
    Early Use and Exploration of Park Headquarters Area 51
Hike 4: Savage River Viewpoint 53
Hike 5: Savage Drainage Stroll 56
Hike 6: Savage River Canyon Loop 58
    Glaciation of the East Side of the Park 60
Hike 7: Primrose Ridge and Mount Margaret 61
    Dall Sheep 63
Hike 8: Sanctuary to Savage River 64
Hike 9: Exploring the Teklanika Campground Area 68
    Teklanika River 69
Hike 10: Teklanika Foothills 71
Hike 11: Igloo Mountain East End 74
    Geology of Igloo and Cathedral Mountains 77
Hike 12: Igloo Mountain West 78
Hike 13: Upper Teklanika River to Sanctuary River 81
    Teklanika Glaciation and Climate Change 85
Hike 14: Calico Creek 86
Hike 15: Cathedral Mountain 90
    Cathedral Mountain Named by Charles Sheldon 92

5

Hike 16: Sable Pass Ridge Walk 94
Hike 17: Tattler Creek and Sable Mountain 97
Hike 18: Polychrome Basin Exploration 101
          Polychrome Area Geology 102
          Adolph Murie's Cabin 104
Hike 19: Polychrome Ridge Walk #1 105
Hike 20: Polychrome Ridge Walk #2 108
Hike 21: Polychrome Bluffs Hike 111
Hike 22: Mom's Polychrome Picnic Loop 115
Hike 23: Polychrome Mountain East End #1 117
Hike 24: Polychrome Mountain East End # 2 120
Hike 25: "Geode Mountain" 123
Hike 26: Toklat East Branch Exploration 126
          Toklat 129
Hike 27: Toklat to Polychrome 130
Hike 28: Around Divide Mountain 134
Hike 29: Toklat to Stony 138
Hike 30: Toklat River Short Walk and Picnic 142
Hike 31: Toklat River to Eielson Visitor Center 144
Hike 32: Highway Pass Perch 148
Hike 33: Hill 5860 Traverse 150
Hike 34: Highway Pass and Stony Creek Walks 154
          Stony Area Wildflowers 156
Hike 35: Hill 5014 Climb or Circumnavigation 158
Hike 36: Stony Hill Ridge Walk 161
Hike 37: Stony Hill Circumnavigation 163
Hike 38: Stony Dome Flower Walk and Climb 165
Hike 39: Thorofare Pass Stroll 167
Hike 40: Gravel Mountain 169
Hike 41: North Fork Gorge Creek Valley 172
Hike 42: Hill 4851 175
Hike 43: Thorofare Pass Bench Walk 178
          My Thanks to the Unknown Ranger 180
Hike 44: Exploring Around Eielson Visitor Center 182
Hike 45: Thoro Ridge #1 184
Hike 46: Thoro Ridge #2 187
Hike 47: Around Mount Eielson 189
          Mount Eielson Geology 192

Hike 48: Grassy Top to Eielson Loop	193
Hike 49: Anderson Pass	196
Discovery and Use of Anderson Pass	199
Hike 50: Around Mount Thoro	200
Mount McKinley Geology	203
Hike 51: Mount Galen	204
Hike 52: Moose Creek Dayhike or Backpack	206
Hike 53: Xerxes Ridge	209
Hikes in the Wonder Lake Area map	210
Hike 54: McKinley River Bar Trail	212
Hike 55: Wonder Lake Ridge	214
Hike 56: Tundra Pond Exploration	217
Wonder Lake	218
Hike 57: McGonagall Pass Backpack	220
McGonagall Pass	222
Hike 58: Bound Point	224

Chapter 5: Denali State Park Hike Descriptions

Overview	229
Weather	229
Camping	229
Transportation/Logistics	230
Hiking Conditions	230
Navigating	231
Food Storage	232
More park information	232
Emergencies	233
Hike 59: Troublesome Creek to Byers lake	234
Hike 60: Kesugi Ridge	237
Hike 61: Ermine Hill	239

Appendix A: Information and Reservations	241
Appendix B: Publications and Maps—an Annotated Bibliography	245
Denali maps	245
Denali books	246
Publications containing some information relevant to Denali	249
Bears: Natural history and hiking with them	251
Appendix C: Backpack and Dayhike Summary Tables	253
Bibliography	256

Photo B. **Mt. McKinley and Wonder Lake from the ridge near Reflection Pond.**

Introduction

Philosophy and purpose

I wrote this book to encourage you to "**Get off the bus!**" I know your Denali experience with be enhanced by leaving the bus to hike and to feel, hear and smell the tundra. The Denali National Park bus service makes it easy to do dayhikes or to at least get off the bus for a picnic or short stroll anywhere along the road. I hope this book provides the information that you need to select an outing to match your skills and interest. I strive to provide this information and encouragement as if we were talking while looking at a map.

I prefer to use the native name Denali (meaning "Great One") to refer to Mount McKinley. However, I reluctantly use Mount McKinley to refer to this magnificent mountain in order to avoid confusion since I frequently use "Denali" to refer to "Denali National Park."

Safety is your responsibility.

Hiking in any area of Alaska can be a risky activity. While I have strived to accurately provide information about conditions that may be encountered along the described routes, this book is not a substitute for skills and judgment on your part . You are responsible for acquiring the skills needed for safe wilderness travel and accurately evaluating the conditions in order to have a safe outing. Hence neither the publisher nor I are responsible for your safety and assume no liability in the event of accident, injury, death or property damage along any of the routes listed in this book.

Have a fun and safe outing!!

Please help improve this book

I hope this book meets your expectations. However I know it can be improved. I would appreciate your suggestions, particularly those for additional routes and better ways to describe routes where there are no trails. Do you wish there was a similar book on other areas of Alaska?

Ike Waits
P.O. Box 100200
Anchorage, Alaska 99510-0200
U.S.A.
ikewaits@denaliguidebook.com
www.denaliguidebook.com

Photo C. **Mount McKinley from near Hike 41.**

Chapter 1

Trip Planning and Logistics

Selecting the time for your visit

While Denali National Park is open all year, motor vehicle travel along the park road is only possible from about mid-May until fall snow blocks the road, which can occur as early as mid-September. During the peak summer season (the last weekend of May until mid-September) when the shuttle buses are operating, private motor vehicle traffic beyond the Savage River (mile 14) is strictly limited. From mid-May until the last weekend of May, the road is usually open to vehicle traffic as far as the Teklanika rest stop (mile 30) and no permit is required. In late September the road is also open to vehicle traffic to Teklanika without a permit until the road is blocked by snow.

Here are some additional factors to help you decide when to visit Denali:

Weather: The weather is about the same throughout June, July and August. Statistics indicate June is a bit dryer. Temperatures can vary widely. Freezing temperatures at night are common in May and after late August. During the peak of summer on clear days, the sun can be brutal (for an Alaskan) with temperatures above 70°F so I always carry a hat and sunscreen.

The mid-summer permanent snow level is about 8,000 feet. By late August snow is often covering mountains above 4,700 feet. (Note: The *Alaska Weather Calendar* referenced in Appendix B has Alaska climate information.) After mid-August, expect snowstorms above 3,500 feet elevation which occasionally cause shuttle bus delays until snow on the road melts or is removed.

In early June, snow may remain along portions of routes described in this book, particularly on north-facing slopes and above 4,000 feet.

Daylight: Who needs sleep on a vacation? If you do, bring a dark mask. From May through July, there are more than 16 hours of daylight. After mid-August, nights will be darker and the sun will set around 9:00 PM. By late August, it will be dark enough by 11:00 PM to see the northern lights if they are active on a clear night.

11

Wildlife condition and viewing: Most animals shed their winter fur during June and early July. By August the fur on most animals is in prime condition. Caribou and moose antlers are well developed by mid-August; they start losing their velvet in late August. Grizzly bear fur is blondest in June and July and gets darker as bears prepare for winter. Ptarmigans begin turning white in late August or early September, as do snowshoe hares.

Some of my best viewing of Dall sheep from the road has been in early June when they are still at lower elevations, often along the road in Polychrome Pass. Once the sheep head for higher ground, it is difficult to see more than white dots on the mountain from the road.

Wild flowers and berries: Peak blooming times for the areas along the road are mid-June through early July. Flowers will be blooming later in areas that face north or are at higher elevations. Blueberries are usually ripe after mid-August.

Fall colors: It is tricky to catch the peak fall colors in Denali. The colors can be turning gradually and then go to peak color almost overnight after a freeze. If it snows or rains hard after the leaves turn colors, the leaves will be knocked off the plants. For the best chance of experiencing the fall colors, try to be in Denali the last week of August through the first week of September.

Crowds: Early to mid-June and after mid-August are the least crowded times.

Transportation to the park

You can reach Denali National Park via car, bus, airplane or the Alaska Railroad. Several bus companies operate daily service between Anchorage and Fairbanks with stops at Denali. Contact information is listed in Appendix A for the Alaska Railroad and bus companies. Bus companies usually post information at the Anchorage Visitors Center, hotels, hostels and the Alaska Public Lands Information Center (See Appendix A).

Lodging and campgrounds near the park

There are many hotels, bed and breakfasts, and privately-operated campgrounds near the park entrance. I list the ones I use most frequently in Appendix A. These tend to be very full during the peak of the season so make advance reservations.

When I need to find other campgrounds or lodges outside the park, I turn to *The MILEPOST®* (See Appendix A). Many of the Denali area lodging facilities and campgrounds advertise in *The MILEPOST®*.

Another option is to obtain information from the *Denali Summer Times*, a newspaper tabloid printed each summer that contains articles and many advertisements for services in the Denali area. (See Appendix A.)

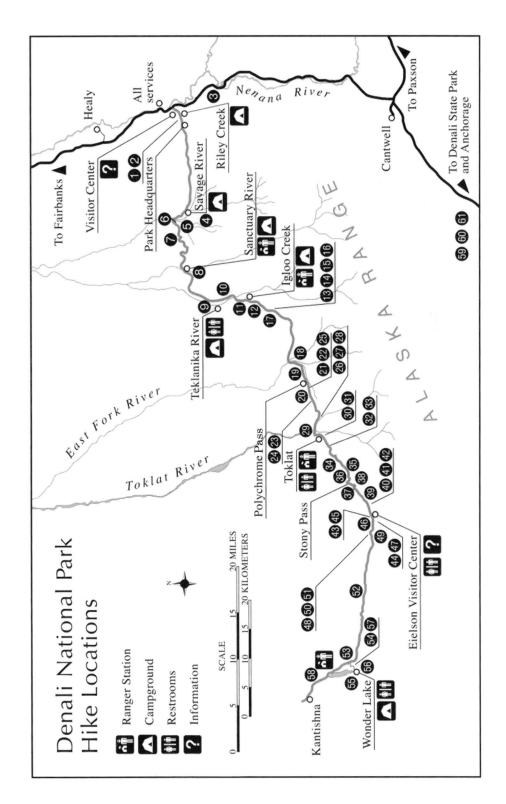

Photo D. **Park bus at Stony Overlook on a clear day.**

Denali shuttle bus is your car in the park

Beginning the last weekend of May (Memorial Day Weekend) through early September, you will need to use the park shuttle bus system to reach most of these hikes. *(photo D)* During the summer season, the Denali National Park road is closed west of Savage River (mile 14) to private vehicles that do not have a special permit. After the shuttle bus service ends, usually early September, and until the road is closed by snow, private vehicles are allowed to drive to the Teklanika rest stop, about 30 miles into the park. Note: The park shuttle buses are not the same as the tour buses that do not allow you to get off and hike.

Advance reservations are available for shuttle bus seats. See Appendix A for reservation information. The shuttle buses run the length of the road departing from the Park Entrance Visitor Center at half-hour intervals beginning at 5:15 AM. The last bus returns to the Park Entrance Visitor Center about 11:00 PM. The round trip to Eielson Visitor Center takes about eight (8) hours and costs $31.45 (2009). A round trip to Wonder Lake takes 11 hours. There is a half-hour stop at the turn around point. When the bus leaves the turn around point, you have a guaranteed seat on the same bus for the return trip. You can remain at the turn around point to hike or picnic and then catch a later bus on a space available basis. At Eielson, there is a sign-up list and bus dispatcher to help get you a bus when you are ready to return.

You may get off to hike at any time. After hiking you will catch a different bus to get back to the park entrance. Seats on the return buses are first come, first served. However buses always leave Eielson with some vacant seats to accommodate hikers along the way. Two or three seats were often available when I stopped the first bus. Occasionally I had to wait for the second bus because the first bus had no seats. Big hiking groups may have to split up to get home. Take a bus schedule with you so you will know when to catch a bus. Buses out of the park are usually operating close to the scheduled times.

The bus drivers and dispatcher at Eielson say it is possible there may not be enough seats on the last scheduled bus out of the park. The risk of not getting a return seat is higher on beautiful days when more people tend to get off the bus to hike and plan to catch one of the last buses out of the park. To avoid being temporarily* stranded, be sure you are on the road in time to have at least two opportunities to

Photo E. **View of Mt. McKinley from Wonder Lake Campground.**

catch a bus. If there are several people in your hiking party, allow even more opportunities to catch a bus and plan on splitting up in order to get enough seats. Early and late in the season, buses are less full.

(***Note**: If you are on the road and trying to catch a bus when the last scheduled bus goes by and there is no space, arrangements will be made to get you out of the park. However it could be several hours before a bus arrives from the park entrance to get you.)

Once you know when you will be in the park, try to make advance reservations for the earliest bus you can stand to catch. Tickets for the unreserved seats may be purchased at the Park Visitor Center two days or less before the travel date. Appendix A describes where to make advance reservations.

Reserving an early bus (between 5:00 and 7:30 AM) allows the most amount of time in the park and generally means you get to Eielson at the time when there is the best chance of seeing Mt. McKinley when the sun illuminates it beautifully. You will also have more time for hiking. Most hikes in this book can be done on the return trip from Eielson if you take an early bus.

The new Eielson Visitor Center opened in 2008. It is built into the hillside to be less intrusive on the landscape and to conserve energy. The Eielson-bound shuttle buses turn around here. You may picnic both inside and outside the center. Restrooms are accessible from outside and are open 24 hours a day. Drinking water is also available. Buses bound for Wonder Lake also make a rest stop at Eielson.

Savage River Shuttle Bus

There is a free Savage River shuttle bus that travels from the park entrance to Savage River at mile 14 to provide access for hikers and campers along this stretch of the park road.

Camper Bus

There is a separate camper bus system to provide transportation to campgrounds and to carry backpackers to drop-off points. People staying at the Sanctuary and Wonder Lake campgrounds may also use the regular shuttle buses or the camper buses to move around inside the park for sightseeing and dayhiking. Camper bus reservations can be made at the same time as campground reservations or when obtaining a backcountry permit for backpacking.

Campgrounds

Advance summer reservations are accepted for spaces in Riley Creek (park entrance), Savage (mile 13), Teklanika (mile 29), and Wonder Lake (mile 85) campgrounds. Wonder Lake is a tent-only campground with access only by camper bus. *(photo E)* If you arrive without reservations, go to the Visitors Center to obtain a campground permit is space is available. Appendix A describes where to make advance reservations.

Riley Creek is the only campground open all year, but flush toilet facilities and water are only available during the summer season. Other campgrounds, except Wonder Lake, are open during the summer season

Photo F. **Lynn and Kathy riding near mile 18 of the park road.**

from late May through early September. Wonder Lake Campground opens in June.

Teklanika Campground is available for tent and RV camping. Campers must store all food, cooking related gear, toiletries and other smelly stuff inside a vehicle or in the metal bear-proof lockers provided at the campground. Drinking water is available. Staying at the Teklanika Campground will give you about an hour's extra sleep each morning if you take one of the early buses. It takes about an hour for the bus to get from the park entrance to Teklanika so you can make reservations for the 6:00 AM bus and catch the bus about 7:00 Am. You drive your vehicle to and from Teklanika but may not drive around while you are camped there. A minimum stay of three nights is required.

Sanctuary, a tent-only campground with 7 sites, cannot be reserved in advance but may be reserved upon arrival at the Park Entrance Visitor Center. Igloo Campground, a historically-popular campground, remained closed as of 2009.

Bicycling

When I camp at Wonder Lake or Teklanika, I often take a mountain bike. By using the bicycle at Wonder Lake I can quickly (compared to walking) reach favorite evening and early morning photography locations. From Teklanika, I often ride to the Igloo Forest (five miles one-way) in the evenings to look for moose, wolves or snowshoe hares. Friends have ridden bicycles from the Savage River ranger station to visit me in Teklanika Campground, about 15 miles one-way *(photo F)*.

Bicycles are allowed anywhere on the park road. Each camper bus can carry two bicycles subject to space availability. Space for bicycles can be reserved at the same time reservations are made for a seat on the camper bus. Sometimes bicycles were carried on the shuttle buses in the rear

Photo G. **Camp site on upper Teklanika River along the Hike 13 route.**

area reserved for wheelchairs if that area was not occupied. Check with the shuttle bus operator on current policy regarding carrying bicycles in empty wheelchair areas.

Backcountry camping permits

You must obtain a backcountry permit to camp overnight outside a campground. *(photo G)* Backcountry permits are only available at the backcountry ranger desk in the Park Wilderness Access Center. Permits are issued on a first come, first served basis. The number of campers permitted in each backcountry permit area is limited. During the peak season and if you have a large group, it will be difficult to get permits for the most popular backpacking areas. Therefore I recommend you plan several possible hikes, be flexible, and be in line well before the permit desk opens.

During peak season you also may have to wait a day or two before any permit areas are open. Spend this time doing some of the dayhikes near the park entrance or get on a regular shuttle bus and do a dayhike.

Camper buses are provided to carry backpackers into the park. Be sure to obtain a camper bus ticket when you obtain the backpacking permit.

Showers

Showers area available at the Riley Creek Mercantile located adjacent to the Riley Creek Campground about one mile inside the park. Some commercial campgrounds near the park entrance also have showers for their campers. See Appendix A.

Chapter 2

Photographing in Denali

Using the bus as your vehicle

Beyond the Savage River (Mile 14) from late May to early September you will be using the Denali Park shuttle buses for transportation and often as your camera platform. If you are a qualified professional photographer, you may be able to participate in the lottery for one of the few permits to use your vehicle in the park. Contact the Denali Park Superintendent to obtain information on the minimum professional qualifications required to participate in the selection process for the limited number of road permits.

While the shuttle bus is not as convenient as a car, I do think the measures to restrict road travel have helped maintain wildlife viewing opportunities along the road.

When requested the bus driver will make short stops for scenic shots from the bus but only the most assertive photographers ask for very many stops for scenic shots. You may get off the bus anytime and stay in an area to make scenic photographs.

Most bus stops are for wildlife viewing (even for sheep or bear "dots" that are too far away to photograph). On stops for distant animals, be sure to look around for scenic shots you can take from the bus while others watch the animal dots. While most drivers will stop the engine if they plan to stop for a while, you may have to request some drivers to stop the engine to minimize vibrations. Fortunately, the bus always stops for wildlife near the road and the driver stops the engine to reduce noise.

For all animals except bears it is best to get off the bus as near as possible to the animals and then work to photograph them on foot. (Note: The driver will not let you off closer than one mile to animals that are near the road.) Photographing bears from the bus is best since park rules require a separation distance of one-fourth of a mile (400 meters) if you do not have a vehicle to jump into. Even with a 600mm lens, bears will be only a small part of the frame at this distance.

Photographing wildlife from the bus

There is no guarantee that animals will be close enough to the road to photograph on any given bus ride! The key to success is to travel the road many times. For example, I usually stay in the park for two weeks and ride the bus everyday during the best light.

Good bear (and other animal) pictures from the bus are possible *(photo H)*. On lucky days bears are within 50 feet of the road and often walk across the road and along the side of the bus. Often the elevation of the bus makes it possible to see animals over the brush. Bears on the move can quickly get so close to the bus that a 300 mm or even 200 mm lens will be too powerful to get the whole bear in the frame. A zoom lens or a spare camera with a shorter lens helps in this situation.

To maximize the time spent photographing bears close to the road, I get off the bus as soon as the driver will allow and catch the next available bus going back toward the bear. (Note: when wildlife are close to the road, the bus driver will not let you off the bus until the bus has traveled a mile from the animal.) When I get on the next bus, I try to sit on the side of the bus that will be near the bear (and hope the animal has not moved). I have my gear ready to shoot as the bus approaches the area where I expect to see the animal again.

While this repeated pass technique might work for other animals that tend to stay in one spot for awhile, I use this technique only for bears because I can usually get close enough on foot for good photographs of other animals.

Photographing wildlife from the bus presents a unique set of technical challenges. Tripods are of little use inside the bus because of limited space and bus vibration. While stopped for wildlife viewing, the driver will usually stop the engine but the bus will shake when people move to get a photograph or better view, particularly when a bear is very close or walking along side the bus.

From mid-June until about the third week of August, most shuttle buses will be nearly full so you will be sharing a window with at least four people because the people who are across the aisle will need to look out your window or you will share theirs. It will be nearly impossible to move around in the bus. In early June, I found many of the buses had vacant seats, particularly the late afternoon buses.

Photo H. **A grizzly on a wet hair day. Photo taken from the bus.**

As long as I am polite and do not monopolize the window space, I find most passengers will see my big lens and try to give me a chance for a shot. This is particularly true when they conclude I am a professional photographer. I've learned to accept missed opportunities when I cannot get window space for the best shots.

I have developed a few techniques to maximize my percentage of good photographs from the bus. I plan on hand holding the camera whenever I shoot from the bus. To increase my shutter speed, I keep one camera body loaded with 400 ISO film. Print film users may have an advantage with the high quality 400 ISO films available.

Because of limited space and lack of a tripod, about 400mm is the longest lens I will try to use. To brace my 300mm f2.8 extended to 420, I discovered the technique of standing in the isle while holding on to the overhead baggage rack with my left arm and bracing the lens in the crook of my left elbow. This position works good if the animal is below the bus and your fellow passengers cooperate to allow your lens a clear path to the window. For animals at eye level or above the bus, the best technique I found was to rest my left arm on the window and then place the lens on my arm. These bracing techniques are difficult to do without autofocus. When I face the challenges of photographing from the Denali shuttle buses again, I hope to be carrying a Canon Image Stabilizer lens!

If I have a window seat rather than an aisle seat, I usually find myself squatting between the seats to have room to maneuver the long lens. Squatting between the seats allows the aisle seat passenger to kneel in the seat and also get a good view.

Even if the animal is staying in one spot, time to photograph animals from the bus will be very short. The bus usually cannot stay by the animal for more than 10 to 15 minutes and sometimes will stay even less time if there are many buses stacked up at the site.

Often the camper buses are less crowded than the shuttle buses. While camper buses run less frequently, I often chose the camper bus for moving around in the park to photograph after leaving my initial shuttle bus. The disadvantages of the camper bus are that windows are smaller and seats are more cramped. However passengers on these busses are usually more willing to accommodate a photographer. Large photo backpacks will not fit in the overhead rack of camper buses but can be placed in the rear of the camper bus with other backpacks.

Opportunities to photograph from your vehicle

Take advantage of the photographic opportunities offered by the first 14 miles of the park road. This section is open to private vehicles from late spring until the road is closed by snow, usually around mid-to-late September. Much of this part of the road passes through prime moose habitat. Fall is a good time to be cruising this area to see bull moose with full racks. In mid-September bull moose sometimes spar near the road. Bear, caribou, fox and ptarmigan may be seen in the area, particularly near the Savage River. I have seen a grizzly in Savage River Campground.

For four days in September after

the bus service ends, 400 private vehicles are allowed into the park each day. Permits to drive in the park on these days are awarded by lottery. After these four days and until the road is closed by snow, the road is open to the Teklanika rest stop (mile 30) for private vehicles. This is a good time of year to photograph bull moose, ptarmigan changing colors, and to hike on Primrose Ridge to look for Dall sheep, all of which can be done within the first 30 miles of the road.

From mid-May to the last weekend of May, the road is usually open to private vehicles as far as the Teklanika Rest Stop (mile 30). The exact time the road is opened for traffic depends on how long it takes to clear the snow and for the road to dry enough for traffic.

Lighting

In June through early July, it is not possible to use the shuttle buses to be in the park within two hours after sunrise or before sunset. After mid-August, the buses that leave the park entrance at 6:00 and 6:30 AM are traveling when the sun is still at a low enough angle to provide good side lighting and reasonably warm tones through Polychrome Pass and most of the way to Eielson Visitor Center. After mid-August, it is possible to catch some of the low-angle, magic light near sunset from Polychrome Pass before you take the last bus returning to the entrance *(photo I)*.

In mid-August, I wanted to photograph Polychrome Pass in the late evening light. Consulting the bus schedule I learned the last bus returning to the park entrance left

Photo I. **Evening view of the Alaska Range from Polychrome Pass.**

Eielson around 6:30 PM and passed through Polychrome Pass about 8:00 PM. There was also a bus from the park entrance that turned around at Polychrome about 9:00 PM and then returned to the park entrance.

While the last buses into the park travel during mid-day when lighting is not the best, they are returning from 7:00 PM to10:00 PM when light is at a sufficiently low angle to provide side lighting *(photo J)*.

Photographing Mount McKinley

The first challenge is to get a clear day or at least a clear morning. Less than one third of the summer visitors see the entire mountain. If Mount McKinley is clear, it is usually early in the morning or late evening. Based on years of observation, I think the best opportunity for seeing Mount McKinley (if you are coming from the park entrance) is to take early morning buses that arrive at Eielson before 11:00 AM. If Mount McKinley is clear in the morning, it usually is shrouded in clouds by noon and remains so until late evening.

Both peaks are visible from the east side of Mount McKinley. For the best possible light on the eastern side of Mount McKinley, take the 6:00 or 6:30 AM bus from the park entrance. On days when Mount McKinley is out, these buses arrive at Stony Pass while the sun is hitting the eastern side of Mount McKinley and the foreground. On days with good views of Mount McKinley, the bus driver usually stops in Stony Pass and lets people off the bus for about 10 minutes to photograph; be prepared to set up a tripod

Photo J. **Spring grizzly cubs taken from the bus in evening light.**

and use this time efficiently. You can also get off the bus and remain in the Stony area to photograph.

Most of the Mount McKinley pictures with the park road and buses in the foreground were taken in morning light from Stony Pass area. *(see photo EE, page 256)* Mount McKinley is about 37 miles from Stony Pass and 33 miles from the Eielson Visitors Center. I use a 28-to-135mm zoom lens most frequently from this area. A 300mm or larger lens will give details of the peaks.

On clear days, the eastern side of Mount McKinley is also visible from several other spots along the road that have good foreground for a moderate telephoto lens shot. Some of my favorite views of the eastern side of Mount. McKinley are from Sable Pass, just past Polychrome rest stop (about mile 47), and near the eastern end of the Toklat River Bridge. *(photo 34C)*

*Even on clear days, captur*ing photographs of Mount McKinley's north face is difficult to do if you start your bus trip from the park entrance. From around 11:00 AM to around 4:00 PM the sun is either directly overhead or a little behind (south) of the Mountain. Mount McKinley also tends to be covered in clouds from around noon until late in the evening.

The best way to photograph Mount McKinley's north face is to camp at Wonder Lake or in the backcountry beyond Eielson. This allows two chances each day to get good light on the north face; early morning as the sun rises in the northeast and late evening as the sun sets in the northwest. Alpine glow often rewards photographers who are early risers or who remain ready after the sunsets.

Photo K. **Mount McKinley and Reflection Pond (see map page 210). Mount Brooks at the far left.**

Photographing the Wonder Lake area

Camping at Wonder Lake Campground is the best way to make photographs of Mount McKinley that include Wonder Lake or Reflection Pond *(photos A and K)*. Take a mountain bike so you can quickly reach Reflection Pond (about a 20-minute ride) or the far end of Wonder Lake (about a 45-minute ride). It takes two to three times longer to walk to these areas. **Note:** Advance reservations to carry a mountain bike on the camper bus are important since the bus only carries two bikes.

Another (but more expensive) way to obtain Wonder Lake area photographs is to stay in a lodge that has the legal right to provide transportation to an area close to Wonder Lake during the evening. Be sure to ask about evening transportation to and from Wonder Lake because some of the lodges are several miles from the lake. Also check the Shuttle Bus schedule as a few buses serve Kantishna but usually do not run late in the evening. Some lodges may have mountain bikes that you can use to reach Wonder Lake in the evening or early morning. See Appendix A.

Camp Denali and North Face Lodge are the closest to Wonder Lake. These lodges have access rights into the park, canoes for use on Wonder Lake and mountain bikes to reach the lake in the evening. These lodges frequently offer photography seminars with professional photographers. Camp Denali and North Face Lodge also have grandfathered rights to bring clients farther into the park for dayhikes, nature studies and photography.

Flower and foliage photography

Mid-June to mid-July is the peak time for wildflowers. Around July 1st, blooms are at their peak in areas along and near the road. Blooms continue later at higher elevations and on north-facing slopes. Consult Verna Pratt's *Wildflowers of Denali National Park* for guidelines on locations and blooming times for specific plants and for lists of plants found in various locations including areas covered by many of the hikes in this book such as the Stony and Thorofare Pass areas. (See Books and Maps appendix.)

If your goal is to catch the fall colors, then plan on visiting the last week of August through the first week of September for the best chance of catching peak color. Early snow or hard rain and wind can rapidly spoil the fall colors.

Wildlife photography times and locations

Many larger animals are still shedding their winter fur during early June. However some of my best viewing of Dall sheep ewes and lambs has been in early June when they are still at lower elevations, often along the road in Polychrome Pass. By August the fur on most animals is in prime condition. Caribou and moose antlers are well developed by mid-August; they start losing their velvet after mid-August. Moose start sparring by the end of August or early September. Grizzly bear fur is blondest in June and July and gets darker as bears prepare for winter. Ptarmigans begin turning white in late August or early September, as do snowshoe hares.

Until about 10:00 AM, light will be the best on animals on the north side of the road (right side of a bus going into the park). After about 5:00 PM, the light will be at a sufficiently low angle to provide side lighting for animals on the south side of the road.

All animals have the right of way in Denali. The rule for your behavior is to avoid doing anything that will alter their behavior. Many non-

Required minimum distance from animals

For safety and to avoid disturbing wildlife, park rules prohibit approaching animals and dens on foot closer than the minimum distances listed below:
- bears: 1/4 mile (0.4 km). (about the length of 36 buses parked end-to-end)
- raptor nests: 300 yards (300 meters)
- wolf dens: 1 mile (1.6 km)
- dens other than wolf: 300 yards (300 meters) from fox, wolverine, lynx or coyote dens
- wolves: 1/4 mile (0.4 km)
- caribou: 75 feet (25 meters)
- moose: 75 feet (25 meters)
- Dall sheep: 75 feet (25 meters)

These distances are subject to annual review. Obtain current information at the park upon your arrival.

Photo L. **Dall sheep ram, the king of the mountain.**

threatening animals will approach a person who is sitting still, including Dall sheep, caribou, and foxes. When this occurs, enjoy it and avoid movement that will startle the animals and alter their behavior. Avoid allowing a bear to come closer than the minimum distance (1/4-mile).

I consider a moose cow with a calf to be as dangerous as a grizzly with cubs. I recommend maintaining more than the minimum 75 feet from a moose cow with calf. I also maintain a larger distance from bull moose during the rutting season.

Mammal photography

Grizzly bears: Photographing bears from the road is usually accomplished in the vicinity of Sable, Highway, Stony or Thorofare passes. In these areas bears are most likely to be found mid-June to mid-September when they are grazing on grass and flowers and then searching for berries until the snow falls. Many of my best shots from the bus have been in Stony Pass and Highway Pass. In the fall, watch for bears feeding in the soapberry patches near the road east of the Toklat River bridge.

In the spring and fall, watch for bears along the first 14 miles of the road. Bears are hunting moose calves in the spring and berries in the fall. In fact, expect to find bears just about anywhere in the park when hiking as they cover a lot of ground searching for food.

Dall sheep: The most easily photographed ewes and lambs are found on Igloo, Cathedral or Polychrome mountains. The north side and Savage River end of Primrose Ridge is also a good place to search for ewes and lambs. Early in the season (late May through mid June) and again in early September, ewes and lambs are often seen along the road in Polychrome Pass or on slopes above the rest area. While eating lunch in mid-June along these ridges, I was joined by some Dall sheep. Rams are tougher to find. I have found them on Primrose Ridge, Polychrome Mountain and Cathedral Mountain *(photo L)*.

Many of the hikes in this book provide access to areas where sheep can be found. Approach sheep slowly and openly and give them time to accept your presence. If you sit still for a while, sheep will often move closer to you. Steep hiking and good route finding is usually required to get good photographs after about mid-June.

Moose: Around the park entrance and along the first 12 miles of the park road are good areas for moose. In early September I was treated to the spectacle of two bull moose sparring in the middle of the highway just east of Savage River Campground. Moose are hard to spot due to thick trees. Take advantage of all the eyes on buses and check out any spot where a tour bus stops. In late August (1998), people were talking about the moose they had already seen just about every time I got on the bus at Teklanika. Near Wonder Lake and around mile 80 on the park road are also good for moose, particularly for photographs of moose in Wonder Lake or some of the tundra ponds visible from the road. *(photo Q)*

Caribou: While caribou can be found just about anywhere in the park, they are more common west of Sable Pass during the July and early August. Some often loiter near Eielson Visitor Center. The Wonder Lake area is good for caribou, especially in the fall. I have seen them walk through the Wonder Lake campground. In mid-August I have shared the trail on Primrose Ridge (mile 17) with caribou bulls. Watch for caribou near the road between Savage and Sanctuary rivers. By late August the caribou fur is a rich chocolate brown accented by a white rump and a white cape around the neck *(photo M)*.

Wolves: In the past two summers, I saw a wolf from the bus about four times in a two week period. Good luck finding a wolf close enough to photograph unless you have professional photographer road permit. I have seen them most frequently in the East Fork of Toklat drainage or in the Stony Creek drainages but too far away for a frame-filling shot even with 600mm lens range. The best I have achieved so far is a full frame shot of female that walked past me on the road. Unfortunately she wore a radio collar. I have not given up as I see many photographs of wolves taken in Denali *(photo N)*.

A wolf can be very near without revealing itself. On a Stony Creek hike, I let my hiking companions get ahead of me so I could visit the brush for a bathroom break. As I entered the head-high brush along the route a wolf startled me when it arose from where it was hiding as my companions walked past. I quickly forgot about my bathroom

Photo M. **Bull caribou, recently shed of velvet, resting near Wonder Lake.**

needs and scrambled to retrieve the telephoto lens from my pack. Alas the wolf was out of range before I was ready to photograph.

The Park Service prohibits hiking in any area with a known wolf den.

Foxes: Foxes can appear any time and anywhere. They are often seen from the bus as they walk along the road looking for squashed ground squirrels. They also use the side of the road as an easy place to walk back to their den with the day's catch of squirrels in their mouth. Occasionally there is a fox den visible from the road but most dens must be found while hiking. Photographing fox dens will require a long lens for detailed pictures of kits since the minimum required separation distance is 300 yards. In the evening foxes are often seen along the riverbank near Teklanika Campground *(photo O)*.

Photo N. **Female wolf howling**

Small mammals: Marmots can be found on many ridges. I have had good luck on Primrose Ridge, along the ridges near the Polychrome Pass rest area and about 200 yards uphill from the Eielson Visitor Center.

Pikas can be found in many rocky areas but they are very hard to see. I had the best luck with pikas in the rock piles along Tattler Creek about 2 miles upstream from the road and north of Stony Hill.

Arctic ground and red squirrels are abundant in most campgrounds.

Snowshoe hares can often be photographed at the Teklanika Campground and along the side of the road in the Igloo Forest west of the Teklanika Bridge. They begin changing colors in late August.

Beavers can be found in many ponds. Check any pond that has a pile of sticks along the shore or check a tundra stream that has been dammed. Ask the rangers if there are still beavers on Horseshoe Lake near the park entrance. Watch for beavers in the ponds between Eielson Visitor Center and Wonder Lake and also in the streams near Wonder Lake.

Bird photography

Golden Eagles: Golden eagles can be seen soaring just about anywhere in the park, particularly near ridges or in valleys adjacent to rocky ridgelines. Look for them along the ridges north of Eielson and through Thorofare Pass.

For several years, golden eagles nested on a cliff below the road just past (west of) the Polychrome Pass summit. Thanks to strict enforcement of the closure area around the nest,

Photo O. **Red fox near Eielson Visitor Center.**

them near Polychrome, Highway, Stony and Thorofare passes.

Ptarmigan are frequently seen along the road and on the brushy gravel bars in the river valleys. These birds will usually allow you to get close enough for good shots with a 300mm lens. They start turning white in late August *(photo P)*.

American golden plovers and long-tailed jaegers are found in Highway and Thorofare Pass areas where they nest. Both are seen frequently from the bus in Highway Pass but the best chance to photograph them is while hiking in these areas.

For other birds in the park, consult *Birds of Mount McKinley, Alaska* by Adolph Murie for a list and possible locations to find the birds.

Photo P. **Ptarmigan family.**

the eagles were not disturbed. In 1999, gyrfalcons took over the nest.

If the nest is active when you visit, you can find the nest by watching where the buses stop for viewing in the dip just before the road curves out of sight after leaving the summit. You will need a big lens (600mm or more) to get any details of nest occupants. The adults often perch on rocks above and across from the nest.

In 2004, an active golden eagle nest was visible above the road east of Eielson (mile 67.5). If the nest is occupied when you visit, you can find the nest by looking for the golden eagles soaring above and finding the "area closed" signs along the road.

Other birds: If you are lucky, gyrfalcons can be found on the tundra or on low peaks such as Stony Hill where they can be photographed. Watch for

Photo Q. **Bull moose at a pond near Wonder Lake the last week of August.**

Chapter 3

Hiking Environment and Preparation

Many hours of daylight

There is plenty of daylight to do dayhikes and still ride the bus both ways in the daylight for maximum wildlife viewing. During most of the summer, you will have at least 12 hours of daylight; in June and July there is much more. Why return to the park entrance hotels at 6:00 PM and spend three or four hours of daylight watching cars and people when you could still be in the park looking for animals, hiking or improving your chance of seeing Mt. McKinley? To assure maximum time in the park, get advance reservations on the earliest shuttle bus you can get out of bed to catch. (See Shuttle Bus Reservations.)

I designed the length of most dayhikes so I could ride the 6:30 AM bus to Eielson and then get off on the way back from Eielson to do the hikes. This approach allowed me the maximum opportunities to see bears and best chance of catching Mt. McKinley out for photographs in the good morning light. I compensated for the long days by taking a few naps on my hikes (and on the bus) and by carrying plenty of food and water.

Denali—a great place to hike without trails

There are very few developed and marked trails in Denali National Park. Most of the hikes in this book are done without developed trails.

I suspect many of you are like me. Before my first summer in Denali (1967), I had little experience hiking without trails. Since then, I have done many hikes without benefit of trails in Denali and in the Brooks Range. I hope this book and the following observations and hints will encourage you to try hiking without trails in Denali.

Denali is a good place to start hiking without trails. Most of the terrain along the road is open tundra so you can see a lot of places to hike. From the road you can often see and judge the difficulty of routes to reach ridges and mountaintops. The brush will rarely be so thick or high that you cannot find a spot to view some of the route ahead. Yes, you may get your feet wet hiking in the tundra until you begin to read the subtle elevation and vegetation signs that indicate where to find the driest hiking.

31

Riverbed walking provides an alternative to tundra hiking. Most river valleys were carved by glaciers and are characterized by meandering channels in broad gravel planes that provide easy walking with good visibility. *(photo S)*

Portions of many of the described hikes follow ridgelines. Scree slopes are often crossed by sheep trails that can be the easiest way to cross the loose rock. *(photo R)*

Help keep Denali trailless

There are places where trails have formed due to animal or human travel. Animals look for the easiest way to get around, through or over obstacles. When I am confronted with obstacles like dense vegetation, a mountain pass or deep ravine, I also look for the easiest way to hike. Frequently animals have already used the route that I find. To me this is what wilderness travelers have done for centuries. When I follow an animal trail, I often find that animals spread out again as soon as they pass the obstacle. This is also a good practice for hikers to follow in order to minimize the creation of human trails.

Trails created primarily by hikers are often called "social trails." These trails form when hikers repeatedly begin from the same spot, often near campgrounds, bus stops or parking areas. In much of Denali, terrain features or wildlife closures do not force hikers to start at the same spot. In these instances please walk along the road to find a different spot to begin your hike away from social trails.

When possible, start your hike walking on rocky surfaces like streambeds. Most rivers and streams in Denali have gravel streambeds that are great places to hike without creating a trail. *(photo S)* When hiking along alpine ridgelines, hike on the non-vegetated surfaces and spread out when hiking on the fragile alpine tundra. Rangers at the backcountry permit desk can provide additional information on how to minimize your impact.

In some cases terrain features, dense vegetation or wildlife closure areas cause hikers to leave the road in a specific location creating a social trail. Some hikes in this book start at these locations. In these instances, use the social trail to get past the obstacle or closure boundary and then spread out to keep the social trail from extending beyond the obstacle.

Guided hikes

If you are timid about hiking without trails, sign up from one of the daily Discovery Hikes led by rangers for a guided introduction to hiking without trails. Many of the Discovery Hikes cover terrain and routes similar to the hikes described in this book. Lodges in the Kantishna area near Wonder Lake also offer some guided hikes. See Appendix A.

Hard to get lost

While the road is frequently out of sight on many of the dayhikes in this book, it would be hard to get lost (i.e. not know where the road is) on any of these hikes. Most routes follow drainages or ridges that either cross or are

Photo R. **Typical sheep trail along a ridge line.**

parallel to the road. If you know that you hiked south from the road, then by heading north you will eventually return to the road. You can always find the road if you have a compass and remember which direction you were going when you left the road and then return by following a direction 180 degrees different. The road is often visible from points along ridges or from the summit.

The only time I have experienced disorientation or route-finding difficulty on any of these dayhikes was when I retraced my route off a mountain. This situation is difficult because often there are several ridges that look similar from above and footsteps are not easy to find in the tundra or rocks on top. I have learned to look backward during rest breaks on the way up and select some landmarks to make it easier to retrace my route.

The most difficult route finding I have encountered occurred while retracing my route on broad mountaintops (such as Sable Mountain) when low clouds obscured visibility. It was difficult to find the correct ridge to follow down. Identifying good landmarks coupled with map reading and compass skills were essential to finding my route under these conditions.

However many of the backpacking routes involve crossing remote mountain passes. The ridges or valleys leading to the correct pass often look like all the others in the area. Without good map reading skills, it is possible to make a mistake finding the described route.

Finding where to start

A sign does not mark the starting point for most of the hikes in this book. Enlist the help of the shuttle bus driver to identify where to get off the bus to start a hike. While many mileposts seem to be missing or are difficult to spot at bus speeds, most bus drivers have been driving in the park for years and know almost by instinct where the milepost should be located. Discuss your hike plans with the bus driver at a rest stop before you get near the area where you decide to hike. At a rest stop, show the driver this book and description of where to get off. Traveling into the park, the bus makes a rest stop before the Teklanika River Bridge and again at Polychrome Pass. You will also have a 30-minute rest stop at Eielson Visitor Center. On the return trip, the rest stops are at the Toklat River Bridge and again at the Teklanika Rest Area.

If you catch an early bus, you can get off the bus on the return trip and still have time for most hikes in this book. Scout the location of the hike on the way out and you will be better prepared to tell the driver when to let you off on the way back.

Trailless hiking pointers

I use the following guidelines when hiking in trailless areas of Denali National Park.

Allow plenty of time! It is easy to underestimate the time it takes to cover a given distance. It takes longer to cover the same distance without a trail than it does on a trail. One mile per hour is a comfortable pace for hiking in the tundra and most other trailless conditions in Denali. This pace is sustainable when I am carrying about 20 pounds of gear and it allows time to enjoy the flowers and catch my breath.

Do not ascend anything you cannot descend. Generally it is harder to descend than to ascend an area that requires some rock scrambling. This guideline is critical if you venture onto some of the mountains that have loose rock formations and exposed slopes.

Find the driest hiking when walking through tundra by looking for the subtle elevation and vegetation changes in the tundra. A slight increase in elevation can reduce the dampness. With practice you will recognize which plants grow in the wettest spots and plan your route around these areas.

"When you start hiking in tundra find the first puddle and jump in because your feet are going to get wet anyway." Ranger Bill Ruth gave me this advice during my first summer in Denali when I asked how to keep my feet dry. Following Bill's advice, or at least accepting wet feet, has led me to concentrate more on the beauty of the tundra and spotting wildlife than on keeping my feet dry.

For easier walking in scree areas,

Photo S. **River gravel bars provide good walking. Teklanika River with Cathedral Mountain in background from Hike 14.**

look for game trails. These trails are often faint but offer the best footing because the trail is flatter and rocks have been packed down so they do not move as much when you walk on them. A trail through the scree is usually made by sheep or migrating caribou *(photo R)*.

The least-brushy routes are usually along ridgelines or gravel bars. The height and amount of vegetation is often reduced by slight changes in elevation. Frequently you can find game trails for routes through brushy areas or tundra but remember moose or caribou do not care if they get their feet wet *(photo S)*.

Look for good hiking in the broad, glacial river valleys south of the park road. The riverbeds are broad planes containing willows, gravel bars and braided stream channels. From a distance the willows may look thick and intimidating. *(photo T)* However I can usually find a route through the willows by following old river channels and gravel bars where the vegetation is not too high or thick. *(photo U)* When this does not work I look for good walking at the base of the bank that separates the tundra from the riverbed vegetation. Often there are game trails or the vegetation is sparse at the base of the tundra bluff. When there is a bend in the river next to a high bank, there is often a game trail along the top of the bank until it is again possible to walk in the riverbed. If the tundra is too high and thick along the top of the bank and the river is not too high to cross, I find it easier and quicker to cross to the other side and continue walking in the riverbed. But I do not mind hiking in wet boots.

Protect the fragile tundra and ridgeline plants and minimize erosion! If you are in a group, avoid walking single file. On ridges and other shallow soil areas, walk on the rocky spots and avoid walking on the vegetation when possible.

Stream crossings

I designed most of the dayhikes to avoid crossing any stream likely to be more than knee deep *(photo V)*. Many of the streams can be stepped across or crossed on rocks. However, some of the backpacking trips require crossing major rivers of the park. I have crossed both branches of the Toklat River near Divide Mountain upstream from the Toklat Bridge, the Sanctuary and Savage rivers near the Alaska Range foothills, the Teklanika River near Cathedral Mountain, and the Thorofare River below Eielson Visitor Center. Don Croner crossed the other rivers described in the backpacking routes.

Photo T. **Sanctuary riverbed (Hikes 8, 13). Hiking through the riverbed willows is often easier than it looks** (photo U) **and usually much easier than hiking in the tundra.**

Due to melting snow, some of the streams and gullies may contain more water in June than later in the summer.

Fortunately, rivers in Denali are often braided and water volume fluctuates diurnally enough to make crossing easier. Water volumes can increase dramatically after a hot day due to glacier melt or after a period of steady rain.

Before attempting a hike with a major river crossing, discuss your plans with the backcountry park rangers and view the stream crossing video in the Park Entrance Visitor Center.

When the water is fast and could be knee deep or more, I use a walking staff or my tripod as a brace. While I remove my socks and roll up my pants, I always wear my boots to protect my tender feet from the rocks. I do not want my balance compromised by rocks hurting my feet.

Hiking with bears

To date, bears in Denali have killed no one and have injured very few people. This good safety record is due to hikers and photographers practicing the hiking and food management rules and recommendations provided by the National Park Service.

When I started hiking with bears in Denali in 1967, I found no guidebooks on hiking in bear country. However rangers and experienced hikers provided the following advice that continues to work well for me:
- remember I am a guest in the bear's home
- avoid surprising bears
- never crowd a bear

Photo U. **Diny finds an open route through willows in the Sanctuary riverbed, Hikes 8 and 13.**

- do not let bears get my food or garbage; and
- above all, do not get between a sow and her cubs.

Currently, there are several books on how to travel in bear country and deal with a threat or an attack. Some of these books are listed in the Books and Maps appendix of this book.

While guidebooks help, I recommend talking to the Denali National Park rangers and watching the backcountry video on hiking in bear country at the Park Entrance Visitor Center. This interactive video covers hiking and camping procedures to avoid bears as well as what to do in the unlikely event of a charge or an attack. You must view the video to get a backcountry camping permit.

Preventing bears from getting food and or garbage is essential to maintain the park's safety record. Once a bear associates humans with easy food, then chances of encounters increase. Allowing bears to get your food or garbage could result in injury for the next hiker and ultimately death for the bear to prevent future human injury. Remember the slogan: "a fed bear is a dead bear."

When picnicking, always keep your food ready to put in your pack in case a bear comes and you have to leave quickly.

Hiking with mosquitoes

To date, Denali mosquitoes have not killed or injured anyone. However, in some areas and during some times of the year, mosquitoes and other flying pests may be annoying. Generally mosquitoes are scarce on ridges or along the broad gravel bars. They seem to be most numerous in locations with both brush and wet areas such as around Wonder Lake.

I deal with these situations by always wearing a long-sleeve shirt and long pants and by carrying a headnet and light gloves in my pack. I do not like to use mosquito repellent. Like the caribou, I also walk or rest on ridges or other spots where there is a breeze to keep the bugs away.

Books and maps to use with this book

The Information Sources appendix at the end of this book contains addresses for obtaining the books and maps described in this section.

Obtain a copy of *The Denali Road Guide: A Roadside Natural History of Denali National Park*. This book contains a description of natural features and references the milepost near which these features are found. Since mileposts are difficult to spot from the bus (and sometimes missing), use this book to keep track of where you are along the road and to help identify where to get off the bus for one of these hikes.

For maps you have two choices, the *Trails Illustrated®* map or the U.S. Geological Survey (USGS) maps. You will benefit from having both types of maps.

For route planning and hiking where there are no trails, I prefer USGS maps because they are more detailed. The USGS maps referenced at the beginning of each hike have a scale of 1 inch = 1 mile (scale 1: 63,360) and contour intervals of 100 feet. Whereas the most detailed side of the *Trails Illustrated®* map has a scale of 1 inch = about 3 miles (1:200,000) with contour intervals of 200 feet. The USGS maps are available at the Visitor Center at the park entrance and from other sources as noted in Books and Maps Appendix.

I use the *Trails Illustrated®* map to see the whole park on one map and make tentative route selections. It is a great map to inspire ideas for future hikes; there is so much to see. Because this map shows the boundaries of backcountry permit areas and of areas permanently closed to hiking, it is indispensable for those who want to plan some alternative backpacking and hiking routes before arriving at the park. I always carry this map to use for orientation and landmark identification when I am on a mountaintop and can see for more miles than the USGS map covers. This waterproof map is nearly indestructible compared to the paper USGS map. The *Trails Illustrated®* map is available at the park visitor center, many bookstores and other sources noted under Information Sources.

Other books to enhance your Denali experience

In the Books and Maps appendix at the end of this book, I describe several of my favorite books about the vegetation, wildlife and geology of the park. I rarely venture into the park without a flower and bird book. I am particularly fond of *Wildflowers of Denali National Park* by Verna and Frank Pratt.

Preparing to hike

Gear: I believe the biggest threat to comfort and safety on any of the dayhikes is getting wet and cold. Therefore I always wear clothes that dry fast (no cotton) and carry a jacket that provides insulation when wet. I wear hiking boots for adequate support in tundra tussocks and scree.

On backpack trips I usually carry either a dry change of clothes or a set of mid- to heavy-weight polyester long underwear in addition to the dayhike gear on the checklist. A tent is essential to protect from rain as well as mosquitoes. A stove is required for cooking since fires are prohibited in the park except in a few campgrounds.

When I am carrying a heavy pack, I always use a walking staff for balance on the uneven tundra. I also carry a walking staff on any hike where I expect to cross a river.

Drinking water: Stream or lake water should be treated, boiled, or filtered before drinking. Carry water on the bus as none of the rest stops before Eielson Visitor Center have water. Water is also available at the campground near the Wonder Lake bus stop.

I start hiking with two quarts of water. When I get off the bus on the return trip from Eielson, I refill my water bottles at Eielson. I also carry a filter to treat water. I try to find clear water because glacial silt clogs my filter.

Other hiking precautions

Perhaps the most important precaution is to leave a hike plan with someone who will contact the

Daypack checklist

- compass and maps
- rain pants and coat
- windbreaker (I use my rain coat.)
- mid-weight pile jacket (or heavy-weight pile jacket in the late fall or early June)
- stocking cap
- sun hat and sun block (it can be 75° F with bright sun)
- two quarts of water and iodine tablets (or a filter) to treat water for refills
- lunch and a lot of snacks
- toilet paper, trowel and bag for used paper
- mosquito headnet and light gloves or repellent
- signaling devices such as flares, smoke or mirror
- a small first aid kit with mole skin and ace bandage
- strong cord for emergency repair; and
- bus schedule

provide an indication of the area to search. However these permits are not monitored in a manner that would trigger a search soon after you are supposed to return. Therefore it is essential to tell reliable people when you will be back and then check in with them immediately upon your return. Failure to check in immediately with them may cause a needless and expensive search to be started.

Emergency help

Do not count on using a cell phone to get help when hiking in most of the area covered in this book. In Denali National Park, your best chance to get help in an emergency is for a member of your party to get to the road. There will be no more than 10 backpackers in each of the back-country units so it is unlikely that another party will discover you. All buses on the park road have radios. Rangers and park maintenance personnel can also get help. Other private vehicles on the road can also help contact a ranger.

If you cannot make it to the road, your best chance of getting help is signaling an airplane or helicopter. I recommend carrying signaling devices that can be seen from the air. These include mirrors, flares and smoke. I also count on my camera flash as a possible signaling device. REI and other outdoor and marine suppliers sell these signaling devices.

Photo V. **Crossing a branch of the East Fork River on Hikes 18 and 21.**

National Park Service to get help if you do not return as planned. Such a precaution is essential when hiking alone and some of your route is out of sight of the road. If you leave a trip plan, then do not deviate from the plan and be sure to check in immediately after returning. Instruct your contact to call the Denali National Park Headquarters at 1-907-683-2294 if you do not check in within a reasonable amount of time after you plan to return.

A backcountry camping permit identifies the general areas where you plan to hike and camp. If you are overdue, this information will

Photo W. **View of Mount McKinley while hiking near the park road between Eielson and Wonder Lake.**

Chapter 4

Denali National Park Hike Descriptions

Hiking times and difficulty ratings

Knowing something about my physical condition and age will help you evaluate the round-trip hiking times and difficulty ratings I have assigned. I researched most of these hike when I was 48 to 57 years old. I am not a jogger and do not work out in a gym. I do stay in reasonable shape by at least walking hard for 15 miles weekly, bicycling 45 miles a week in the summer, cross-country skiing several hours eight-to 15 times a winter, and backpacking or day hiking six to 10 times a year (more when researching this book).

Hiking times: The hiking times and distances are for the round trip. Time includes brief stops for some quick photographs, lunch, and rests. I did not include time for stops longer than 15 minutes for photography or wildlife observation. People with a primary objective of speed and who are in great shape will be able to do these hikes faster.

Hiking difficulty: Hiking difficulty ratings are subjective. Hike descriptions identify the features that contributed to the ratings. An *easy* rating means most of the footing is good, little bushwhacking in vegetation above knee level is required, and stream crossings do not require wading. A hike is rated *moderate* if conditions encountered include some combination of bushwhacking through waist-high tundra, steep grades, stream crossings which require wading, or difficult walking due to scree. A *difficult* hike will include some combination of steep and rocky terrain, dense and high vegetation or a major river to cross where water is likely to be more than knee deep.

Route-finding difficulty: An *easy* rating means the route is clearly visible from the road or it would be nearly impossible to miss the route. A *moderate* rating indicates a need to find a faint game or human trail, to select the best ridge to ascend or descend, or to negotiate a route around or through rocky terrain or through longer stretches of brushy tundra or spruce forest. Some map reading skills may be needed on a moderate rated hike. Good skills in using a map and compass or Global Positioning System

41

Photo X. **Emily hiking toward Primrose Ridge near mile 17 (Hike 7).**

(GPS) receiver are required to select the appropriate pass or ridges for *difficult* routes. Experience finding the best paths through rocky or broken terrain is needed on *difficult* routes.

GPS trailhead coordinates: A GPS receiver is not required to find the hike starting points. Since the GPS has become more common, I provide the latitude and longitude coordinates for many of the hike starting points, particularly those that are not near an easily identified place. Coordinates are in degrees and minutes and referenced to the 1927 North American Datum (NAD 27) used on the U.S.G.S. maps. Be sure to set your GPS to this datum or your reading may be up to 200 meters off.

IMPORTANT SAFETY NOTE:

While the reference maps used in the hiking descriptions are taken from USGS contour maps, do not rely soley on them for navigation!

Obtain original, full color maps from the sources listed in Appendix A before starting your trip!

Selecting a hike

Dayhikes and backpacks: This book will help you plan dayhikes or backpacking trips to suit your ability, interest and time. Many of the dayhike routes can also be extended into a backpacking trip as noted in the "variations" section of hike descriptions. The beginning point of most dayhikes also offers opportunities for much shorter strolls away from the road for a picnic or to experience the tundra. Another option is to simply walk along the river gravel bars.

Either Don Croner or I have done all the hikes in this book. I researched the dayhikes and some backpacks. Don Croner researched some of the backpacking routes.

Wildlife closure areas: Some areas of the park are permanently closed to hiking or have been closed for many years. Other areas are closed temporarily to protect wildlife activity such as nests and dens or to keep people away from a fresh kill that will attract bears. Temporary closures are usually marked with white cardboard signs along the road or in the area. In addition most bus drivers know where the current closed areas are and will remind you to stay out of the closed areas if you get off the bus near one.

Some hikes in this book follow the boundary of, or open corridors through, permanent closure areas. Other hikes may be affected by temporary closures. Closure areas are mainly marked with signs along the road so map reading skills are required to avoid straying into closed areas once you leave the road.

Since closure conditions can

Photo Y. **Hoary marmot on Primrose Ridge (Hike 7).**

change from year-to-year and day-to-day, I recommend you check your plans with the backcountry ranger desk before deciding where you will hike. The backcountry ranger desk is located in the Wilderness Access Center. There is a large map displaying the closure areas at the backcountry ranger desk and smaller maps are available to take with you. You may also wish to write Park Headquarters for a copy of this map to help plan some alternative hikes before you arrive.

TIP: You can quickly compare key characteristics of all hikes in this book by using the tables on pages 253-255.

Denali National Park Entrance Area Hikes

There is a network of footpaths in the park entrance area. These trails offer good routes between the major visitor attractions and park facilities as well as opportunities to see wildlife such as moose, snowshoe hares, squirrels and, in the evening if you are lucky, a lynx.

My favorites are the Horseshoe Lake and Mt. Healy Overlook trails. The Horseshoe Lake trail leads to a lake where you are likely to see beavers and moose. The Mt. Healy Overlook trail begins with a walk through the forest and climbs to an overlook with a view of the entire park entrance area.

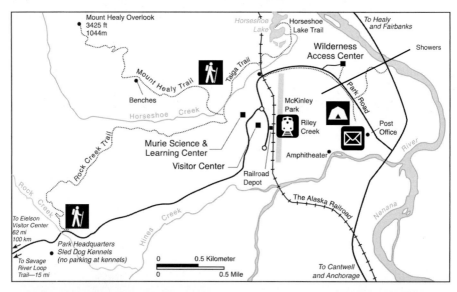

1

Horseshoe Lake

Location: Denali Park Entrance
Hike Length: 1.5 miles (2.4 km)
Hiking Time: 2 hours
Elevation Gain: 200 feet
Hiking Difficulty: Easy
Route Finding Difficulty: Easy
USGS Map: Healy (C-4)

(facing page) Photo 1A.
Beaver

(above) Photo 1B.
Moose

Highlights

I like this hike in the late evening when there is the best chance of seeing beavers and moose at the lake. The slight elevation change provides an opportunity to stretch my legs and get some air in my lungs after a long day of travel to reach the park.

Route description

The trailhead is located at about mile 0.9 on the park road where it crosses the Alaska Railroad tracks. There is a small parking lot at the trailhead. The Roadside Trail provides access from the Visitor Center and Riley Creek Campground.

Follow the trail down to the lake. The trail is flat for a short distance to a point that overlooks the lake. From this point the trail descends steeply to the lake so be sure to wear shoes with good traction. Return along the same route.

2

Mount Healy Overlook Trail

Location: Denali Park Entrance
Hike Length: Overlook 4 miles (6.4 km)
Hiking Time: 3 to 4 hours
Elevation Gain: 1,700 feet
Hiking Difficulty: Moderate
Route Finding Difficulty: Easy
USGS Map: Healy (C-4)

Highlights

The hike to Mount Healy above the park entrance provides a good introduction to the Denali region. It was one of my first hikes when I worked at the park hotel in 1967. The trail climbs through a wide variety of vegetation representative of the area, from boreal forest across the timberline to alpine tundra. After a number of switchbacks, the trail reaches the rocky overlook with a sweeping view of the Alaska Range from Mount Deborah (12,339') 60 miles to the east to Mount McKinley (20,320') 90 miles to the west. In the foreground, about 8 miles to the southeast, is Mount Fellows (4,212'), named after Dr. Robert Fellows, a scientist killed in 1949 while doing geological research in the park. Directly to the south of Mount Fellows, the Yanert Fork River enters the Nenana River from the east. From the overlook, the hotel area is visible across the river and further north, the entrance to the Nenana Gorge.

Looking due south to the first ridge across the road and to the right of Riley Creek, a large boulder can been seen at about the 3,400-foot level. This granite boulder was carried from its source near the crest of the Alaska Range by the Browne glacial advance and dropped at its current location when the ice receded, indicating that the glacier had reached to at least this level. Such rocks are known as glacial erratics and are important to geologists who attempt to trace the paths of ancient glaciers.

Route description

The trailhead is located at about mile 0.9 on the park road where it crosses the Alaska Railroad tracks. There is a small parking lot at the trailhead. The Roadside Trail provides access from the Visitor Center and Riley Creek Campground.

It is about two miles to the overlook but after about one mile there is a scenic viewpoint.

Cautions

Good footgear and stamina are required. Take a windbreaker and water. In the trees near the hotel watch for cow moose and calves and do not approach them. I consider a cow moose with a calf more dangerous than a bear.

Vegetation and Animals Along Mount Healy Overlook Trail

The first of the vegetation zones passed through is a forest of spruce and aspen with an understory of willows. The trail is lined with shrubs and flowers typical of the boreal forest: prickly rose, bluebells, spiraea, Labrador tea, fireweed, northern shooting stars, twin flowers and at least two poisonous plants, death camas and monkshood.

Lynx, which feed on snowshoe rabbits, may be present in the area but are rarely observed. Birds common to the boreal forest include the spruce grouse, Bohemian waxwings, three-toed woodpeckers, boreal chickadees, the nocturnal great-horned owl and gray-cheeked, hermit, varied and Swainson's thrushes.

After the spruce aspen forest is a transition zone of grassy tundra interspersed with clumps of willows and alders where moose are often seen feeding. Above this is a thin belt of low bush tundra dominated by dwarf birch and willows. Near this zone, the trail goes by an outcropping of schist, a metamorphic rock shot through with quartz veins and shiny little flakes of mica. Pikas *(photo 2)*, small animals that resemble a cross between a rabbit and a mouse, are often seen in these rocky outcroppings. Listen for their call, a single "yank" sound. Next is alpine tundra with mats of mountain avens, dwarf willows, bearberry, blueberry, and crowberry, sprinkled with northern anemones, alpine arnicas, and various louseworts and saxifrages.

In the rocks along the overlook ridge only the heartiest species of alpine plants are found: purple mountain saxifrage, golden saxifrage, arctic poppy, dwarf rock jasmine, dwarf hawk's beard, and dwarf arctic butterweed.

– Don Croner

Photo 2. **Pika.**

3

Triple Lakes

Location: Parks Highway mile 231
Hike Length: 5 miles (8 km)
Hiking Time: 4 hours
Elevation Gain: 600 feet
Hiking Difficulty: Easy
Route Finding Difficulty: Easy
Backcountry Permit Area: 1
USGS Map: Healy C-4

Highlights

This route is a good day hike or backpack. It provides an opportunity to experience hiking in an environment different than the open tundra found on most hikes further in the park. Moose are occasionally seen in the area. Beavers can be seen in some of the lakes. Look for denizens of lakes and ponds like the lesser yellowlegs and the northern phalarope, and numerous species of ducks, including mallards, oldsquaw, and bufflehead. Triple Lakes were one of my favorite quick backpacks when I worked at the park hotel. *(photo 3A)*

Route description

The trailhead is at the south entrance to Denali National Park at the north end of the Nenana River Bridge at mile 231.3 on the George Parks Highway. There is a turnout available for parking. In 2009 there was no shuttle bus to this trailhead from the Park entrance. Hopefully there will be a shuttle bus in future summers.

Hiking to the end of the third lake is about a 5 mile round trip. The well-established trail is easy to follow through the forest and along the lakes. A few camping spots are available near each lake.

About halfway along the third lake, look for a faint, old social trail that leads up to the ridge. This ridge gives a good view of the Triple Lakes Valleys. *(photos 3B & 3C)* The old trail to Triple Lakes came from the north along this ridge. In the summer of 2004, I met some people who were doing a traverse along the old route that begins at the southern end of the railroad bridge over Riley Creek. The last time I tried the northern route, I found the trail very wet at the north end on the climb out of the Riley Creek valley. *(photo 3C)*

Variation: Try hiking the old route to Triple Lakes. The north trailhead is located south of the railroad trestle and on the west side of the tracks just before the tracks cut through a high bank of gravel. The trail descends to the forest area along Riley Creek and continues a short distance along the creek. As the trail climbs out of the valley, the vegetation becomes more open and often crosses wet tundra. Views of the Nenana River valley are available as the trail climbs. Follow the ridgeline until the first lake is visible and the trail drops down to the lake.

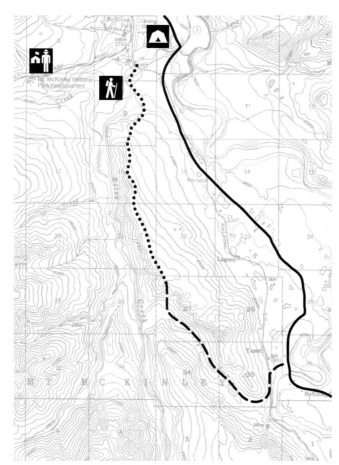

Hike 3
Contour interval 100 feet.
Grid = 1 mile.

Small dots represent the old trail from the north. See text.

In 1995, the north end of this trail had long sections of wet areas along the route toward the ridgeline and was beginning to be overgrown after it left the forest along Riley Creek. While we could easily find the route, we decided not to continue after traveling about 1 mile from Riley Creek. If you plan to do more than explore the area along Riley Creek, ask the rangers about the current trail conditions before hiking this end of the route.

There are two ways to reach the north end of this route. Wade Riley Creek or walk in the forest parallel to the railroad tracks from the south where the Parks Highway crosses under the tracks (mile 236.7) south of the Riley Creek highway bridge. Do not use the railroad bridge as a route to the trail from Riley Creek Campground. The bridge has clearly posted "no trespassing" signs.

Cautions

Make some noise as you travel through the forest. Exercise caution if crossing the railroad tracks on the variation of this hike.

(top) Photo 3A. **View of Triple Lakes valley from ridge above the northernmost lake.**

(above) Photo 3B. **Old trail from the northernmost lake to rideline and old route to Triple Lakes. See Variations.**

(right) Photo 3C. **Alaska cotton, a sure sign of wet hiking.**

Early Use and Exploration of Park Headquarters Area

The Yanert Fork is named after Sergeant William Yanert, U.S. Army, who led a reconnaissance party to near here in 1898. Yanert made the first recorded crossing of Broad Pass, the gap through the Alaska Range followed by the George Parks Highway (named after pioneer Alaskan George Parks) and the Alaska Railroad. According to some accounts, Yanert was the first white man to set foot in what is now Denali National Park. Indians had long before used Broad Pass to travel between the Cook Inlet Region and the Interior, and Yanert used their trails whenever possible. The Yanert party was an offshoot of a larger survey party led by George H. Eldridge and Robert Muldrow that determined for the first time the true position and altitude of Mt. McKinley.

The first white man to ascend the Nenana River from the north was probably prospector, explorer and trader Arthur Harper. In 1875 Harper floated from the headwaters of the Tanana to the Yukon, the first white man to do so, and in 1878 he ascended the Tanana to near the present site of Fairbanks. During one of these journeys he made a side trip up the Nenana; exactly how far is not known. Harper is credited with discovering gold in the Yukon and Tanana drainages, thus setting off any number of gold rushes into the Interior.

Harper is also believed to be the first white man to describe Mt. McKinley from the north. In a letter to F.W. Nelson of the U.S. Biological Survey, Harper reported "having seen a giant ice mountain off to the south which was plainly visible from the Tanana…one of the most

Photo 3D. **Tours buses in front of the old Mout McKinley Park Hotel. Photo courtesy National Park Service.**

remarkable things they had seen on the trip." Harper married an Athapascan named Jennie Albert from Nulato, and on their honeymoon they poled a boat 1,050 miles up the Yukon to Ft. Selkirk in Canada. The Harpers had eight children. The youngest of them, Walter, would accompany the 1913 Hudson Stuck mountain-climbing expedition and become the first man to set foot on the true summit of Mt. McKinley.

On either side of the Nenana River, just above the gorge, archaeologists have located two ancient hunting camps of the Tanana Athapascans, the Native people who inhabited this area before the arrival of Europeans. The sites were used as hunting camps during late summer and fall for several hundred years and perhaps much longer before these Indians first came into contact with white men. The camps were ideally located to observe and intercept animals moving through the Nenana valley. Remains of sheep, caribou, black bear (now very seldom seen in this area), hoary marmots and ground squirrels have been found, along with fire pits for cooking and heating, boiling pits for rendering fat, and butchering and meat processing areas. These In-Indians apparently used snares, spears, and bows and arrows to hunt. Weapon points made of raw copper and chalcedony available only south of the Alaska Range and obsidian believed to be from the valley of the Koyukuk River hundreds of miles to the north in the Brooks Range indicate widespread travel and trading among native peoples prior the arrival of white men.

Explorer William H. Dall, who officially named the Alaska Range, although he only saw it from the mouth of the Tanana River far to the north, and incidentally, for whom the Dall sheep is named, encountered a band of Tanana Athapascans who may have never seen a white man before while traveling up the Yukon in 1866 and left us this account: "Of their mode of living nothing is known, except that they obtain their subsistence principally by hunting deer [caribou]…their dress consisted of pointed parkas which were ornamented with beads of quill and smeared with red ochre. All the men wore dentalium nose-ornaments. The hair was allowed to grow to full length, parted in the middle, and each lock smeared with a mixture of grease and ochre, then gathered behind the head by a fillet of dentalium shells, with the whole head finally powdered with fine cut swan's down which adhered to the hair." The descendants of these people still live in the region, scattered at various places along the Parks Highway, including the towns of Cantwell and Nenana, and in more remote villages.

– Don Croner

4

Savage River Viewpoint

Location: Mile 12.8
Savage River Campground
Time on bus (one way): 30 minutes
Hike Length: 7 miles (11.2 km)
Hiking Time: 8 hours
Elevation Gain: 1,600 feet (486 m)
Hiking Difficulty: Moderate plus
Route Finding Difficulty: Moderate
Backcountry Permit Area: 4
U.S.G.S. Map: Healy (C-5)

Highlights

I did this hike to get a different view of the Savage River and Jenny Creek drainages. To my delight, Mount McKinley was also visible while walking across the low tundra ridge to reach the foot of the mountains. We surprised a couple of caribou along the way. I enjoyed threading my way through the fairytale environment in the spruce forest at the base of the mountains. Wildflowers line the upper part of the drainage that the return route follows down from the viewpoint. In mid-August, I enjoyed blueberries and low-bush cranberries when I paused to catch my breath on the climb. *(photo 4A)*

This hike provides practice at finding routes to avoid or to get through areas of waist-high brush. The return route provides practice finding game trails through the brush in river drainages.

Route description

See map on page 55.

Travel to the Savage River campground by car or on the Savage Shuttle Bus. This hike begins at the south side of campground where there is a closed road. Follow this closed road to the point where Jenny Creek flows into Savage River. Find the place where the tundra bluff along the south side of Jenny Creek intersects with the tundra bluff along the east side of the Savage River plane. (Note: You will be returning along a game trail at the base of the bluff bordering the Savage River riverbed.)

Walk upstream along Jenny Creek and find a place to cross. Before crossing the creek, study the low ridge that runs south toward the mountains and determine the best (e.g. least brushy) way to reach the ridgeline. Cross the creek. While I crossed the creek without getting water in my boots, wading may be necessary if the creek is higher. *(photo 4B)*

After crossing the creek, walk upstream at the base of the bluff. Then climb the bluff (about 10 feet high) at the spot that you selected to begin walking through the tundra to reach the low ridge. Once on the tundra ridge, it is easy to find good walking through predominately knee-high tundra while avoiding most of the higher brush. Follow the ridgeline until you reach the willows that border the spruce forest. Look for the easiest way to get through the willows and into the forest where walking is easier. Before entering the forest, study the mountains and determine where you want to exit the forest. Select a point on the mountain to serve as a landmark as you go through the forest. (My goal was to exit the forest to the west of the drainage that flows from the mountains. My landmark was a spot on the ridge above the west side of the drainage.)

Once through the spruce forest, select your route up the ridge. While this climb is steep, footing is good in the tundra. At times, I chose to zigzag up the slope and varied my route to climb the least steep areas.

From the top, study the return route and determine where you plan to hike to get through the narrowest part of the spruce forest (much easier than the forest crossing above). Your goal is to get to the low bluff that separates the broad Savage River floodplain from the adjacent tundra.

The best way to spot this bluff line is to look for the difference in vegetation. The bluff is about 1/2-mile (.8 km) or more from the water. At the base of this bluff, I found a game trail leading all the way back to Jenny Creek. (Note: Whenever I am faced with travel along a brushy river, I always look for, and usually find, a game trail at the base of the tundra bluff next to the riverbed. See also *Trailless Hiking Pointers* in Chapter 3.)

Walk to the saddle south of the high point and descend into the drainage. In a dry August, water was still available in this stream. Walk along the west side until the canyon begins to open. Select a route west around the toe of the slope to maintain your elevation above the thicker brush. Walk until you reach a low ridge running northwest toward the thinnest part of the spruce forest. Descend this ridge and walk along the south border of the spruce forest until you reach the spot where you plan to head north through the forest.

Once through the forest continue walking north without going any closer to the water until you can see the tundra bluff.

(Note: if after you exit the spruce forest you find yourself in tundra like on the ridge at the beginning of this hike, you may need to walk west to find the bluff.)

Walk along the base of the bluff and look for a game trail. Even if you do not find a game trail, walking at or near the base of the bluff is still easier than walking closer to the river. Follow the bluff north to Jenny Creek.

Variations: Rather than do a loop, follow the bluff (return) route both ways. This route is less brushy and the spruce forest is thinner. If you do not want to climb to the viewpoint, walk along the tundra ridge at the start of this loop until you reach the spruce forest. Then walk west toward Savage River until you hit the tundra bluff return route.

Cautions

Be ready to sing or talk a lot along most of this route because brush can easily hide a bear.

(upper left) Photo 4A.
Diny nearing the summit of Hike 4. The light gravel area at right center is the junction of Jenny Creek with Savage River where this hike starts.

(left) Photo 4B.
Crossing Jenny Creek.

(upper right) Photo 5A.
Willow ptarmigan.

5

Savage Drainage Stroll

Location: Mile 14.8
Time on bus (one way): 45 minutes
Hike Length: 3 miles (4.8 km)
Hiking Time: 3 hours
Elevation Gain: 100 feet
Hiking Difficulty: Easy or moderate
Route Finding Difficulty: Easy
Backcountry Permit Area: 4
U.S.G.S. Map: Healy (C-5)

Highlights

This is a great hike to see what it is like to hike in Denali without following a developed trail like the one downstream from the Savage River Bridge (Hike 6). Ptarmigan are usually found in the brush along this route and caribou frequent the area. I did this hike to photograph caribou that were resting near the small ridge in the middle of the valley. Fall colors are great along this route. The small ridge at the end of this hike is a great place to picnic or to photograph the Savage River drainage. *(photos 5A and 5B)*

The stream crossing is easy but requires wading water that will usually go over your boot tops. The length and the moderate difficulty rating noted above are for the route shown on the map. If you do not want to cross the creek, just walk upstream as far as you like.

Route description

Travel to the Savage River Bridge by car or on the Savage Shuttle Bus. Walk to the west side of the bridge. The route travels along the edge of smaller stream that joins the Savage River just upstream of the bridge. Before descending to the streambed, look for bears in the area. Also ask the ranger at the gate if there have been any bears in the area that day.

Descend to the streambed level and look for the best route through knee-high brush along the creek. Walk upstream until you reach a point across from the small ridge to the east. Look for the best place to cross the clear creek; the wider spots will be shallower. Cross the creek and head through the knee-high brush to the ridge. Once on the ridge, walk to the south side at the top for great view and picnic spot. Return along the same route.

Variations: To sample hiking and develop your route finding in the higher tundra brush, walk farther upstream along the western-most branch of the stream and then return to the road across the tundra.

Cautions

If you want to keep your boots dry, bring other shoes to cross the creek.

Photo 5B. **View of Savage River Valley. The turnaround point for Hike 5 is the low ridge at the mid-right center beyond the main river. A great place for a picnic.**

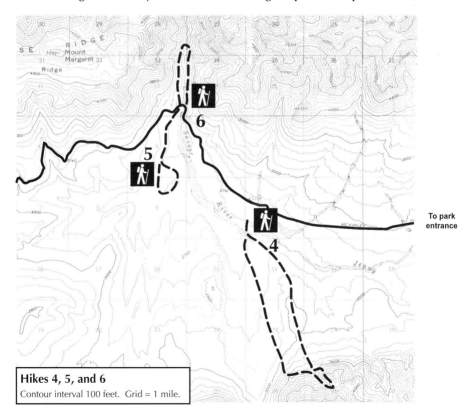

To park entrance

Hikes 4, 5, and 6
Contour interval 100 feet. Grid = 1 mile.

Savage River Canyon Loop

Location: Mile 14.8
Time on bus (one way): 45 minutes
Hike Length: 2 miles (3.2 km)
Hiking Time: 1.5 hours
Elevation Gain: 50 feet
Hiking Difficulty: Easy
Route Finding Difficulty: Easy
Backcountry Permit Areas: 25 & 26
USGS Maps: Healy (C-5), (D-5)

Highlights

This recently-constructed trail in the Savage River Canyon is easy walking for most people. Dall sheep are often seen high on Primrose Ridge to the west. Some lucky hikers see sheep descend for a drink or to cross the river. I hike this trail to look for ptarmigan in the brush along the river and hoary marmots and collared pikas in the rocks along the trail. At the northern end of this loop, hikers use an undeveloped route on the western side of the river to hike through the canyon. *(photos 6A, 6B)*

Route description

See map on page 55.
Travel to the Savage River Bridge by car or on the Savage Shuttle Bus. The trail begins at the northern end of the parking lot. *(photo 6C)* Follow the trail for about a mile until it reaches a bridge across Savage River. Cross the bridge and return on the trail along the western bank of the river. Along the return, there are some side trails to the river and benches to rest. Look for ptarmigan in the willows near the river. The trail ends at the bridge.

Variations: Continue along the western side of the canyon on the undeveloped trail to explore the canyon or go backpacking. Near the north end of the canyon, the undeveloped trail gets harder to follow in the brush but it is not essential to find the path to get through the canyon.

Cautions

Visibility is good on the developed hiking loop. Enjoy!

Photo 6A. **Collared pika in the rocks at the beginning of the Savage Canyon loop trail.**

Photo 6B. **Dall sheep jumping the river in Savage Canyon.**

Photo 6C. **Savage Canyon loop trail.**

Glaciation of the East Side of the Park

The valleys of the Yanert Fork, the Nenana, and Riley Creek, to the right of the Nenana, have been scoured and gouged by glaciers that have advanced at least seven times during the last five million years. The two earliest of these advances, the so-called Nenana Gravel and Teklanika River glaciations, occurred from two-to-five million years ago when the Outside Range, of which Mt. Healy is a part, had not been uplifted to its present height and the Nenana canyon had not yet been formed.

These glaciations have left only scattered and indistinct traces. By the time of the Browne glaciation, 1.5 to two million years ago, the Outside Range had been uplifted to near its present configuration, and the Nenana River, eroding a path through the mountains faster than they were rising, had created the incision that would become the modern-day Nenana Gorge. During the Browne glaciation, huge glaciers swept down the valleys of the Yanert Fork, the Nenana, and Riley Creek, through the Nenana canyon, and past the present site of the town of Healy to the old settlement of Browne, 27 miles north of the park entrance. A lobe of the Browne glacier also may have advanced westward along the path of the road into the valley of the Savage River.

During the last glacial episode, the Riley Creek glaciation, which ended about 10,000 years ago, ice advanced down the valleys of the Yanert Fork and the Nenana almost as far as the park hotel. The terminal moraine—rocks and gravel bulldozed into piles and ridges by the advancing snout of a glacier—of the Riley Creek glaciation can easily be seen where the railroad bed cuts through it directly south of the Riley Creek trestle.

The high, light-colored bluffs on the far bank of the Nenana River directly to the east are glacial outwash from the Riley Creek glaciation which the Nenana has since cut through. Large glaciers still exist at the headwaters of the Yanert Fork and the Nenana, but substantial as they may be, they are but remnants of the huge ice flows that once swept through this area.

—Don Croner

7

Primrose Ridge & Mount Margaret

Location: Mile 16.5
GPS: N63° 43.9' W149° 20.1'
Time on bus (one way): 45 minutes
Hike Length: 7 miles (11.2 km)
Hiking Time: 6.5 hours
Elevation Gain: 1,900 feet
Hiking Difficulty: Easy
Route Finding Difficulty: Easy
Backcountry Permit Area: 26
USGS Maps: Healy (C-5), (D-5)

Highlights

As we started this hike, Mount McKinley was visible so I knew it would be a good day! We paused frequently to enjoy blueberries (early August). The ridge below the summit of Mount Margaret is a long, wide plateau with easy hiking. Judging from the number of flowers still present in August, the flowers must be spectacular in the peak season (late June to mid-July). From the top, we could see the Healy area plus the north and south Savage and Sanctuary River valleys.

Marmots were the first animals to greet us. While most marmots disappeared before I could photograph them with my telephoto lens, one big marmot ran straight at us. He stopped at the foot of my tripod, too close to photograph with my telephoto lens. *(photo Y, page 43)* We spent a few hours watching Dall sheep rams near the Savage River end of Primrose Ridge. On the way down, we shared the ridge with two caribou bulls that at times stopped our progress by using our path.

Route description

Take the Savage River Shuttle bus or drive to the parking lot at the Savage River Bridge. Walk west on the road about 1.8 miles (2.5 km). It took me about 40 minutes walking at a brisk pace. Watch for a ridgeline that comes down to the road and terminates in two rock outcrops near the road. *(photo 7A)* Climb onto the ridgeline near the rock outcrops and hike up the ridge following the easiest walking. When possible, please walk on the rocky surface along the ridge to minimize impact on the vegetation. Even in September, I found a small stream running near where the ridgeline reaches the broad plane of Primrose Ridge. Be sure to note some landmarks so you can retrace your route down.

Once you are on Primrose Ridge, head northwest toward the rock outcrop that is the summit of Mount Margaret. Alternatively, head east toward the rocky outcrop that is above Savage River. Retrace your steps to return to the road.

If you get confused about the location of the route down, walk to the edge of the Primrose ridge until you see the road, turnout loop with toilets and this route. The ridge directly above the turnout loop is a good alternative to descend or ascend. Do not drop off Primrose ridge in the drainage west of the turnout loop as the bushwhacking will be rough.

Variations: The main variations on this hike are different routes to reach or descend from the summit ridge. An alternate route is to take the ridge above the turnout at mile 17 shown as "B" on the hike map. Thread your way through a short stretch of alders across the road from the western end of the turnout and follow the ridge to the top. You can also detour around most of the alders by leaving the road east of the turnout loop. *(photo X, page 42)*

Cautions

At the beginning of these hikes, make a lot of noise and watch for bears in the brush near the road. Do not try to descend from the eastern end of Primrose Ridge directly above the Savage River unless you can clearly see a route to avoid cliffs and loose rock. In early September, water was available in small meadow ponds on top. This water should be purified or filtered before drinking. To be safe, bring plenty of water so you can spend the day enjoying this ridge. It is often windy and there is little shelter so bring a warm jacket and windbreaker.

Photo 7A. **A ridge that provides access to the top of Primrose Ridge and Mount Margaret.**

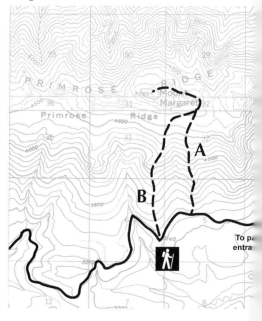

Hike 7
Contour interval 100 feet. Grid = 1 mile.

Dall Sheep

Bands of Dall sheep rams feed on the vegetated slopes above the valley floors near the headwaters of Sanctuary and Teklanika rivers. After spending the winter on the Outside Range north of the park road where snowfall is lighter and winds expose vegetation on the ridges, many sheep, especially rams, move south for the summer to the headwaters of streams flowing out of the Alaska Range.

Toward the end of May, sheep are sometimes seen crossing the two-to-three mile expanse of rolling tundra between Primrose Ridge and the foothills of the Alaska Range. Since they are vulnerable to predators when they leave their rocky redoubts, sheep cross the open tundra as quickly as possible. In June of 1940, naturalist Adolph Murie saw a band of 64 sheep cross the tundra from Sanctuary canyon to Double Mountain, between the Teklanika and Sanctuary rivers. He noted that when they finally reached Double Mountain, they "galloped up the slope in high spirits, seemingly relieved to have made the crossing."

During the summer, rams band up by themselves in hierarchical groups and ignore ewes and lambs. Most rams return to the Outside (north) Range in August and September. During the mating season in November and December, the fraternal relationships enjoyed by the rams over the summer break down and individuals engage in head-bashing conflicts to see which will service the ewes.

—Don Croner

Photo 7B. **Dall sheep rams enjoying the view from Primrose Ridge.**

8

Sanctuary to Savage River

Location: Sanctuary River Bridge
Time on bus (one way): 1 hour
Hike Length: 15 miles (24 km)
Hiking Time: 3 days
Elevation Gain: 1,100 feet
Hiking Difficulty: Easy to Moderate
Route Finding Difficulty: Easy
Backcountry Permit Areas: 4, 5
USGS Map: Healy (C-5)

Highlights

This backpack is a good introduction to trailless hiking in Denali. It offers relatively easy hiking along riverbeds on most of the trip. The crossing between two river drainages provides the experience of cross-country hiking in a variety of conditions, from waist-high brush to finding a route across short, wet areas. Some map reading skill is required to locate where to cross between the two drainages and to avoid any wildlife closure area.

Although I did this hike on an extended Memorial Day weekend more than 15 years ago, some events remain fresh in my mind. One was crossing the Sanctuary River sooner than planned in order to get past a bear safely. We also saw ptarmigan and caribou. As we returned along the eastern side of the Savage River, we found faint evidence of a route that apparently was used by wagons, or perhaps early motor vehicles, to take visitors into the Savage River area. Most of all I remember the pleasure of being out there with a couple of close friends after a long winter.

Route description

Get off the bus at the Sanctuary Campground. You can chose to walk along the east or west side of the Sanctuary River. I have done both.

To walk on the west side, cross the Sanctuary River Bridge. Walk along the road a short distance until you find an easy place to reach the riverbed. Follow the edge of the riverbed south. When the river cuts against the bank, there is usually a game trail on the bank through the forest to get around this area. The forested area continues for about 3 miles. After the forested area, higher cut banks are encountered. If the water is not high, it may be possible to walk along the edge of the river at the bottom of the cut bank. *(photo 8C)* Otherwise you will need to climb onto the top of the bank and bushwhack through waist high tundra until you can walk in the riverbed again. *(photos T and U)*

To travel along the east side of the river, walk through the campground and look for a social trail that heads south through the forest along the riverbank. This trail leads to the riverbed at the south edge of the forest. At this point select the easiest walking through the riverbed vegetation. I usually can thread my way through the vegetation following old channels and gravel bars that have not overgrown.

Photo 8A. **Bull caribou**

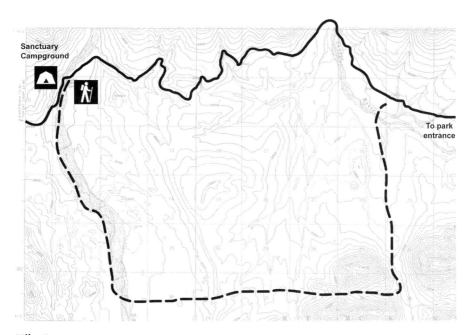

Hike 8
Contour interval 100 feet. Grid = 1 mile.

Photo 8B. **Upper Sanctuary River after several days of rain.** Photo by D. B. Geeseman.

Photo 8C. **Hiking along a high bank on the Sanctuary River.**

On either side of the river when vegetation is too thick in the riverbed, I head for the bank that separates the riverbed from the tundra. Often there are game trails or the vegetation is sparser at the base of the tundra bluff. When a bend in the river is next to a high bank, there is usually a game trail along the top of the bank until it is again possible to walk in the riverbed.

When the water is low enough to easily cross the river braids, I often cross back and forth to find the easiest walking in the riverbed. I find it quicker to cross the river to get around a cut bank than to bushwhack for extended distances in waist-high tundra on top of the bank. I do not mind hiking in wet boots, particularly on sunny days. *(photo 8D)*

When you reach the foothills of the ridges that separate the Sanctuary and Savage rivers, head east to reach the Savage River. The brush is mostly thigh-high or less. Wet areas and short stretches of taller brush are found when crossing the small drainages between these two rivers. Head for the low saddle south of hill 4232 that leads to the Savage River.

Return to the road by following the Savage River until you reach the Savage River Campground. Near the campground, you will see a route from the riverbank to the campground that has been used by campers and vehicles. You can also continue up the drainage to the east of the campground until you reach the road.

Variations: Take extra days to allow for dayhikes up either the Savage or Sanctuary rivers, or both! We spent our extra day hiking up the Savage River.

Cautions

Watch for bears and make noise, particularly while walking in the riverbed vegetation or near the tundra bank where you cannot see above the riverbank.

Sanctuary and Savage River crossings are required. In medium water, I crossed the Sanctuary river braids many times in spots where the water was less than calf-deep and occasionally knee-deep. However, friends hiked this river in flood stage and found it difficult to find a dry place to walk anywhere in the riverbed. *(photo 8B)* Crossing the river would be more difficult in high water conditions.

Some of the area between the Sanctuary and Savage rivers may be closed to hiking. The crossing route described above was south of the closed area in 2004. Check with the rangers to make sure the closure area has not been extended south far enough to include this route.

Photo 8D. **Crossing a Sanctuary River channel.**

9

Exploring the Teklanika Campground Area

Location: Teklanika Campground
Time on bus (one way): 1.5 hours
Hike Length: 1/2 to 4 miles (.8 to 6.4 km)
Hiking Time: 1 to 4 hours
Elevation Gain: little
Hiking Difficulty: Easy
Route Finding Difficulty: Easy
Backcountry Permit Areas: 6, 29
USGS Map: Healy (C-6)

Highlights

Opportunities for dayhikes or short evening strolls are plentiful near Teklanika Campground. Walking either direction along the river provides opportunities to look for tracks and to see bears and other smaller wildlife such as foxes or ptarmigan families in the brush along the riverbanks or snowshoe hares in the spruce forest. After a long day on the bus it feels good to walk while along the river listening to the water and watching the sunset *(photo 9C)*.

Photo 9A. **Teklanika River between the campground and bridge (located where the river narrows at top left).**

Ask the campground host for Ask Ask the campground host for hiking ideas in addition to the following.

Routes

One of my favorites is to get off the bus at the Teklanika Bridge and follow the faint social trail along the east bluff back to camp. It is about two miles *(photo 9A)*. Keep a watch for bears.

A short stroll downstream from the campground leads to a cliff jutting into the riverbed; a good place to enjoy the sunset and watch for wildlife along the gravel bars in both directions.

Friends have walked along the river downstream to the canyon below Mount Wright. They returned by walking across the tundra back to the road and then to the campground. Along the way they saw grizzlies. If you do this hike, watch to see if traffic is stopping along the road. Traffic stopping is a good indicator that a bear or other animals are in the area.

Across the road from the campground, you have an opportunity

Photo 9B. **View of the Teklanika Campground and River from a small hill across the road.**

to explore the taiga forest. Walking among the trees is easy. Go inland as far as you want to go and then select a route south parallel to the road. Return to the road when you are ready. I had a delightful time in this forest while trying to find an owl that was hooting. It is a good idea to take a compass with you since the trees block views of landmarks and make it hard to hear where the road is located.

A small ridge across the road provides a good view of the campground and the Teklanika River valley. *(photo 9B)* Walk along the road toward the park entrance until you see a small ridge on your right. Watch for a clearing where you can see the ridge and then look for a social trail through the brush that leads to the ridge. This ridge is less than 1/4-mile from the road. Once on the ridge you can walk east along the ridge to explore. I have hiked to the hills across the tundra from the end of the ridge.

Old roadbeds leading from the campground are easy walking and provide opportunities to see snowshoe hares or just for an evening stroll. My favorite starts near the campground host's site and parallels the park road. When this path becomes too faint to follow, you can go through the forest toward the road or head in the opposite direction to the river for your return to camp.

Teklanika River

According to Grant Pearson, one of the early park superintendents, Teklanika is an Athapascan word meaning "much river bed, little river." (Bus drivers frequently have a slightly different but similar version of the translation.) Like most of the north flowing rivers in the park, the Teklanika is heavily laden with glacial silt created when glaciers grind rocks into fine powder. This silt quickly clogs stream channels, causing the river to change course. Over thousands of years the river has shifted back and forth across the valley floor innumerable times, laying down broad, flat river bars; hence the "much river bed, little river."

– Don Croner

Photo 9C. **Hike 9.** Early morning reflection along the river near Teklanika Campground.

Photo 10A. **Enjoying the view of Double Mountain on Hike 10.**

10

Teklanika Foothills

Location: Teklanika Rest Stop Mile 30.3
GPS: N63° 38.9' W149° 33.5'
Time on bus (one way): 1.5 hours
Hike Length: 4 miles (6.4 km)
Hiking Time: 4.5 hours
Elevation Gain: 1,200 feet
Hiking Difficulty: Moderate
Route Finding Difficulty: Moderate
Backcountry Permit Area: 6
USGS Map: Healy (C-6).

Highlights

From the Teklanika Campground or rest area, the jumbled and colorful ridge and peak #3992 look enticing. This peak and adjacent ridges provide an opportunity to explore Cantwell Formation conglomerates.

The view of the Teklanika River headwaters, the panorama view of the Teklanika Campground area and the closer inspection of craggy Double Mountain delighted me *(photo 10A)*. To the north, Mount Wright, Primrose Ridge and Mount Healy Ridge were visible from the peak.

As I started down, a grizzly sow and spring cub rewarded my efforts by appearing on an adjacent ridge.

In the fall, blueberries can be found in the tundra between the road and ridge. Teklanika campers will appreciate this information since it is hard to find blueberries in the taiga forest near the campground.

Route description

Get off the bus at the Teklanika Rest Stop. Walk along the road about one-half mile to reach a place where the road makes a 90-degree turn and there is a gap in the trees (GPS Coordinate: N63° 38.9' W149° 33.5'). At this point study the ridgelines of this route as well as the tundra area. The route follows the ridgeline with exposed areas of light-colored soil and rock. *(photo 10B)* Look for grizzly bears and find some landmarks to guide your route through the tundra. Some of the route passes through waist-high brush with pockets of mud and water between some tussocks.

Head for the first small hump in the tundra. While on the hump look for small lakes to the north shown on the USGS map. From the hump, veer south to follow the sparse spruce line toward the thicker spruce near the drainage that comes from the north side of the ridge that you will follow. As you near the drainage look for a place to cross to the south side. Willows in the drainage are chest-high. Walking along the bank on the south side of the drainage is much easier than along the north side. Continue along the south side of the drainage until you reach the foot of the ridge with light colored outcrops and a small cave visible in a cliff about halfway up the ridge. Climb this ridge to reach the summit ridge.

Once on the north-south summit ridge, head south for an easy walk to peak 3992.

Photo 10B. **View of the ridge (center of photo) followed on Hike 10 as seen from the road. Summit of hike is at top right.**

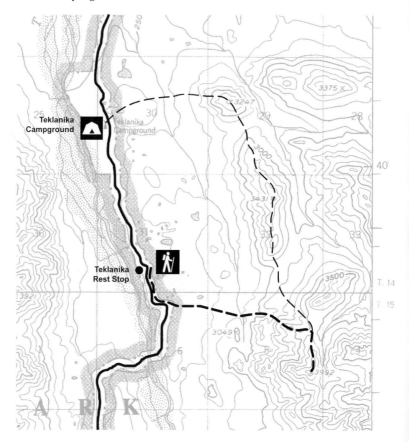

Hike 10
Contour interval
100 feet.
Grid = 1 mile.

Return the same way or select a different route further north. Remember the area south of peak 3992 (toward Double Mountain) is often in a wildlife closure area.

Variations: From the Teklanika Campground you can go cross-country rather than walking along the road. From the campground, walk north (toward the park entrance) a short distance until you see a social trail that goes up a small bluff on the east side of the road. Climb up this bluff and walk to the east end of the short ridge behind. From this point select a route to reach the ridgeline that contains peak 3431 located about two miles northwest of peak 3992. Continue south along this ridgeline to reach the routes described above (See Alternate Route on map).

Crossing the saddle between peaks 3431 and 3992 looked like a good backpacking route between the Teklanika and Sanctuary River drainage. Drainages to the east and west of the summit ridge offer good places to camp out of sight of the road. Water was plentiful in mid-June but hikes to nearby lakes for water may be required later in the season.

Cautions

Since it is difficult to see grizzly bears due to the vegetation along the tundra part of this route, watch for bears and make noise as you walk. The ridgeline due west of this peak, which is an interesting, jumbled mess of loose and tilted conglomerates, is not a good hiking route. The conglomerates in this area are loose and look unstable to me. On the south and east side of summit 3992, I found major cracks and soft spots in the soils that indicated enough deep instability to keep me off these areas.

Photo 11A. **The meadow (center) leading to the ridgeline is the Hike 11 route to the eastern summit of Igloo (top right).**

11

Igloo Mountain East End

Location: Mile 34, Igloo Campground
GPS: N63° 36.6' W149° 34.9'
Time on bus (one way): 1.5 hours
Hike Length: 3 miles (4.8 km)
Hiking Time: 4 hours
Elevation Gain: 1,700 ft.
Hiking Difficulty: Easy
Route Finding Difficulty: Moderate
Backcountry Permit Area: 29
USGS Map: Healy (C-6)

Highlights

Igloo Mountain is well known as a home for Dall sheep. Even though we did not see any sheep from the road, I was confident we would at least see some ewes and lambs during our hike. We found four ewes and their lambs sunning themselves in a sheltered, rocky area near the top and another ewe was grazing in the meadow along our return route.

The fragrant meadow route to the summit ridge tested our motivation to reach the top by tempting us to stop to enjoy the flowers or perhaps a nap *(photo 11A)*. Once on top, the views south and west of mountains, cliffs, alpine meadows, and geological striations offers some of the richest texture and lushest green I have seen in the park *(photo 11D)*. Our sense of accomplishment was enhanced by

Photo 11B. **The forested part of the Igloo Mountain summit route passes to the left of the small hill at right center.**

finding and following the unmarked trail from the road through the boreal forest to reach the meadow that provided the route up Igloo.

My greatest highlights on this hike were hearing Travers (age 14) say; "I didn't know anyone climbed mountains just for fun" and then watching him figure out the route and beat us all to the top. Now if I could only get him to carry some of my gear!

Route description

The bus driver will undoubtedly begin talking about Igloo and Cathedral mountains after you cross the Teklanika River Bridge. As you approach Igloo Mountain (or even from the Teklanika rest stop), look for the wide green strip leading up the northeast side of Igloo Mountain *(photo 11A)*. This strip is the meadow that you will follow to the summit ridge. As you near the Igloo Ranger Station and just as the meadow is going out of sight, look for the small hill (about 100 feet high) at the base of Igloo Mountain that is clearly visible above the trees. The trail to the meadow goes between this small hill and the base of Igloo Mountain. Use this hill as a landmark when you are on the unmarked trail to the meadow.

The route begins on an unmarked path near the Igloo Creek Campground. Get off the bus at Igloo Campground. Walk along the ranger cabin side of the road back toward the park entrance until you find milepost 34. Continue about 26 paces beyond the milepost watching for a faint, unmarked path leaving the road through the vegetation *(photo 11C)*. This path is located where the road begins to curve to the right. (The trailhead is about 30 paces from the 20 MPH speed limit sign.) Initially the trail goes into the forest about 50 feet and then begins to head to your right (north) around the foot of Igloo Mountain and passes to the left of the small hill mentioned above *(photo 11B)*. The path stays in the forest until it begins to gain elevation to cross the saddle between the small hill and the foot of Igloo Mountain. The path has some short wet spots.

If you lose the path, alter your route toward Igloo Mountain instead of toward the road. When Igloo Mountain begins to rise out of the valley, contour around toward the meadow. Do not climb too high on Igloo until you can see the meadow that is your route to the top.

Follow the meadow toward the ridge at the head of the meadow. (I selected a route a little left of the

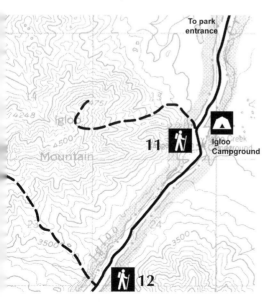

Hikes 11 and 12
Contour interval 100 feet.   Grid = 1 mile.

Photo 11C. **Beginning of the forest path for Hike 11 to eastern summit of Igloo Mountain.**

meadow's center.) At the top of the meadow, climb onto the ridge at the head of the meadow and follow it to the summit ridge of Igloo Mountain. You will see the final route to the summit ridge that is worn into bare soil and scree by people and sheep using this route. Once on top, it is an easy ridge walk to the eastern summit of Igloo Mountain (4,751').

Variations: I talked to rangers who had traversed the length of Igloo Mountain. However only hikers experienced with steep scree slopes, rock scrambling and route finding should do this traverse. See the Hike 6 description for a route to the west end of Igloo.

Cautions

Make a lot of noise and watch for bear and moose during the hike through the boreal forest and until you get into the meadow. The forest trail is narrow and bordered by shoulder-high bushes and grasses. If the bushes are wet, wear rain gear or expect to get completely wet. While this route provides easy access to Igloo with minor scree crossings at the top, most of the surrounding cliffs, rock outcrops and steep scree gullies look unstable. Do not risk a fall trying to get a better sheep picture.

Photo 11D. (next page) **Napping on the eastern summit of Igloo. Western summit of Igloo is the pointed peak at top center. Sable Mountain is the rounded mountain on the horizon at left center. (Hike 17.)**

Geology of Igloo and Cathedral Mountains

Both Cathedral and Igloo mountains consist largely of basalt, an igneous rock formed when volcanoes spew out molten material known as magma. As the Kula tectonic plate was moving north about 60 million years ago, it was subducted, or forced underneath, the North American plate. As the Kula plate sank deep into the mantle of the earth, perhaps tens of miles, its leading edge melted. The molten magma seeped to the surface through the overriding North American plate and spread out over the landscape, creating a deposit known as the Teklanika Formation. The Kula plate was eventually subducted completely. The Pacific plate, following directly behind the Kula, first collided with the North American plate and then about 30 million years ago, for reasons unknown, began sliding westward along what is known as a strike-slip fault. As a result of these tectonic stresses, the Teklanika formation was broken up along fault lines into many segments which then tilted, one end of a block rising and the other falling, resulting in mountains like Cathedral and Igloo.

This effect can easily be seen directly across the valley of the Teklanika on Double Mountain, which resembles a somewhat battered layer cake tipped on its side. The top layer of the mountain is the dark brown rock of the Teklanika formation, while the bottom layer is the gray sandstones, shale and conglomerates of the Cantwell formation. Notice how both formations have been tipped to the south.

– Don Croner

12

Igloo Mountain West

Location: Mile 36
GPS: N63° 35.7' W149° 36.4'
Time on bus (one way): 1.75 hours
Hike Length: 3 miles (4.8 km)
Hiking Time: 5 hours
Elevation Gain: 1,500 feet
Hiking Difficulty: Moderate
Route Finding Difficulty: Moderate
Backcountry Permit Area: 29
USGS Map: Healy (C-6)

Highlights

The highlights for us were the geology and ripe blue berries (early August). We found some colorful (and muddy) clays, geodes and interesting conglomerate formations along the final ridge. The views south of the colors and geology of Cathedral Mountain and views to the north from Igloo Ridge beg to be photographed in better weather *(photo 12B)*. I hope to repeat this hike when the wind and rain don't drive my camera into hiding. After seeing fresh bear poop near the saddle, we bantered nervously (and loudly) about why the bear went over the mountain and wondered if it was just over the ridge. (It wasn't!) Tracks along the route and on the ridge indicted use by caribou and sheep.

This route offers another way to reach the peaks of Igloo Mountain (see variations). Because of the elevation and habitat changes, this route offers a variety of flowers in season.

Route description

This route starts about mile 36 where you can see the southwest end of the top of Igloo Mountain <u>and</u> you are across from the first major drainage joining Igloo Creek from the west. This drainage is the first drainage from the west that is shown in blue on the USGS Healy (C-6) in Section 23 and first drainage shown in blue on the *Trails Illustrated®* map. The route is up the ridge that begins at the 30-foot soft earth bluff to the right of where this drainage joins Igloo Creek *(photo 12A)*.

The mile 36 marker is not easy to find. Igloo Creek Bridge near the campground is at mile 34.2. After the Igloo Creek Bridge at the campground, begin watching on the downhill side of the road (right side on east-bound buses) for the first major drainage that has gabions (wire cages filled with rocks). These gabions are on a drainage that comes from Cathedral Mountain and ends in Igloo Creek. Note: There is a second group of gabions further up the road so be sure to get off the bus at the first gabions. If you reach the second bridge on Igloo Creek, you have gone too far.

Before leaving the road and descending to Igloo Creek, look for bears in the Igloo Creek bottom and along the hiking route.

Follow the gravel bed of the Cathedral drainage from the road through the brush to reach Igloo

Photo 12A. **View from the road of the ridge followed on Hike 12. After crossig Igloo Creek, climb onto the ridge at the earth bluff at left center.**

Photo 12B. **Emily on a rainy hike to the west end of Igloo Mountain (Hike 12). Teklanika River and Double Mountain are at top left center. The park road, Cathedral Mountain, and Igloo Canyon are at right-center.**

Photo 12C. **Scrambling across Igloo Creek on slick boulders on Hike 12.**

Creek. Then walk upsream along the creek to reach the bluff described above where you begin the ridge walk. As an alternative, you can begin climbing the ridge across from the spot where you first reach Igloo Creek but you will hit more brush than on the route beginning at the earth bluff.

We crossed Igloo Creek via some large boulders less than 100 feet upstream from the earth bluff. These boulders were slick *(photo 12C)*. Water level and stream width on Igloo Creek will vary with rainfall so it may not always be possible to find a place to cross without wading. However there should always be a place to cross that is less than knee deep and 15 feet wide.

From the bottom of the earth bluff, pick the best route through a short stretch of waist-high brush and head for the lower brush higher along the ridgeline.

Follow the ridge toward the western end of Igloo Mountain. Once you see a mound of white earth with some vegetation in the direction of the saddle at the west end of Igloo, select a route that veers left off the main ridgeline toward the saddle. The best route goes to the right of the white mound without losing elevation. Retrace the route to return to the road.

Variations: Because of stormy weather our primary destination was the saddle at the foot of the Igloo Mountain summit ridge. In the future, I plan to use this route to reach the west summit of Igloo Mountain. The route up to the summit ridge looked like an easy scree scramble and there were footprints leading up this slope. Two rangers used this route to begin a west-to-east traverse of Igloo Mountain. (See Hike 11.)

I think this hike would provide a backpacking route into the Big Creek drainage behind Igloo Mountain. My opinion is based on what I saw from the saddle, map information, and my previous experience using Tattler Creek Pass to reach Big Creek.

Cautions

Watch for bears and moose, particularly in the high brush along Igloo Creek and the lower part of the ridge. Make a lot of noise when you are walking along Igloo Creek. If you continue on to Igloo Mountain summit, remember where you went up and do not climb anything that you cannot descend. Rocks on Igloo Mountain are often loose. Do not scramble on cliffs or exposed slopes. Watch for slick rocks if you try to boulder-hop across Igloo Creek.

13

Upper Teklanika River to Sanctuary River

Location: Begin Mile 38, end Mile 23
GPS: N63° 33.5' W149° 38.7'
Time on bus (one way): 2 hours
Hike Length: 35 miles (56 km)
Hiking Time: Allow 5 days
Elevation Gain: 2,300 feet
Hiking Difficulty: Difficult
Route Finding Difficulty: Difficult
Backcountry Permit Areas: 5, 6
USGS Maps: Healy (B-5), (B-6), (C-5), (C-6)

Photo 13A. **This path from the road is the start of hikes 13, 14, 15 and 16.**

Highlights

This is a strenuous hike through the summer home of Dall sheep in the rugged mountains at the headwaters of the Teklanika and Sanctuary rivers. Both headwaters offer beautiful places to camp. A glacier once extended from the head of Refuge Valley at least 15 miles down the main valley of the Sanctuary. Its marks are clearly visible on the valley's sides.

In addition to spectacular glacier-carved scenery, there are excellent chances to see bears and caribou. Caribou that have wintered to the west and north migrate in the spring through the pass followed by this hike.

In the headwaters pass watch for the rare white-tailed ptarmigan, which are noticeably smaller than willow and rock ptarmigan. Their summer plumage matches almost perfectly the gray Paleozoic slates of this area, making them hard to see unless they move.

Since Teklanika River is closed to hiking above the bridge for about three miles, the beginning of this route is one of the best ways to get to the upper Teklanika River area.

Route description

Ask the bus driver to let you off at the last outward curve (about 50 yards) before the bus reaches the sign marking the boundary of the Sable Pass closed area. Here you can see past the south end of Cathedral Mountain. Look the area over for bears, particularly along Igloo Creek.

From the wide spot on the curve before the road reaches the closed

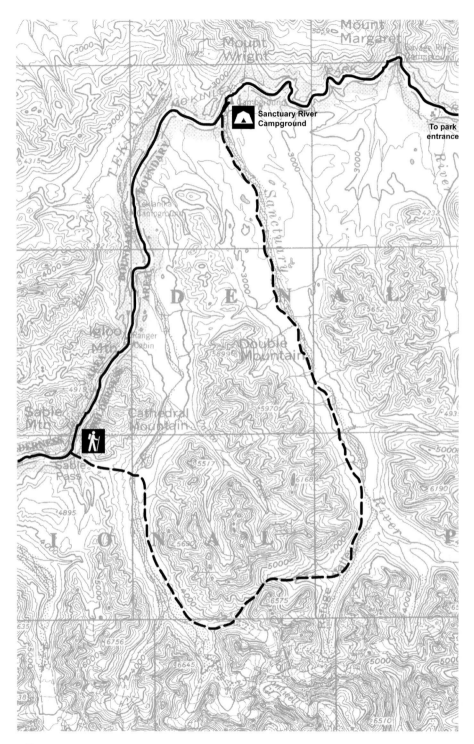

Hike 13
Contour interval 200 feet. Grid = 6 miles.

area sign, select a route down to Igloo Creek. There is a faint trail leading down an easy and mostly open slope to Igloo Creek. Make noise while you are in the brush along Igloo Creek. Cross Igloo Creek at a wide, shallow spot about 200 feet downstream from the yellow bank *(photo 13A)*. (I have managed to cross here without getting any water in my hiking boots. However the water may be a little deeper if it has been raining.)

After crossing Igloo Creek, find the social trail up the bank out of the creek bottom. People and animals that are traveling past the west end of Cathedral have made this trail. Select a route across a grassy divide and down a brushy bank to the valley of the Teklanika. Bears are very common in this area. Be alert. Follow the braided gravel bars of the Teklanika about six miles south to where the river breaks up into three branches.

Photo 13B. **Starting up the eastern-most branch of the Teklanika River.** Photo by D. B. Geeseman.

To continue to the headwaters of the Sanctuary, cross the Teklanika and continue along the eastern-most branch of the Teklanika into a canyon until it branches, then follow the branch to the left, a clear water stream that trends to the northeast up a steep, rocky ravine leading to an unnamed 5400' pass *(photos 13B and 13C)*.

The Sanctuary side of the pass is fairly steep. Follow caribou trails down to the unnamed creek that flows east into Refuge Valley. Climb onto the bench to the south of the creek and follow it to Refuge Valley. Stay high on the bench to avoid the worst of the ravines that drop down into the canyon. Do not follow the creek bed itself. High waterfalls eventually block the canyon.

From where Refuge Valley meets the main valley, it is about a 15-mile hike to the road. I have walked along both sides of the Sanctuary. Walking along either side requires finding routes through streambed vegetation and occasionally walking in waist high tundra to get around places where the river flows against high cut banks. Visibility is often limited along the river because of willows and alders and this is prime bear country so make noise.

When selecting a route in the streambed, I usually can thread my way through the vegetation following old channels that have not overgrown and walking along gravel bars that are not overgrown. When this does not work, I look for good walking at the base of the bank that separates the tundra from the riverbed. Often there are game trails or the vegetation is sparser at the base of the tundra bluff. When these trails encounter a bend in the river next to a high bank, there is often a game trail along the top of the bank until it is again possible to walk in the riverbed.

When the water is low enough to easily cross the river braids, I often cross back and forth to find the easiest walking in the riverbed. I find it quicker to cross the river to get around a cut bank than to bushwhack for extended distances in waist high tundra on top of the bank. But I do not mind hiking in wet boots. See Sanctuary River photos T and U in Chapter 3 and also photos in Hike 8.

Variation: Explore the upper Teklanika River on a long dayhike or backpack outing by following the beginning of this hike and then returning to the road along the same route. Plan a backpack to the headwaters of either river and spend time dayhiking to explore the surrounding valleys. The headwaters of the Sanctuary and Teklanika rivers are in different backcountry permit areas, so you will need to make the decision not to cross the pass before you obtain the backcountry camping permit.

Caution

Because of stream crossings, remoteness and the pass crossing, this is a hike for experienced hikers in good shape, with good map reading skills, and with plenty of time. Watch for bears in the brush.

Photo 13C. **Eastern branch of the Teklanika River seen from above the side stream that leads to the pass to Refuge Valley of the Sanctuary River (Hike 13)** . Photo by D. B. Geeseman.

Photo 13D. **Mountains at the headwaters of the Teklanika River.**

Teklanika Glaciation and Climate Change

The glaciers visible at the headwaters of Teklanika River are remnants of the huge ice flows that once carved out the valley of the Teklanika. During the last ice age ending about 10,000 years ago, these glaciers came together and swept down the valley at least 12 miles to near where the park road now crosses the river. This glacier carved through the sedimentary rocks of the Cantwell formation at the head of the valley and then the volcanic basalts of the Teklanika formation, leaving the characteristically U-shaped glacial valley. Glaciers during earlier ice ages may have reached as far as the Teklanika campground, scouring out the U-shaped valley of the upper river.

As the last glacier receded it left unvegetated glacier rubble in its wake. As you hike, notice how spruce trees have now extended south up the river bottom to around Calico Creek and up the sides of the glacial-scoured alley. About 14,000 years ago, when weather conditions were much more severe, spruce trees were found only much further north in small, isolated pockets along the Yukon and Tanana rivers. The country from the edge of the ice here in the Denali region north into the Interior was covered with "tundra steppe" (also known as "mammoth steppe," since it supported the woolly mammoth) consisting of grasses, sedges, artemsia, various plantains, dandelions and assorted members of the mustard family.

Starting about 14,000 years ago, a sudden change of climate took place and low bush tundra, characterized by dwarf birch, alders, willows and heather, began to overtake the tundra steppe, first along the rivers of the Interior and then slowing moving south. Spruce-aspen-birch forests also began to expand, quickly taking over the river bottoms and following them south. Spruce forests may have reached up the valley of the Nenana as far as the park entrance and the foothills of the Outside Range by as early as 8,500 years ago. Migrating south through the canyons of the Outside Range, spruce forests were probably established in the upper valleys of rivers like the Teklanika and Sanctuary by 6,000 years ago. Today there is no tundra steppe left in the park. The rolling hills between the Sanctuary and Teklanika rivers are covered with low brush tundra dominated by dwarf birch, and spruce trees continue their inexorable march up the valleys.

– Don Croner

14

Calico Creek

Location: Begins at Mile 38
GPS: N63° 33.5' W149° 38.7'
Time on bus (one way): 2 hours
Hike Length: 9 miles (14.4 km)
Hiking Time: Allow 3 days
Elevation Gain: -500 feet
Hiking Difficulty: Difficult
Route Finding Difficulty: Moderate
Backcountry Permit Area: 6
USGS Maps: Healy (C-5), (C-6)

Photo 14A. **View of Calico Creek valley as a storm approaches.**

Highlights

Seeing the rich colors on the east side of Cathedral Mountain is one of the delights of this trip *(photo S in chapter 3)*. Along the way expect to encounter bears and caribou. Since a wolf pack has lived in this drainage for several years, watch for wolf tracks. If you get lucky, perhaps you can hear some howling or see a wolf.

The spruce forest along the east side of the Teklanika River and north of Calico Creek offers the opportunity (and challenge) to explore this environment. Watch for moose in the forest area. During a late August or early September trip, the fall colors and berries are a treat.

Our plans to explore the upper Calico Creek drainage were thwarted by snow in September *(photo 14A)*.

Route description

Ask the bus driver to let you off at the last outward curve (about 50 yards) before the bus reaches the sign marking the boundary of the Sable Pass closed area. At this point you can see past the south end of Cathedral Mountain. Look the area over for bears, particularly down in Igloo Creek bottom.

From the wide spot on the curve before the road reaches the closed area sign, select a route down to Igloo Creek. There is a faint trail leading down an easy and mostly open slope to Igloo Creek *(photo 13A)*. Make noise while you are in the brush along Igloo Creek. Cross Igloo Creek at a wide, shallow spot about 200 feet downstream from the yellow bank. (I have managed to cross here without getting any water in my hiking boots. The water may be a little deeper if it has been raining.)

After crossing Igloo Creek, find the social trail up the bank out of the Igloo Creek bottom. People and animals that are traveling past the west end of Cathedral have made this trail. Select a route across a grassy divide and down a brushy bank to the valley of the Teklanika. Bears are very com-

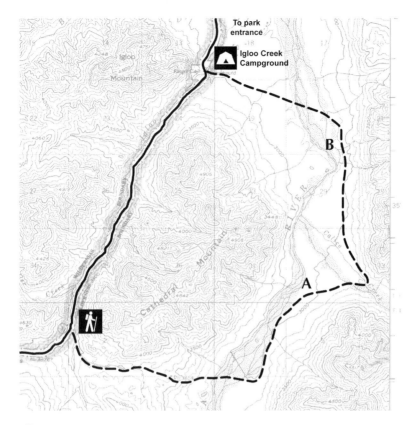

Hike 14
Contour interval 100 feet. Grid = 1 mile.

Photo 14B. **Teklanika River valley seen from Igloo Mountain on Hike 11. Calico Creek is shown at upper right. Double Mountain is at the top, left-center. The last half of Hike 14 begins at Calico Creek and ends at the park road (X on photo).**

mon in this area. Be alert.

I recommend crossing the Teklanika as soon as possible. We were able to cross without encountering water more than knee-deep. Near Calico Creek the river is less braided.

Continue downstream along the river. Look for game trails along the bank above the gravel bars. Watch for bears. Once you can see the Calico Creek valley (Point A on map), select a route across the tundra toward where the Calico Creek valley narrows. While this route occasionally encounters short stretches of brush that are chest high, you can usually find game trails through or routes around the worst spots *(photo 14C)*.

After exploring Calico Creek, head north through the spruce forest until you think you have passed the sharp bend along the narrow part of the Teklanika River (Point B on map). We found walking through the spruce forest well away from the river to be the easiest route. We zigzagged through the forest following game trails. We made the mistake of not going far enough downstream before turning toward the river and first encountered the river upstream of the sharp bend. Hiking along the river at this point was much wetter than back in the forest so we retreated into the forest and continued downstream.

Downstream from the river bend, an island divides the river. We used this island as a camping spot and "stepping stone" to cross the river. In 2000, the eastern channel was ankle deep. The western channel carried most of the current, did not have as many braids and looked intimidating because the bottom was not visible in the deeper spots.

After much searching and debate we selected a place and route to cross. We crossed the western channel early in the morning about mid-way down the island *(photo 14D)* We were expecting much deeper water when we started across but encountered only a short stretch of water over knee deep. (Whew!!!) Skill at reading a river is essential to find a good spot to cross in this area.

If you are unsure about crossing the Teklanika River in a place that may have higher water than your upstream crossing, then retrace your steps after exploring Calico Creek. The area downstream from the island to the bridge is closed to hiking.

Once across the river, head downstream along the high bank looking for a ravine to provide an easy route up onto the tundra. Walk across the tundra toward Igloo Campground

Photo 14C. **Hiking cross-country from Teklanika River to Calico Creek.**

Photo 14D. **Teklanika River from the island described in Hike 14. We crossed the wide area at the left.**

(photo 14B). To stay out of the closed area, head a little left of the northern peak of Igloo Mountain. The area on both sides of Igloo Creek near the campground may also be closed to hiking. Avoid this area by continuing in the tundra parallel to the creek until you can get to the road without walking down in the creek bottom.

Variation: Remain on the western side of the river and circumnavigate Cathedral Mountain. I did a backpack around Cathedral before I began keeping good notes. However I do remember negotiating a lot of spruce forests and brushy tundra to reach Igloo Campground. A strong, experienced and gonzo hiker could probably do the Cathedral circumnavigation in a long day.

Caution

Because of stream crossings and route finding through forests and brush, this is a hike for experienced hikers in good shape and with good map reading skills. Watch for bears and make noise in the brush.

15

Cathedral Mountain

Location: Mile 38
GPS: N63° 33.5' W149° 38.7'
Time on bus (one way): 2 hours
Hike Length: 3 miles (4.8 km)
Hiking Time: 3-5 hours
Elevation Gain:1,200 feet
Hiking Difficulty: Moderate
Route Finding Difficulty: Moderate
Backcountry Permit Area: 6
USGS Map: Healy (C-6)

Highlights

Cathedral Mountain, like Igloo Mountain, is a good place to look for Dall sheep, particularly ewes and lambs and occasionally rams *(photo 15A)*. Watch for caribou on the lower part of the route. The summit provides panoramic views of the Alaska Range, especially the glacier-carved areas of the upper Teklanika River valley. Hiking along the extensive summit ridgeline is easy. The rock colors on the back of Cathedral seem more vivid than the colors seen from the road. The high meadows are great for enjoying flowers or a nap. In late August, blueberries are plentiful at the beginning of this hike in the small drainage on the side of Cathedral above Igloo Creek.

While in the Igloo Creek area, keep an especially sharp eye peeled for the olive-green arctic warbler. This world traveler spends its winters in Southeast Asia, but is particularly partial to Igloo Creek as a nesting ground during the summer. Harlequin ducks are often seen in Igloo Creek itself.

Route description

Ask the bus driver to let you off at the last outward curve (about 50 yards) before the bus reaches the sign marking the boundary of the Sable Pass closed area. At this point you can see past the south end of Cathedral Mountain. Look for bears; particularly down in Igloo Creek bottom. Also look for bears in the small drainage on Cathedral directly across from you. Your hiking route follows the right side of this drainage until you reach the saddle at the head of the drainage.

From the wide spot on the curve before the road reaches the closed area sign, select a route down to Igloo Creek. There is a faint trail leading down an easy and mostly-open slope to Igloo Creek. Make noise while you are in the bushes along Igloo Creek. Cross Igloo Creek at a wide, shallow spot about 200 feet downstream from the yellow bank. *(See Photo 13A.)* (I have managed to cross here without getting any water in my hiking boots. The water may be a little deeper if it has been raining.)

Find the social trail up the bank out of the Igloo Creek bottom. People and animals that are traveling past the west end of Cathedral have made this trail. Once on top of the bank follow this trail for a short distance (less than 200 feet) until you can easily contour

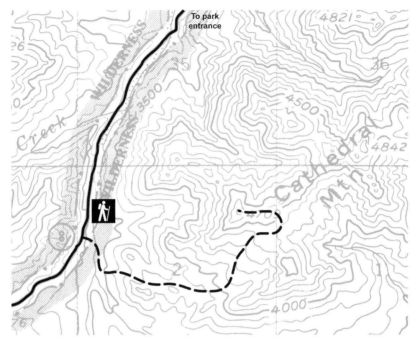

Hike 15
Contour Interval 100 feet. Grid = 1 mile.

Photo 15A. **Dall sheep nursery herd on Cathedral Mountain.**

Cathedral Mountain Named by Charles Sheldon

Cathedral Mountain is the name given to the jumbled mass of ridges and peaks to the east of the road near Igloo Campground. Probably the first white man to climb these peaks was big game hunter and conservationist Charles Sheldon during his 1906 visit to the Denali region. Camped on the Toklat River hunting sheep, Sheldon saw hundreds of ewes, lambs and young rams, but he soon despaired of finding any of the big, mature Dall rams for which he was looking.

Noticing several peaks to the east through Sable Pass, Sheldon set off by himself to explore them. He was soon struck by their appearance. "Never have I seen a mountain of that height more beautiful, with its startling conformation, jagged crests, deep canyons, irregular spires and variegated colors." he says in his classic book *The Wilderness of Denali*. He immediately christened the peaks Cathedral Mountain.

Just as important, Sheldon found the big rams. "After an arduous exploration of the country for more than eighty miles, including many days of toilsome tramping over rough mountains, at last I had found old rams," he exalted. Out of a band of thirteen, he shot seven specimens for the Museum of Natural History in New York and for his own personal collection. The hunt was the culmination of the year's trip: "I sat there smoking my pipe and enjoying the exhilaration following the stalk, while the beauty of the landscape about me was intensified by my wrought up senses."

Sheldon fought for years to have the Denali region designated a national park and he finally succeeded in 1917. Interestingly, he was the first to suggest the name Denali National Park, which was overridden in favor of the name Mt. McKinley National Park. The name was finally changed to Denali in 1980.

Thanks to Sheldon's effort, Dall sheep are commonly seen today on the flanks of the mountain from the park road.

– Don Croner

Photo 15C. **After crossing Igloo Creek, Hike 15 continues up the drainage at left toward the lighter area at top-left center.**

to the left across the toe of the ridgeline to reach the drainage on the other side of this ridge *(photo 15C)*. Head up the right side of the drainage toward the saddle. Cross this drainage near the top and walk toward the dirt on the left at the head of the saddle. Once at this saddle, you will see another saddle with grayish white soils. Head for this grayish white area without losing any altitude. When you reach the grayish- white area, you will see a broad grassy route up Cathedral. Select a path up this route near the middle. Follow the meadow to the summit ridge.

Remember the landmarks so you can find your way back down. If you get confused on the return, you can continue down the grassy meadow to the pass at the foot of Cathedral and then follow a social trail back to Igloo Creek.

Once on the summit ridge, you can hike in either direction looking for sheep or enjoying the view.

Variations: Hikers experienced with steep scree slopes can return to the road by descending one of the drainages where the route down is visible.

Backpackers can find places to camp in the meadows along the east side near the top. There were some small ponds in July but finding water may be difficult at times.

To explore the geology without climbing the mountain, try walking from the road up one of the three canyons that penetrate into the interior of Cathedral Mountain. The first of these canyons starts 1.8 miles past Igloo Campground. Watch for bears in these canyons and in the brush near Igloo Creek.

Cautions

Be alert for bears in the Igloo Creek brush and on the brushy, lower flanks of the mountain. Rocks on Cathedral are very unstable. Stay on the gentler slopes and ridgelines along this route. Do not attempt to climb any rock outcrops or scramble around on cliffs to get closer to sheep. Even though this route is close to the road and the road is frequently visible, people on the road are unlikely to see you, or a signal, from where you might end up after a fall.

(previous page) Photo 15B. **Dall sheep**

16

Sable Pass Ridge Walk

Location: Mile 38
GPS: N63° 33.5' W149° 38.7'
Time on bus (one way): 2 hours
Hike Length: up to 7 miles (11.2 km)
Hiking Time: 5-7 hours
Elevation Gain: 1,300 feet
Hiking Difficulty: Easy
Route Finding Difficulty: Easy
Backcountry Permit Areas:
Border of 6 and 7
USGS Map: Healy (C-6)

Highlights

For years I wanted to see what was behind (south of) the Sable Pass closed area. From this ridgeline hike along the closed area boundary, I could see this mystery area of rolling tundra plus the Teklanika River headwaters and multi-colored back side of Cathedral Mountain *(photo 16A)*. Flowers were abundant as well as large areas of Alaska cotton *(photo 16B)*.

Because of the Sable Pass reputation for bear traffic, I expected to see a bear. I was prepared to turn around or detour into the Teklanika valley if a bear came near my path along this ridge. I took frequent breaks to enjoy flowers (early July) and scan for bears. After several "bears" became bushes or rocks when viewed with binoculars, three blond spots 3/4 mile away proved to be a sow with cubs. The bears seemed to be grazing and playing in one spot rather than heading toward my route. From past experience I knew these bears could reach my route in less than 15 minutes if they decided to travel my way. During the balance of this hike, I kept track of the bears from my ridge vantage point and hoped they would not come my way. The bears stayed in the same area until I lost sight of them as I returned to the road at the end of my hike.

Route description

First make sure this route is open to hiking since, during some of the summers, there were temporary closures in the Igloo drainage that would prevent this hike.

Ask the bus driver to let you off at the last outward curve (about 50 yards) before the bus reaches the sign marking the boundary of the Sable Pass closed area. At this point you can see past the south end of Cathedral Mountain. Look the area over for bears; particularly down in Igloo Creek bottom. Also look for a yellow bank (about 20 feet high) across Igloo Creek that forms the end of the ridge that is the route for this hike.

Select a route down to Igloo Creek from the wide spot on the curve before the road reaches the closed area sign. There is a faint trail leading down an easy and mostly open slope to Igloo Creek. *(See photo 13A.)* Make noise while you are in the bushes along Igloo Creek. Cross Igloo Creek

at a wide, shallow spot about 200 feet downstream from the yellow bank. (I have managed to cross here without getting any water in my hiking boots. The water is often a little deeper if it has been raining.)

In 2000, the area at the base of the yellow cliff was posted as closed to hiking. So it was necessary to begin this hike by walking along the social trail at the base of Cathedral Mountain for about half a mile. At this point, cross the drainage and climb onto the ridgeline that serves as the boundary

Photo 16A. **Teklanika River viewed from the end of Hike 16.**

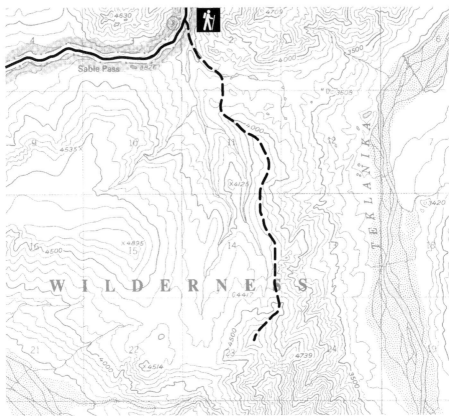

Hike 16
Countour interval 100 feet. Grid = 1 mile.

Photo 16B. **Flowers and rolling tundra along route of Hike 16.**

of the closure area. If you are in doubt about the exact location of the ridgeline (boundary of backcountry area 7), stay on the eastern edge of the ridgeline and do not take a route that drops into the drainage to the west that is permanently closed to hiking.

Follow the ridge as far as you want to hike.

Variations: Based on my observations and the topographic map, it looks easy to continue on to hill 5419. Another option is to select a return route that allows exploration of the meadows and ponds at the base of Cathedral Mountain.

Cautions

Early in the hike, brush along Igloo Creek and rolling terrain can hide bears. Examine the area from the road and make lot of noise when you are in this area. Along the ridge, views of the distance are good, but there are swales that can hide a bear.

17

Tattler Creek and Sable Mountain

Location: Mile 38
GPS: N63° 34' W149° 38.2'
Time on bus (one way): 2 hours
Hike Length: 5 miles (8 km)
Hiking Time: 6 to 8 hours
Elevation Gain: 2,500 feet to summit
Hiking Difficulty: Moderate
Route Finding Difficulty: Easy
Backcountry Permit Area: 29
USGS Map: Healy (C-6)

Highlights

Sable is one of the highest peaks to easily reach on a dayhike. The panoramic summit view is still fresh in my memory from a clear day 20 years ago. The view seems to encompasses the entire Denali region: 150 miles of the crest of the Alaska Range from Mt. Deborah (12,339') in the east to Mt. McKinley in the west; the broad basin between the Alaska Range and the Outside Range running 35 miles east towards the park entrance; the Kantishna Hills far to the northwest; and the series of ridges and peaks rolling off to the north with the great Interior beyond. The immediate foreground is a study in contrasts: the tumbled mass of Cathedral Mountain, the high, rolling tundra hills of Sable Pass, and the flat basin along the branches of the East Fork River, each branch leading to glaciers resembling fingers on a hand.

During my second trek to the summit (1996), it rained and clouds swirled around me obscuring the valleys below. As I headed down, the sun poked through holes in the clouds providing a spectacular patchwork of light and shadow highlighting the contrast between the wet tundra greens and the red, gold and brown soils of nearby mountains. I met three people coming up the mountain. As we spoke, our efforts and perseverance in the rain were rewarded by Mt. McKinley revealing its summit through a hole in the clouds.

Sheep have been visible every time I have hiked in this area. Bears frequent the Tattler Creek part of this route. A number of birds can be found along Tattle Creek, including the arctic warbler, which summers here and winters in Southeast Asia, the northern wheatear, which crosses all of Asia to reach its wintering grounds in Africa, the mysterious Townsend's solitaire and, of course, the wandering tattler, from which Tattler Creek apparently got its name. I spent an hour photographing pikas in the rocks along upper Tattler Creek.

Route description

Ask the bus driver to let you off at Tattler Creek.

Both of the routes to the summit begin by following Tattler Creek. Walk up Tattler Creek. Make lots of noise as you pass through the brush as bears frequent this area. About 1/4 mile from the road, the creek passes

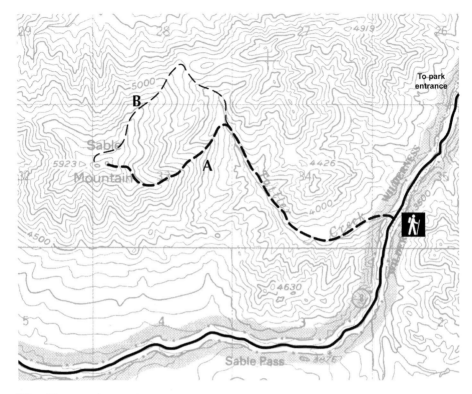

Hike 17
Contour interval 100 feet. Grid = 1 mile.

through a narrow, rocky canyon about 30 feet deep. Go around this canyon by climbing onto the bench on the right side. You will see where others have climbed out of the creek bed to get on the bench. From here on, Tattler Creek is easy walking and mostly open but make noise and watch for bears.

Route A to the summit, which I followed in 1996, is a little shorter but a slightly steeper way *(photo 17A)*. This route involves climbing out of Tattler Creek onto the ridge along the left (west) side of the creek about 2 miles upstream from the road. A bonus for taking this steeper route is the view of Sable Pass, Polychrome Pass and Mt. McKinley (if it is out) once you get on the ridge and while continuing to the summit.

Summit Route B continues to the saddle at the head of Tattler Creek and then heads west up the ridge to the summit. (I used this route my first time.) This route is less steep but slightly longer. Mount McKinley is blocked from view along this route until you reach the summit but there is a clear view of the seldom seen Big Creek drainage to the north on the final summit climb.

To use Route A, continue upstream about two miles until you see the first ridge on the west side of the Tattle Creek composed of gray soils where it hits the creek instead of the reddish soils you have been passing. This ridge of gray soils is the same color as Sable Mountain and the ridge is an obvious extension of Sable Mountain. On the upstream side of this ridge you will find a drainage that begins on Sable Mountain. Follow the ridge along the left side of this drainage up to the summit ridge. The footing on this ridge is good. When you achieve the summit plateau, be sure to note where you will need to start down when you return. It is easy to get confused about which ridge to take, particularly if you are in the clouds.

To use Route B, continue walking up Tattler Creek and climb to the saddle at the head of this creek. Once on the saddle, follow the ridgeline up to the top of Sable Mountain.

To return, retrace your steps or combine routes A and B into a loop.

Variations: For a shorter, less strenuous trip, you can get a good view of Sable and Polychrome Pass areas and Mount McKinley by just climbing up to the ridge on the west side of the creek. The easiest place to get on the ridge is a little over a mile up Tattler Creek. Watch for a wide grassy valley coming in from the left. Select a route up this valley to reach the low point of the ridgeline.

I have also climbed to the ridgeline on the east side of Tattler Creek and then followed this ridge back to the road. I used the USGS map to select a route out of the creek toward the point labeled 4426 in square 34 on the map. This dayhike allows exploration of the creek and provides a great view of Cathedral Mountain as well as Igloo and Tattler Creek valleys.

A few years ago, I began a four-day backpacking trip in backcountry permit area 29 at Tattler Creek and finished on the road between the Teklanika River and Igloo Campground. At the headwaters of Tattler Creek, I crossed the pass to reach the Big Creek drainage. After dayhikes up Sable Mountain and exploring the Big Creek headwaters, I continued downstream past Igloo Mountain until I reached the first low saddle through the north ridge of Igloo Mountain. The USGS map shows a small lake in this saddle. I followed a game trail through the saddle.

Once through the saddle, do not head directly to the road because you will be crossing wet areas that are the headwaters of two small creeks. Instead veer south toward Igloo Campground while you still have some elevation and can select a route using the highest ground to reach the road.

Photo 17 A. **View of Tattler Creek from Route A of Hike 17.**

Photo 17B. **View downstream of Tattler Creek from the beginning of Route A of Hike 17. Note the light-colored tent in the lower right of the photo—it's a good indication of the scale of the landscape.**

Cautions

This is bear country so make noise, watch for them and be prepared to alter your route or retreat. Two years ago, Lynn and I hiked up Tattler Creek about two miles and then decided to climb up the east side of the creek. After gaining about 100 feet in elevation, we paused for breath and looked down to where we started our climb. There was a bear! Lynn and I looked at each other and wondered if we had passed the bear or if it had been behind us.

There is no water after you leave Tattler Creek valley unless you can find some melting snow in north-facing spots early in the season.

18

Polychrome Basin Exploration

Location: Mile 43.4
Time on bus (one way): 2.5 hours
Hike Length: 11 miles (19.2 km)
Hiking Time: 12 hours to three days
Elevation Gain: 400 to 1,000 feet
Hiking Difficulty: Moderate
Route Finding Difficulty: Easy
Backcountry Permit Area: 8
USGS Maps: Healy (B-6), (C-6)

Highlights

If you're hesitant about traveling into the more remote backcountry, this area offers a day or overnight hike that never ventures too far out of sight of Polychrome Overlook on the park road *(photo 18A)*. This area provides frequent opportunity to view wildlife. The McKinley caribou herd migration funnels through this area during their east-west migrations. Bears and caribou are common. Sheep are found in the foothills of the Alaska Range, especially the north-south trending hills that overlook the headwaters of the East Fork Toklat River. Many of my wolf sightings from the bus have been in the East Fork drainage. In *The Wolves of Mount McKinley,* Adolph Murie reported his studies of wolves in this drainage. Golden plovers and ptarmigan frequent the tundra between the road and foothills.

Route description

Start this hike at the East Fork Bridge. After crossing the westernmost branches of the river, hike south to the foothills along the river branch that is the east boundary of back-country permit unit 8. *(See photo V in chapter 3.)*

(In the summer of 2002, the valley of the eastern-most branch of the East Fork and the broad tundra areas west of this branch to the edge of the next branch were closed to hiking. Do not hike in this area unless you have checked to make sure your route is not in a closed area. Also carry a map showing the current closure areas.)

Once past the restricted area you can proceed up any of the valleys toward the glaciers and find a camping spot. Remember to select a spot where your tent cannot be seen from the road. Return along the same route if you do not follow the foothills route described below.

For a longer, more strenuous backpack, travel west along the foothills of the Alaska Range. Continue to the western-most branch of the East Fork and then head back to the road. Allow three days for this route because you will be crossing several drainages and to provide time for exploring or climbing the ridges to see if Mount McKinley is visible. Each drainage crossing requires route finding through tundra and some elevation changes.

Variations: (See Polychrome Bluffs Hike #21.)

Extend this route to return via the Toklat River using Hike 27.

Polychrome Area Geology

The brilliantly-colored red, yellow and brown rocks of the mountains to the north and south are basalts and rhyolites of the Teklanika formation, laid down about 60 million years ago when volcanoes erupted in this area. The names of Polychrome Pass, mountain and overlook refer to these colorful rocks. C.E. Giffin of the U.S. Geological Survey first suggested the name "Polychrome".

During the last ice age (ending about 10,000 years ago), much of this basin was filled with a glacier that extended down to about the East Fork Bridge. The remaining glaciers at the head of the East Fork branches are but remnants of the earlier, large glacier. One of the landmarks of the basin is a huge chunk of limestone easily visible from both the foothills and the overlook. This rock was carried by the glacier from its source along the crest of the Alaska Range and deposited here when the ice receded. A rock deposited by glaciers like this is called an "erratic."

– Don Croner

Photo 18A. **View from the Polychrome Rest Stop of the area traversed on Hike 18. Distance to the foothills is about 3 miles.**

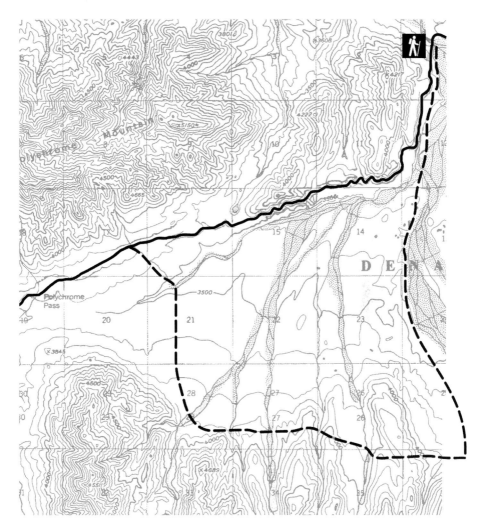

Hike 18
Contour interval 100 feet. Grid = 1 mile.

Cautions

This hike might be affected by temporary closures. Stream crossings may require wading water about knee deep so be sure to carry a walking staff. Map reading skills are required to assure you stay out of any closure areas, particularly if you hike along the south boundary of the closure area to explore the eastern-most valley of the river.

Adolph Murie's Cabin

Famed naturalist Adolph Murie used the cabin, which is visible to the east from the Polychrome Pass road across the East Fork. In the '30s and '40s, he was doing research that led to his book *The Wolves of Mt. McKinley*. **The cabin is not available for public use.**

The Polychrome basin is one of the best places in the park to look for wolves. The wolf den studied by Adolph Murie, located on a bluff to the left (east) of the main fork of the East Branch about two miles above the bridge, has been used on and off for decades and might currently be occupied. Consequently much of the area along the eastern-most branch of the East Fork is closed to hiking.

Wolves are great travelers, routinely hunting across an area 50 miles wide and occasionally traveling much greater distances. They are often seen moving through Sable Pass to the east and Polychrome Pass to the west on their way to their hunting grounds. According to Murie, the main food items of wolves are caribou, both calves and adults, followed by sheep, ground squirrels, marmots and mice.

In one dramatic incident in recent years, a pack of wolves chased down and killed a bull caribou a hundred yards from the road along the east branch of the Toklat just west of here. No sooner did they have the animal down than a female bear and two cubs came along and chased them off the kill. The wolves retreated to some nearby hills and watched for hours as the bears ate their hard-earned meal. The episode occurred directly in front of the rest stop used by tour buses and was witnessed by hundreds of people. If you camp in the Polychrome basin area, you just might hear what is still one of the most dramatic of all sounds—the howling of wolves.

–Don Croner

Photo 18B. **Female wolf.**

19

Polychrome Ridge Walk #1

Location: Mile 45.9, Polychrome Pass
GPS: N63° 32.20' W149° 49.1'
Time on bus (one way): 3.5 hours
Hike Length: 2.5 miles (4 km)
Hiking Time: 2.5 hours
Elevation Gain: 500 feet
Hiking Difficulty: Easy
Route Finding Difficulty: Easy
Backcountry Permit Area: 31
USGS Map: Healy (C-6)

Highlights

I like this hike because there is only a short climb at the beginning followed by easy ridge walking with a downhill finish 500 feet lower than where I started. From the high point of this hike I had a box seat view of the East Fork Toklat River valley, Sable Pass and the Polychrome glaciers among multi-colored hills to the south (*photos 18A and 19B*). I'll bet the top third of Mt. McKinley is visible on a clear day. I heard pikas and saw marmots on the ridge. In June, I have seen sheep on this ridge. From the road, I have also seen bear and caribou on the ridge. The ridge is a good place to use binoculars to search for wolves, bears and caribou that frequent the East Fork valley.

Route description

Get off the bus at the Polychrome Pass summit. Walk east along the road toward the park entrance for about 1/4 mile until you reach the sharp corner where part of the old road is visible in the saddle about 20 feet north of the existing road. Many bus drivers point out the old road. From the rest stop you will pass one road curve in and one curve out. The hike begins at the second inward road curve where the old road is visible. Begin by climbing the ridge to the east of the old road. When hiking on the ridge, walk on the gravel areas and try to stay off the fragile vegetation. Once on the ridge, walk north toward hill 4217. (*photo 19A*)

Just before you start the final hike to the summit of hill 4217, you will reach a shallow saddle. The route down to the road begins in this saddle. After checking the view from hill 4217 return to the lowest point of this saddle. Start your hike down and follow the right side of the drainage to stay out of the brush. When the drainage narrows near the bottom, hike on the side hill above the brush. When the road is in sight, the best route to the road through the waist-high brush is along the low ridgeline to your right. (I found it easy to thread my way through the brush.) The hike ends about 1/2 mile from the East Fork Toklat River Bridge.

Variations: If you do not feel comfortable descending to the road as described above, return the way you came. Another option is to descend off the west side of this route to the stream. Walk up this stream to return to the spot where you started this hike

Photo 19A. **View north from along the ridge traversed on Hike 19.**

or continue hiking west over the small hill to the road.

From the map and my observations, I believe you can also descend to the East Fork River along the ridges to the east or west of hill 4217. Before deciding to try this route, read the cautions section of Polychrome Ridge Walk #2 (Hike 20) concerning following the river back to the road.

Cautions

If you are unsure of your ability to find the route down as described, retrace your route to reach the road. Do not descend to the road anywhere else along the eastern (road) side of this ridge because of steep terrain, cliffs and unstable scree and soil.

Photo 19B. **East Fork River braids from Polychrome Pass. Rain darkened the gravel bars producing this spectacular contrast between the water and gravel.**

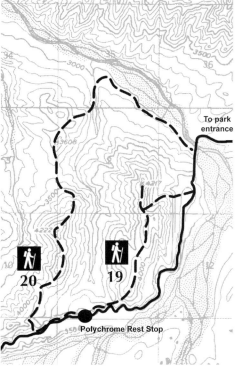

Photo 20A. **Kathy and Travers heading to the creek below. The route for Hike 20 crosses the flat plane toward the East Fork river just beyond Kathy's head (white hat). Note the 180-degree folds in the Cantwell Formation anticline seen in the cliff, left of center.**

Hikes 19 and 20
Contour interval 100 feet. Grid = 1 mile.

20

Polychrome Ridge Walk #2

Location: Polychrome Pass
GPS: N63° 32.1' W149° 50.4'
Time on bus (one way): 2.5 hours
Hike Length: 4.5 miles (7.2 km)
Hiking Time: 5 hours
Elevation Gain: 600 feet
Hiking Difficulty: Moderate
Route Finding Difficulty: Moderate.
Backcountry Permit Area: 31
USGS Map: Healy (C-6)

Highlights

While eating lunch on the ridge, we watched a grizzly sow and two cubs grazing on the slopes of Polychrome Mountain across the valley. When not watching golden eagles or checking out the alpine flowers, we marveled at the geologic formations and colors of the soil and rocks that give the area its name. Later in the hike as I viewed the swirling, 180-degree folds (anticline) *(photo 20A)* in the Cantwell Formation rock along the East Fork Toklat River, I felt insignificant relative to the force and time required to bend rocks in such graceful arches.

Based on sightings during previous hikes in the area and sheep sign visible on this hike, I would expect to see Dall sheep on the ridge early and late in the season (early June and September). I have seen bears along the ridge and behind Polychrome Rest Area. From 1995 to 1998, golden eagles were nesting on a cliff below the road across the road from the beginning point of this hike and were frequently visible perched on the rocky cliffs. In 1999, gyrfalcons took over this nest. In 2004, this nest was occupied so it will be interesting to see what happens in the future. Marmots also live in the rocks on the south side of the road and along the ridgeline at the beginning of this hike.

Route description

When you cross the East Fork River Bridge on the bus, examine the river channel downstream (north) to see if the river is running against the west bank where you will be walking at the end of this hike. (See Cautions below for what to do if the water is against the bank.)

Get off the bus at Polychrome Pass. Walk west along the road about one-half mile until the road drops into a shallow drainage and just before it veers sharply left along a cliff. On the south side of the road, the drainage drops steeply down between two rocky outcrops. On the north side of the road there is a faint game or social trail leading up the ridgeline along the right bank of the drainage. Walk up the right bank of the drainage heading for the skyline. Stay on the bare soils and off the vegetation as much as possible. Your goal is to gain enough elevation to get above the willows to the north before you cut across to the low saddle of the ridgeline that you will follow on this hike.

Photo 20B. **Lunch with a view of Mount Polychrome on Hike 20.**

Once on the saddle, walk up the ridgeline. The initial climb is through scree. The best route is on the left (west) side where there is a faint game trail. Once past the scree walk along the ridge toward the pyramid-shaped peak (hill 4222 on the USGS map).

The south side of the pyramid-shaped peak is too steep and rocky for a direct approach. It is best to reach the summit from the back (north) side. To reach the backside, begin angling up the east slope toward the backside side of the mountain just about where the lighter rock on the ridge begins to turn into the browner summit rock. A faint trail traversing the scree on the east side of the peak indicates sheep and possibly other hikers followed the same route to the back (north) side of the peak. Once in back, it is a grassy walk to the peak, a great place for lunch (*photo 20B*).

From the peak scout your route north across the saddle to the grayish soils of the next high point on this route (hill 3608 on the USGS map). Walk down the ridge until you find a place to descend off the ridge and cross the saddle. (We descended along a shallow ravine about half mile down from the peak.) Select the shortest possible route to cross the saddle with the least elevation loss. (The brush in the saddle is about thigh high but easy to weave through.) Once across the saddle, head for the next high point along the ridge (hill 3608 on the USGS map). Continue past this point through a shallow saddle and then descend along the spur ridge northeast to the creek (*photo 20A*).

Once at the creek continue downstream toward the East Fork River. (See Variation below for an alternate return route.) There was (1996) a faint game trail on the east side of the creek. Walk downstream watching for a distinct drop in the height of the right (east) stream bank from more than 20 feet high to about six feet high. At this point climb out of the steam bed and bushwhack easterly toward the East Fork River. It is easy to find a route through the thigh-high brush *(photo 20A)*. Once on the East Fork River bed, walk upstream until you reach the bridge.

We expected to reach the road on the downstream side of the bridge by scrambling 20 feet up the loose rock of the bank. From the bus, it looked possible to do this scramble. When we reached this cliff, Travers (a fearless teenager) was willing to scramble up this bank, but I did not want to risk a skin-scraping slide on the loose rock. However no one wanted to wade the knee-deep cold water to go under the bridge for an easier climb out on the upstream side of the bridge.

Consequently we chose to backtrack about 100 yards and climb over the ridge above the bridge and reach the road west of the bridge, a route I had done several years ago. (Because the route down to the road from the ridge above the road is difficult to find, do not try this unless you are skilled at backcountry route-finding.) Next time if the water is knee deep or less, I will wade under the bridge rather than do the route we chose since it would be a lot quicker and easier.

Variations: For a shorter hike, after dropping into the stream bed from hill 3608, return to the road by following the creek upstream to reach the road near Polychrome Pass. From the ridge, the walking looked easy along this creek. You can shorten this hike even more by descending to the small creek along the ridge (east) from the pyramid-shaped peak (hill 4222 on USGS map) and then returning upstream to the road.

Cautions

Even though the basic route is easy to see, I rate the route-finding difficulty as moderate due to the need to find faint trails in scree and select the best routes through some stretches of thigh-high tundra. Near the East Fork River Bridge, hiking and route finding may become moderate to difficult. Reaching the road at the bridge requires either scrambling up a loose rocky bank (20 feet high) on the downstream side of the bridge, or wading under the bridge to reach the road from the upstream side of the bridge, or climbing out and over the ridge to reach the road to the west of the bridge which is the most strenuous and difficult route finding option.

The river channel under the west end of the bridge may vary from year to year. If you plan to wade under the bridge, examine the river as you pass the area on the bus before you begin the hike.

21

Polychrome Bluffs Hike

Location: Mile 47.5 (about 2 miles west of Polychrome Pass summit)
GPS: N63° 31.7' W149° 52.7'
Time on bus (one way): 3.5 hours
Hike Length: 4 miles (6.4 km)
Hiking Time: 3 to 4 hours
Elevation Gain: 200 climb feet at end
Hiking Difficulty: Moderate
Route Finding Difficulty: Easy
Backcountry Permit Area: 8
USGS Map: Healy (C-6)

Highlights

The small streambed at the beginning of this route is an intimate garden path through the tundra. It provides a gravel path to reach the Polychrome tundra plain or the bottom of the Polychrome Bluffs without bushwhacking or scrambling down steep banks.

On this hike I have frequently seen caribou, bear, ptarmigan, snowshoe hares, northern harriers and soaring golden eagles. Along the foot of the bluffs I heard pikas but did not take the time to find them. Golden plovers can be found in June and July further out on the tundra plain. The willows and tundra adjacent to the streambeds provides additional birding opportunities. Small streams flowing down tundra banks were a delight to photograph *(photo 21B)*.

Photo 21A. **East end of Mount Polychrome as seen from the road; use this landmark to find the start of hikes 21, 22, 23, 24 and 25.**

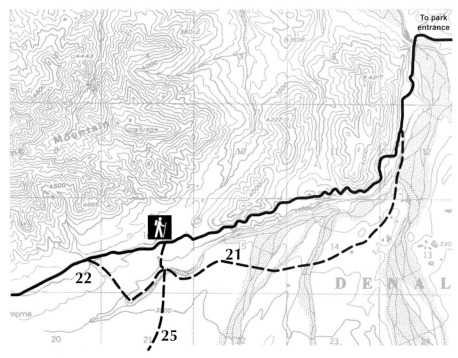

Hikes 21, 22 and 25
Contour interval 100 feet. Grid = 1 mile. Full Hike 25 map on page 131.

Route description

Begin this hike at the first gravel drainage that flows south from Polychrome Mountain to the road (in square 16 on USGS map). This drainage is <u>not shown</u> in blue on either the USGS or *Trails Illustrated*® map. It is east of the Polychrome Mountain drainage shown in blue on the USGS map (square 17) or *Trails Illustrated*® Map.

Tell the bus driver you want to get off a little west of Mile 47 where a creek crosses the road. A distinguishing landmark for this creek is a small off-road parking spot on the north side of the road at the creek. If you are riding the bus west (into the park), talk with the bus driver about where you want to get off during the Teklanika rest stop.

Photo 21B. **Tundra stream flowing into the East Fork River on Hike 21**

Prepare to stop the bus after the road leaves the cliffs of Polychrome Pass. A good landmark for deciding when to stop the bus is the first big open area you see on the north side after the road leaves the cliffs of Polychrome Pass. At this point, you will also be able to see the rust-colored cliffs at the top of the east end of Polychrome Mountain (Hill 5150 on Healy (C-6) map) *(photo 21A)*. If you are riding the bus out of the park, talk to the driver about where you want to get off while at the Toklat rest stop.

Follow the streambed downstream until it joins the western-most branch of the East Fork Toklat River. Make a lot of noise and watch for bears in the brush! Periodically find a gap in the vegetation along the bank and climb out of the streambed to look for bears, caribou, tundra flowers and berries in season.

Upon reaching the western-most branch of the East Fork Toklat River, you have two options. You can climb the bluff (about 20 feet high) across the stream and explore the tundra plain while heading east. Before choosing to venture very far onto the tundra plains, make sure you know if any of the area is closed to hiking as some of the area at the eastern end of this hike has been closed in the past. The other option is to head downstream and explore the foot of the Polychrome Bluffs.

Both routes will require some stream crossings, most of which can be done without wading. As you proceed downstream, the main channel gets bigger. Expect to wade across the final channel to reach the road. Crossing the final chanel may involve knee-deep water about 10 feet wide. My friend used a hiking staff and I used my camera tripod for stability on the final crossing *(photo V)*.

Because I like exploring the tundra and watchng for birds, I have always hiked in the tundra on the south side of the main channels rather that along the bottom of the Polychrome Bluffs. Also based on my observations, I concluded it would be difficult to avoid wading by hiking next to the foot of Polychrome Bluffs because the stream channel frequently runs next to the bluff.

You can continue to the East Fork Toklat Bridge or elect to climb to the road when you see it about 200 feet above the streambed. To reach the road before the bridge, watch for a route that you can scramble up. To minimize bushwhacking, do not climb the bank unless you can see the road since the road sometimes is about half a mile from the river bank.

Variations: Walk down to the west branch of the East Fork Toklat River and then return to the road by walking back along the creek. The area where the small creek joins the west branch of the East Fork Toklat is a wide delta that offers views to the south and on hot days some tall brush might provide shade. To enjoy a view to the north of Polychrome Bluffs and Mountain, picnic on the stream bank along the south side of the west branch of the East Fork Toklat.

Photo 22A. **This young caribou came to investigate Mom and I and then bolted away.**

Cautions

Watch for bears. Scout the area before leaving the road. For the first half-mile of this hike you cannot see what is in the tundra on either side of the stream because brush on the streambank obscures the view. Make lots of noise while walking in this area. Periodically find gaps in the vegetation and climb onto the bank (about three feet high) and look around for bears.

Be prepared to wade streams near the end of this hike. If early in this hike you find the need to wade rather than step across streams, then consider retracing your steps rather than continuing toward the bridge because the water will get deeper and wider as you proceed downstream.

Photo 22B. **Willow Ptarmigan**

22

Mom's Polychrome Picnic Loop

Location: Mile 47.5 (2 miles west of Polychrome Pass summit)
GPS: N63° 31.7' W149° 52.7'
Time on bus (one way): 3.5 hours
Hike Length: 2 miles (3.2 km)
Hiking Time: 2 hours
Elevation Gain: 200 feet at end
Hiking Difficulty: Easy
Route Finding Difficulty: Easy
Backcountry Permit Area: 8
USGS Map: Healy (C-6)

Highlights

This route is like a garden path through the tundra. It has trickling streams, grassy banks, ptarmigan *(photo 22B)*, arctic ground squirrels, snowshoe hare and easy walking. I have frequently seen caribou, bear, northern harriers and soaring golden eagles along this route *(photo 22A)*. Mom enjoys and finds the route easy to negotiate *(photo 22C)*. There are plenty of picnic spots along the west branch of the East Fork Toklat River with views to the north and south and far enough from the road to eliminate traffic noise. This is a quick loop hike to get some air and enjoy one of the most beautiful spots in the park.

Route description

This hike begins at the first gravel drainage that flows south from Polychrome Mountain and crosses the road (in square 16 on the USGS map) before continuing to the East Fork drainage. The drainage followed at the beginning of this hike is east of the drainage shown in blue in square 17 on the USGS map and on the *Trails Illustrated®* Map. However the end of this hike is the drainage shown in blue shown on these maps.

If you are riding the bus west, talk to your bus driver during the Teklanika rest stop about where you want to get off the bus. Tell the driver you want to get off beyond Polychrome Pass and a little west of mile 47 where a creek crosses the road. A distinguishing landmark for this creek is a small off-road parking spot on the north side of the road at the creek. Prepare to stop the bus after the road leaves the cliffs of Polychrome Pass. A good landmark for deciding when to stop the bus is the first big open area you see on the north side after the road leaves the cliffs of Polychrome Pass.

At this point, you will also be able to see the rust-colored cliffs at the top of the east end of Polychrome Mountain (hill 5150 on Healy (C-6) map). *(See photo 21A.)* If you are riding the bus out of the park, talk to the driver about where you want to get off while you are at the Toklat rest stop.

Before starting down the streambed, scout the area for bears. Walk downstream making plenty of noise. In about half a mile the streambed broadens to a wide delta before it enters the west branch of the East Fork Toklat.

Photo 22C. **Mom enjoying the streamside stroll on Hike 22.**

Follow the right (west) edge of the delta and continue west parallel to the stream. You will see a grassy area with some clumps of higher brush at the foot of a 10- to 20-foot bank at the edge of the tundra. Walk west along the grassy area. You will encounter some hummocks and minor stream crossings.

Once you reach the next drainage from the north, follow this drainage back to the road. Again make noise as you walk along the creek bed back to the road.

Variations: Extend the hike by exploring the tundra plain across the west branch of the East Fork Toklat River. Another option is to take a short hike upstream from the starting point into the Polychrome Mountain canyon to see some interesting geology. (See Hike 24.)

Cautions

Watch for bears. Scout the area before leaving the road. For the first half a mile of this hike you cannot see what is in the tundra on either side of the stream because of brush on the stream bank. Make a lot of noise while walking in this area. Periodically find gaps in the vegetation and climb onto the bank (about three feet high) and look around for bears. Follow the same approach when returning to the road along the next streambed.

23

Polychrome Mountain East End #1

Location: Mile 47.5, about 2 miles west of Polychrome Pass summit
GPS: N63° 31.7' W149° 52'
Time on bus (one way): 3.5 hours
Hike Length: 4 miles (6.4 km)
Hiking Time: 4 hours
Elevation Gain: 1,500 feet
Hiking Difficulty: Moderate
Route Finding Difficulty: Moderate
Backcountry Permit Area: 31
USGS Map: Healy (C-6)

Highlights

Sometimes I get lucky. During my second summer researching this book, I returned to this mountain because of the flower covered slopes on the north side plus the beautiful 360-degree panorama view that I discovered the previous summer *(photo 23C)*. This time an additional reward was an hour spent photographing a young Dall sheep ram resting among the flowers and rocks near the summit *(photo 23A)*. The ram was still there when I reluctantly quit photographing and continued to the summit. From the summit I used binoculars to watch six more rams on adjacent ridges. On the way up, pikas chirped as I passed their hiding places in the scree. During my lunch, a golden eagle soared above the cliffs. (See also highlights of Hike 24.)

Route description

See map on page 120.

During the Teklanika rest stop, talk to your bus driver about where you want to get off the bus. Tell the driver you want to get off beyond Polychrome Pass and a little west of mile 47. After the Polychrome Pass road summit (mile 46) prepare to stop the bus after the road leaves the cliffs of Polychrome Pass. A good landmark for deciding when to stop the bus is the first big open area you see on the north side after the road leaves the cliffs of Polychrome Pass. At this point, you will also be able to see the rust colored cliffs at the top of the east end of Polychrome Mountain (hill 5150 on Healy (C-6) map) which is your destination. (See *photo 21A*.)

Photo 23A. **This young ram was a patient model. What a fine day!**

Photo 23B. **Hike 23 route follows the drainage to the left and behind the dark, conical outcrop (top right) at the east end of Mount Polychrome.**

If you are riding a bus going out of the park, talk to the driver about where you want to get off during the Toklat rest stop. Tell the driver you want off before mile 47 which is just before the road starts along the Polychrome cliffs.

From mile 47, walk west until you find a place where the road makes about a 90-degree turn to the north followed quickly by another turn west. This jog is shown at the eastern edge of square 16 on the USGS map. You have gone too far if you get to the first gravel drainage which flows south from Polychrome Mountain and crosses the road and continues to the East Fork drainage (in square 16 on USGS map). (Note: This first Mt Polychrome drainage is <u>east</u> of the one shown in blue on the USGS or *Trails Illustrated®* map.)

Where the road turns west at the north end of the jog, find a break in the brush and hike north into the tundra heading for higher ground. The brush is about waist high near the road but becomes knee high and easy to get through. Head toward the prominent dark reddish brown rocky peak at the eastern end of Polychrome Mountain ridge *(photo 23B)*. Your route will eventually take you to the left and behind this peak to gain the main ridge. Check your route across the tundra by watching for the tundra pond on your right (east). Take time to check the pond for ducks and wildlife. I saw bufflehead and mallard ducks on this pond.

Continue north until you reach a grassy swale that is about 20 feet lower in elevation. Follow this swale northeasterly toward where it joins the drainage from the pond. Continue following this drainage until you have gone far enough north to see up the drainage which originates behind the dark reddish-brown peak at the eastern end of Polychrome Mountain. Your goal is to follow the drainage originating behind this reddish brown peak to reach the saddle that connects the peak to the main ridge of Polychrome Mountain *(photo 23B)*.

To get behind the reddish-brown peak, rather than follow the bed of the drainage that is brushy, initially select a route up the ridge on the south side of the drainage. Get on this ridge by

Photo 23C. **Enjoying the meadow and view on the summit at the east end of Mount Polychrome.**

walking up the wide gravel drainage on the left side of the ridge. Near the toe of this ridge there is a grassy swale that leads up the bank onto the ridge. Once you are far enough up the ridge to see the saddle behind the peak and the drainage is mainly grassy, drop into the drainage and continue walking up the drainage toward the saddle behind the peak. The final route to the saddle is loose dirt and scree. Try to stay on the gravel and soil instead of walking on the vegetation. Once on the saddle follow the ridge connecting to the main Polychrome Mountain ridge. You will see the grassy sloping north side of this mountain. Follow the Polychrome Mountain ridgeline to the summit (hill 5150 on the USGS map).

Variations: Make this a loop hike by combining with Hike 24. Through mid-June, snow underlain by ice on the north side of this mountain may make it difficult to make the traverse for a loop hike without risking a long slide to the rocks below.

Cautions

Route-finding difficulty is moderate because of the tundra crossing required to get to the drainage leading to the summit ridge. Once you have made it to the drainage, route finding is easy. While there is scree along the final route to the summit, it is stable and there is no exposure. However, you may not be visible from the road if you become disabled so watch your step. Do not attempt any scrambling on the cliffs along the south face of Polychrome Mountain.

Bears are common in the tundra area. I saw bear scat on the summit ridgeline.

24

Polychrome Mountain East End

Location: Mile 47.5, About 2 miles west of Polychrome Pass summit
GPS: N63° 31.7' W149° 52.7'
Time on bus (one way): 3.5 Hours
Hike Length: 4.5 miles (7.2 km)
Hiking Time: 5 hours
Elevation Gain: 1,500 feet
Hiking Difficulty: Moderate
Route Finding Difficulty: Easy
Backcountry Permit Area: 31
USGS Map: Healy (C-6)

Highlights

Because there are cliffs and bare rock on the front (south) side of Mt. Polychrome, I was expecting a narrow ridge of bare rock on the top. The flower-covered meadow on the back (north) side was a delightful surprise. *(photo 23C)* The slope of the meadow was just right for taking a nap. While clouds obscured Mt. McKinley, from past hikes on nearby peaks I believe the top third of Mt. McKinley would be visible on a clear day. Even without Mt. McKinley, the expansive view north along the East Fork drainage reveals routes and inspires dreams of hiking deeper into the wilderness. From the saddle I saw three rams across the valley. On subsequent hikes I photographed rams and ewes in this area. In the canyon at the beginning of

Hikes 23 and 24
Contour interval 100 feet. Grid = 1 mile

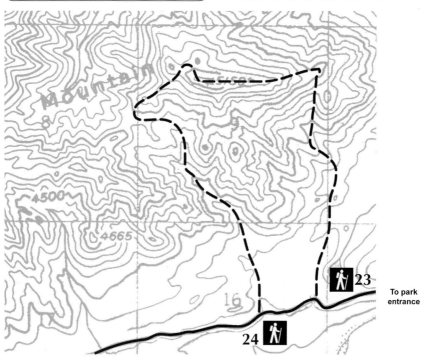

Photo 24A. **Follow this creek to reach the eastern summit of Mount Polychrome described in Hike 24**

this hike, patches of dwarf fireweed added contrast and color to the rocky streambed and canyon walls. Ground squirrels had a lively discussion about my passage along this canyon.

The changing geology and colored soils along this route will fascinate the geology first graders (like me) and the experts. People from an Alaska rock hound club were camped near this drainage to do some geology research.

Route description

Begin this hike at the first gravel drainage that flows south from Polychrome Mountain to the road (in square 16 on USGS map) and then continues to the main East Fork drainage. This drainage is not shown in blue on either the USGS or *Trails Illustrated*® map. It is east of the Polychrome Mountain drainage shown in blue on the USGS map (in square 17) or *Trails Illustrated*® Map.

If you are riding the bus west, talk to your bus driver during the Teklanika rest stop about where you want to get off the bus. Tell the driver you want to get off beyond Polychrome Pass (mile 46) and a little west of mile 47 where a creek crosses the road. A distinguishing landmark for this creek is a small off-road parking spot on the north side of the road and the west side of the creek.

Prepare to stop the bus after the road leaves the cliffs of Polychrome Pass. A good landmark for deciding when to stop the bus is the first big open area you see on the north side after the road leaves the cliffs of Polychrome Pass. At this point, you will also be able to see the rust-colored cliffs at the top of the east end of Polychrome Mountain (hill 5150 on Healy (C-6) map). (See *photo 21A*.) If you are riding the bus out of the park, talk to the driver about where you want to get off while at the Toklat rest stop.

The gravel streambed is about 20 feet wide where it crosses the road *(photo 24A)*. In early July there was water in the stream, but there may not be water if it has been a dry summer. Looking upstream, you will see the streambed disappear into a canyon at the base of Polychrome Mountain. From the road, you cannot see your destination, the saddle between the east end of Polychrome Mountain (hill 5150) and the rest of Polychrome Mountain to the west.

Walk up this streambed. For the first half-mile, the stream banks and brush on both banks will make it hard to see bears so make some noise. At the head of the valley just below the saddle, you will see a saddle that is divided by a mound of rock. Walk up the last drainage to the right (east) of the rock mound to reach the right side of the saddle.

As you walk east up the ridgeline from the saddle you will encounter a rock formation that blocks the ridge. I followed a sheep trail around the south side of this formation. Next you will find another cliff with white clay at its base. Pick your way across the jumble of boulders and clay to reach the east side of this cliff. There you will find a route up some loose but easy to negotiate scree to the ridgeline. When you reach this ridgeline you will discover the wonderful meadow on the backside and an easy stroll to the summit. Return to the road the way you came.

Variations: Combine this hike with Hike 17 to make a loop. Through mid-June, snow underlain by ice on the north side of this mountain may make it difficult to make the traverse for a loop hike without risking a long slide to the rocks below.

Cautions

This route requires adequate boots and route-finding skills to negotiate short stretches of scree and loose gravel. The scree along the final route to the summit is stable and there is no exposure. You may not be visible from the road if you become disabled so watch your step. Do not attempt any scrambling on the cliffs of the south face of Polychrome Mountain because the rock is unstable. This is why the route goes around rather than over the rock outcrops along the final summit ridgeline above the saddle.

Bears are common in the tundra area beside the creek. I saw bear scat on the summit ridgeline.

Photo 25A. **Geode on Geode Mountain, Hike 25.**

25

Geode Mountain

Location: Mile 47.5
GPS: N63° 31.7' W149° 52.7'
Time on bus (one way): 3.5 hours
Hike Length: 6.5 miles (10.4 km)
Hiking Time: 7 hours
Elevation Gain: 1,700 feet
Hiking Difficulty: Easy
Route Finding Difficulty: Moderate
Backcountry Permit Area: 8
USGS Maps: Healy (B-6), (C-6)

Highlights

A comment by Lee Lipscomb, a Denali bus driver and avid hiker, enticed me to hike this mountain. Lee called this unnamed mountain "Geode Mountain." I have always been interested in the multi-colored mountains and geology of this area and wanted to scout locations for future photography trips. So I celebrated my 57th birthday testing myself with this climb and finding out if there were geodes on top. If you find any geodes please leave them for others to enjoy. *(photo 25A)*

Caribou and bears frequently travel through the Polychrome valley. Wildflowers are abundant along the way and on the slopes of the mountain. In mid-June a surfbird family was on the summit ridge. *(photo 25B)* Golden eagles were nesting on a cliff nearby. Mt McKinley is visible from the top and the view of the Toklat and Polychrome geology is spectacular. *(photo 25C)*

Route Description

See map on page 131.

This hike begins at the first gravel drainage that flows south from Polychrome Mountain and crosses the road (in square 16 on the USGS map) before continuing to the East Fork drainage. The drainage followed at the beginning of this hike is east of the drainage shown in blue in square 17 on the USGS map and on the *Trails Illustrated*™ Map.

If you are riding the bus west, talk to your bus driver during the Teklanika rest stop about where you want to get off the bus. Tell the driver you want to get off beyond Polychrome Pass (mile 46) and a little west of mile 47 where a creek crosses the road. A distinguishing landmark for this creek is a small off-road parking spot on the north side of the road and the west side of the creek. Prepare to stop the bus after the road leaves

Photo 25B. **Surfbird on Geode Mountain in mid-June.**

the cliffs of Polychrome Pass. A good landmark for deciding when to stop the bus is the first big open area you see on the north side after the road leaves the cliffs of Polychrome Pass. At this point, you will also be able to see the rust-colored cliffs at the top of the east end of Polychrome Mountain (hill 5150 on Healy (C-6) map). *(See photo 21A)* If you are riding the bus out of the park, talk to the driver about where you want to get off while you are at the Toklat rest stop.

While on the road, examine Geode Mountain, the lumpy green mountain on the west side of Polychrome Valley. The route follows the slope up the eastern front of the mountain. Select a route that looks good to you. Also look for bears in the brush along the approach to the mountain. *(photo 25D)*

From the road, follow the gravel streambed until it joins the East Fork drainage flowing east. The brush on both sides of this drainage is high so make noise. At the bottom, cross the main stream to get to the tundra bluff. I was able to jump across the stream. Look for a game trail up the bluff in a notch a little way downstream. This game trail is a good (but not essential) way to begin finding the easiest walk through the knee-high tundra and around areas with higher brush while heading to Geode Mountain.

I was able to thread my way through the tundra by finding open areas and small drainages while continuing to make progress toward the canyon to the east of Geode Mountain. Once I reached the canyon, I followed a game trail west along the toe of Geode Mountain until I came to the

Photo 25C. **View of Polychrome Valley from near summit of Hike 25. The valley at center is the return route down.**

Photo 25D. **Geode Mountain is the lumpy mountain in the foreground to the right edge of the photo. Hike 25 climbs the ridge at the right edge of the photo and returns from the canyon at the left-center.**

route that I followed to the top. I used this roundabout approach, rather than a more direct route to the toe of the mountain, in order to avoid crossing most of the higher brush in the drainage at the base of it.

In June, I filtered water from one of the small clear streams descending the northeastern toe of Geode Mountain. Clear water is also available in the drainage followed by the return route of this hike.

Once at the base of Geode Mountain, follow the easiest walking to the top ridgeline. Once on the ridgeline, walk south around the drainage headwaters to reach the ridgeline on the far side that is the route down. Near the top and along the ridgeline, look on the ground and in the rock outcrops for geodes that have broken open naturally. Please do not break rocks or carry any geodes away.

Descend the ridgeline adjacent to the drainage or walk down the drainage. Follow the drainage until it reaches the junction with the main river. Exit the main canyon and return to the road. It took me about an hour of non-stop hiking to reach the road.

Variations: The valley followed on the route down, with its flowers, interesting geology and streams, is a great dayhike destination. Allow more time to explore this area by doing this hike as a backpack. See Hike 27 for information on following the streambed south in the main canyon.

Cautions

The Toklat drainage side of the Geode Mountain ridgeline is very steep with loose rock and large drops in the drainages. I do not recommend ascending or descending on the western (Toklat) side of the Geode Mountain ridgeline.

26

Toklat East Branch Exploration

Location: Mile 51
Time on bus (one way): 3 hours
Hike Length: 3 (4.8 km) to 20 miles (32 km)
Hiking Time: 3 hours to 3+ days
Elevation Gain: 200 to 800 feet
Hiking Difficulty: Easy
Route Finding Difficulty: Easy
Backcountry Permit Area: 9
USGS Maps: Healy (B-6), (C-6)

Highlights

If you have a limited amount of time but still wish to visit some pristine backcountry, try this day or overnight hike into the mountains along the crest of the Alaska Range. The hike up the valley itself is fairly easy and does not require crossing any major glacial streams. The valley offers beautiful scenery and good chances to see sheep, caribou, bears, and occasionally wolves and foxes. Ptarmigan families are often seen in the brush along the riverbed. About seven miles from the road the river splits into two forks, each of which starts at an unnamed glacier flowing down from the crest of the Alaska Range. The small valley that swings to the left is particularly scenic and a good place to see sheep. *(photo 26C)*

Route description

Start this hike at milepost 51, about 5 miles past the Polychrome rest stop. Climb down a brushy bank to a ravine that flows into the valley of the East Branch of the Toklat. Bus drivers call this ravine "I Scream Gulch." Hike south on the broad Toklat gravel bars as far as you want to go. *(photo 26A)* Be especially alert for bears in this lower part of the valley. They like to feed on the roots of pea vines (Hedysarum alpinum) that flourish on the river bars.

After about three miles the Toklat valley begins to narrow. The strikingly-colored mountains on the left (east) consist of volcanic rocks of the Teklanika Formation created about 60 million years ago when volcanoes erupted here and buried the area under thousands of feet of lava. Sheep are often seen on the high bench to the left. For the next two miles or so there are a number of good camping spots where clear streams flow out of the mountains on the left. About 7 miles from the road the river splits into two forks, each of which start at the snouts of unnamed glaciers flowing down from the crest of the Alaska Range. The passes at the heads of these valleys are natural wind funnels. If you camp overnight, be prepared for strong winds.

Variations: The main variation on this hike is the distance you chose to walk up the valley. If you do not mind stream crossings, try one of my all-time favorite hikes, a loop around Divide Mountain (Hike 28). Another option is to combine this hike with a crossing into the Polychrome basin (Hike 27).

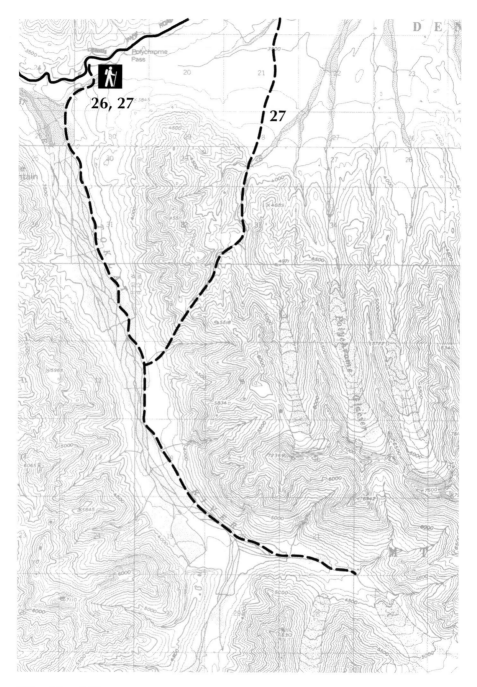

Hikes 26 and 27
Contour interval 100 feet. Grid = 1 mile.

Photo 26A. **This view from the road shows the ravine that is the initial route of hikes 26 and 27 where it enters the east branch of the Toklat River (braided river in the distance).**

Cautions

Bears are the main concern. Be extra careful if you walk along the east side of the Toklat within a couple miles of the bridge instead of starting the hike as described. Bears love the brush between the river and road near the bridge, particularly after mid-August when the soapberries are ripe. So exercise caution and make noise because bears are hard to see in this area.

Photo 26B. **Willow ptarmigan**

Photo 26C. **Enjoying the view at the Toklat headwaters.**

Toklat

Most sources claim that "Toklat" is an Indian word for dishwater. However, Judge James Wickersham of Fairbanks, who in 1903 led the first party to attempt an ascent of Mt. McKinley, pooh-poohs this idea. He states on good authority that "Toklat" was the name given by the Athapascans to another river altogether, the current-day Cosna River northwest of the park. Through an amusing series of errors on the part of the early explorers of the Denali region and topographers, the name Toklat came to be applied to this river here in the park. Its original name, according to the sources cited by Wickersham in his classic book *Old Yukon*, was "Totlot," which in Athapascan means "headwaters" or "water source."

27

Toklat to Polychrome

Location: Mile 51
Time on bus (one way): 3 hours
Hike Length: 10 miles (16 km)
Hiking Time: 2 days
Elevation Gain: 1,500 feet
Hiking Difficulty: Diffult
Route Finding Difficulty: Moderate to Difficult
Backcountry Permit Areas: 8 & 9
USGS Maps: Healy (B-6), (C-6)

Highlights

Views of the Toklat valley and of multi-colored mountains on the Polychrome side are stunning. Tracks in the pass indicate sheep use this route. I have seen caribou, bear, marmots and ptarmigan along this route. The changes in elevation and terrain produce a wide variety of wildflowers. While camped at the base of the mountains on the Toklat side, marmots whistled me to sleep.

A major highlight was accomplishing this hike after years of looking at the map and wondering if it were possible for me to do this route. From the map and previous scouting hikes, I knew the western (Toklat) side of this pass is extremely rugged; containing cliffs made of loose rock, steep scree slopes and drainages with large drops. While backpacking in the Toklat River valley, I studied the mountains and saw a route that looked feasible if I could get past a rock outcrop at the top. This was the route that I had identified as possible on the map so I decided to try it on my return from the Toklat headwaters.

Route Description

Ask the bus driver to let you off at the ravine that provides a good access route to the Toklat River near mile 51. Some drivers call this ravine "I scream gulch." When approaching the ravine from the east, it is located before the "porcupine forest area." This is the access route that I use to start (or finish) a hike up the east side of the eastern branch of the Toklat River (Hike 26). *(photo 26A)*

Before leaving the road, examine the ravine and Toklat River valley for bears. Follow the ravine to the Toklat. Select the easiest walking along the Toklat and head upstream.

When you are across from the pass on the south side of Divide Mountain, begin looking at the ridges of the mountains above you. To me, the route for this hike stands out as the widest, grassy slope that reaches almost to the top of the mountain range. *(photo 27A)* With binoculars I could also see a game trail leading up the grassy part of the slope.

I camped between the large drainage adjacent to this route and the next small drainage to the south. Even though July had been hot and dry, clear water was available upstream in the small drainage and also in the drainage further to the south. I enjoyed marmots whistling to each other from rock outcrops above my camp.

Photo 27A. **On Hike 27, follow the diagonal ridge (bottom right to top left) to reach the pass to the Polychrome drainage. Scene as viewed from the Toklat riverbed.**

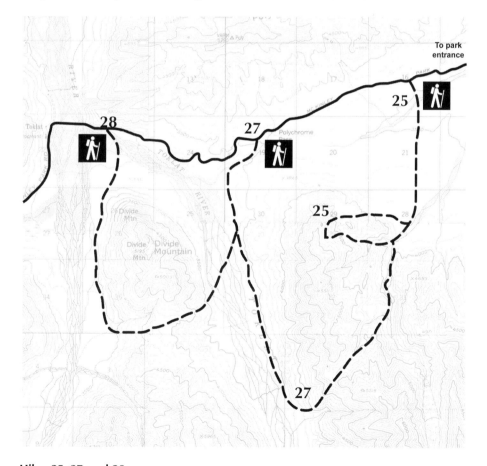

Hikes 25, 27, and 28
Contour interval 100 feet. Grid = 1 mile.

Photo 27B. **View form the pass of the ridgeline I followed up from the Toklat River. I hiked along the other side of the ridgeline at the top. Note the light colored soil that serves as a landmark for selecting the route to descend into the Toklat drainage. See "Variations" under Hike 27.**

Select the easiest walking to climb the ridge. As the ridge narrows at the top, the sheep trail becomes more obvious. Just before the first rock outcrop, I noticed the sheep trail went across the scree slope on the south side below the outcrop. I followed this trail as it continued across the scree below the ridgeline. In about 100 feet I came to a drainage that was full of dried gray clay. The deep (6 inches) sheep tracks in the dried mud indicate this area will be muddy when wet. While the sheep tracks went up this dried mud area, I crossed it and followed the adjacent ridge to the top. The sheep trail was stable and I did not feel exposed to a fall along this route.

Without my pack, I walked back along the spine of the final ridge to see if I could negotiate the rock outcrops. I had to scoot down on my rear end several times while hunting for adequate hand and foot holds in the loose rock. I then climbed back up over the rock outcrops. Since a slip would mean a sliding drop of 6 to 10 feet, I would not be comfortable negotiating these outcrops of loose rock while alone and wearing a backpack. To me it is much safer and easier to go around these outcrops. (photo 27B)

When leaving the pass, contour east on the south side of the drainage leading toward the Polychrome area and then follow a ridgeline to the creek bed. This creek had clear water beginning near the top. From the pass it is also possible to walk in the creek instead of walking above the creek. However the creek eventually enters a narrow canyon with steep, unstable walls, slick rocks and drops of 4 to 6 feet. Before the canyon narrows, the drainage curves sharply to the north and there is another drainage entering from the southeast with a high plateau above. At this point climb southeast out of the main streambed onto the plateau and then follows a broad ridge to the junction with the main stream. *(photo 27C)*

Just before the side stream joins the main river, climb up the north bank of the side stream to reach the west bank above the main river. Walk north along the bank above the main river until you see the main canyon is wide and easy walking to the mouth of the canyon. (Note: I made the mistake of walking down the main riverbed and was soon in a narrow canyon with unstable walls wading in fast, murky, often knee-deep water with difficult footing.)

At the mouth of the main canyon, the drainage entering on the west side is the last chance for clear water until near the road. After leaving the main canyon, look for the gravel drainage that leads up to the road. Use this drainage as a goal as you select a route through the tundra toward the road. I managed to pick up a game trail that generally headed northeast following a swale through the higher willows. When I was almost south of the gravel drainage I began heading toward the road following the best walking through the knee to thigh-high vegetation. I found it easy to find openings through the vegetation and maintain a relatively straight course.

Variations: If time permits, add more days to explore the Polychrome or Toklat sides or combine this route with a trip around Divide Mountain.

If you chose to do this trip in reverse, start at the same place as Hike 25 "Geode Mountain." Once at the pass and starting down ridge to the Toklat, look for the gray soil area along the ridgeline. *(photo 27B)* The sheep trail bypassing the rock outcrops begins by dropping down on the south side of this gray area about 20 feet. The sheep trail is much harder to find from this angle because it goes through the area of dried (hopefully) mud, so the best procedure is to contour along at the base of the rock outcrops until you can clearly see the trail below the last outcrops.

Cautions

Bears travel the riverbed and tundra areas of this hike. While visibility is generally good, a sow and two cubs surprised me in an area where I thought visibility was good. They already knew I was there and were moving out of my path.

Photo 27C. **View of the drainage followed on the Polychrome side of Hike 27.**

28

Around Divide Mountain

Location: Mile 53
Time on bus (one way): 3 hours
Hike Length: 7.5 miles (12 km)
Hiking Time: 8 hours
Elevation Gain: 1,000 ft.
Hiking Difficulty: Moderate to Difficult
Route Finding Difficulty: Easy
Backcountry Permit Areas: 9 & 10
USGS Maps: Mt. McKinley (B-1), (C-1), Healy (B-6), (C-6)

Highlights

Views of the geology and colors at the headwaters of both branches of the Toklat are highlights. Someday I hope to return to photograph the views from this pass in the early morning and evening light. *(photo 28A)* Wildflowers are abundant along the route over the pass. Ptarmigan, caribou, wolves and bears frequent the Toklat River gravel bars and adjacent banks. Tracks on game trails in the pass indicate caribou frequently use this pass. Dall sheep are often seen on the slopes of Divide Mountain, particularly in mid-June and after late August.

Hunter and naturalist Charles Sheldon named Divide Mountain when he camped here while sheep hunting in 1906. In order to protect the Dall sheep that were being over hunted, Sheldon became the driving force behind the creation of the park in 1917.

Route Description

See map on page 131.

Get off the bus at the east end of the Toklat River Bridge. While on the road, examine the river upstream to locate an area with the most and widest braids. (All the braids of the east branch of the river join just upstream from the bridge making it difficult to cross near the bridge.) Also look for bears in the brush between the road and gravel bar. Bears frequent this area, particularly in the fall when the soapberries are ripe.

To find a multi-braided place to cross, I walked upstream until I was just about due east from where Divide Mountain begins to rise out of the riverbed. I managed to cross most of the braids at points were the water was calf-deep or less but one braid had a knee-deep channel about 3 feet wide. When water levels are high, the "difficult" rating of this hike applies. *(photo 28B)*

Once across the river, walk west around the bottom of Divide Mountain. Walking is easy at the base of the mountain. Walk upstream along the flat plane selecting the easiest path through the occasional knee-high brush. As you get close to the drainage that is north of the route over the saddle, you will see this drainage is full of head-high willows. Cross through these willows on the west (river) side where the willows are thinner. Proceed up the southern edge of these willows until you reach the foot of the ridge that is the route over the saddle. Thread your way

Photo 28A. **View up the western branch of the Toklat River from saddle south of Divide Mountain.**

through a short stretch of willows to reach the foot of the ridge.

When I did this trip in mid-July after about a week of hot weather and no rain, finding a clear stream for drinking water along the west side of Divide was difficult. After listening carefully, I discovered a running stream in the willows of the drainage described above. Hopefully this is indicates the stream will be running most of the time. The streambed is reddish orange from mineral deposits but the water was clear, did not clog my water filter and tasted fine.

Once on the ridge, continue to the top of the pass and around the southern end of the high point in the center of the pass. It took me about 1.5 hours to do this climb with a full backpack. On the east side of the pass, there was water in the headwaters of the stream to the south.

Since my plans were to continue up the eastern branch of the Toklat, I chose to descend the southern ridgeline as shown. It is possible to descend other ridgelines to the north to shorten a day trip. As a general rule, I do not descend in a streambed unless I can see it all the way down in order to avoid difficult drops and poor footing. *(photo 28C)*

While descending, identify the best places to cross the river and also look for bears along the route to the road. After crossing the river, walk downstream until you reach the drainage paralleling the road. (If you decide to start this hike here, the bus drivers call this "I scream gulch.") The area near and in this drainage is brushy so make noise. While this side drainage is brushy, I consider this route less brushy than the area along the Toklat River downstream to the bridge.

Follow the drainage until you can see the road above and find a place to climb out to the road or follow the drainage until it crosses the road. I usually climb out when I can see the road and can see a reasonable route up the bank.

Photo 28B. **Toklat River braids where Hike 28 begins. In June Dall sheep often cross the river here to get to Divide Mountain and the ridges above the Toklat River. They return in the fall.**

Variations: Doing this hike as a backpack trip allows more flexibility to do river crossings at times when the water is lowest and allows more time to enjoy the flowers and views. I did this hike as the first part of a backpack trip up the eastern branch of the Toklat. It could also be done as part of a trip on the western branch of the Toklat.

I would normally get off the bus and start this hike from the gravel bank between the two concrete bridges across Toklat River. However in 2004, this area was closed to hiking due to a nearby wolf den. If the area is not closed, try this start and cross the western branch of the Toklat near Divide Mountain.

Cautions

You will have to cross the Toklat River. Water levels vary daily, lower in the morning and higher in late afternoon. The hotter the day, the larger the daily changes in water level due to increased glacier melt. A few days of rain can also significantly increase water levels.

Bears frequent the Toklat River bars and vegetation along its banks. While I consider visibility generally good on this hike, I have been surprised by bears that were in a dip or behind some brush. These occasions reminded me to make noise even when I think visibility is good.

Photo 28C. **View of ridgelines that can be used to descend from the saddle south of Divide Mountain to the eastern branch of the Toklat River.**

Photo 29A. **Whitish gentian was abundant along the higher elevations of Hike 29.**

29

Toklat to Stony

Location: Mile 53
Time on bus (one way): 3 hours
Hike Length: 15 miles (24 km)
Hiking Time: 3 days
Elevation Gain: 700
Hiking Difficulty: Moderate to Difficult
Route Finding Difficulty: Moderate
Backcountry Permit Areas: 32, 33, 39
USGS Maps: Mt. McKinley (B-1), (C-1)

Highlights

The view from my camp at the saddle between Toklat and Stony included rugged multi-colored cliffs with golden eagles soaring above, a reflecting pond bordered by Alaska cotton grass and a lone bull caribou resting high on the slopes above. My second campsite featured a commanding view of the Stony Creek drainage and an unexpected view of Mount McKinley's peaks. In mid-July one of my favorite flowers, whitish gentian, was abundant at both of my campsites. *(photos 29A,D)* A spruce grouse family surprised me in the forest during my climb from the Toklat River.

Route Description

If you are on an eastbound bus, get off at the Toklat River rest stop. Westbound buses also stop here.

Follow the edge of the Toklat riverbank south past the employee housing area. Walk through the gravel pit area along the edge of the metal sheet piling used to keep the river out of a gravel storage area. Walk towards the point that juts into the riverbed at the end of the metal sheet piling. If the river is not flowing against this point, walk around this point on the Toklat gravel bar. If the river is flowing too fast against the point, there is a low spot about 100 yards (100 meters) south where you can climb over the point and reach the gravel riverbed on the other side. Continue downstream past the two major drainages entering from the west.

When I did this hike, a major branch of the Toklat was flowing against the high bluffs visible downstream. So I decided to climb out of the riverbed rather than to try either walking along the river's edge at the bottom of the bluffs or crossing the river and then re-crossing it at the mouth of Sheldon Creek.

After I scrambled up the high bank and entered the forest above the river, I thought it would be easier to walk west through the forest until I reached the toe of the ridge at edge of the forest and then walk north toward Sheldon Creek. As I traveled away from the bluff, I began to encounter patches of head-high willows among the spruce trees. Usually I could find a way to get through the willows with only a few feet of hard going or I could detour around the edges while I maintained progress toward the western edge of the forest. When I reached the western edge of the forest, I did not find a game trail or tempting route north to Sheldon

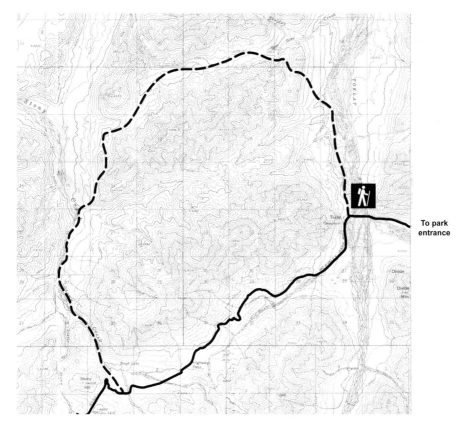

Hike 29
Contour interval 100 feet. Grid = 1 mile.

Creek through the waist to head-high vegetation at the toe of the ridge. So I continued climbing through the pass south of hill 4006 to reach Bear Draw. The beauty of this small pass with its clear water stream and wild flowers delighted me.

Bear Draw is a small stream full of head-high willows. To avoid this brush, walk along the south slope above Bear Draw while maintaining an elevation about the same as the headwaters of Bear Draw. This route crosses several drainages that are easy to cross and encounters patches of willows that are easy to negotiate. At a point where the bottom of Bear Draw becomes wide and grassy, drop down and continue walking west toward the pond at the pass and enjoy the wildflowers. *(photo 29C)*

If you camp in the pass, it is difficult to find rocks or bare dirt on which to operate a camp stove on the tundra slope south of the pond. The best option is to cook in the gravel bed of a drainage southwest of the pond. *(photo 29B)*

Continue west either by contouring or following the streambed. After the first major drainage west of the pond, the gravel streambed gets wider. I chose to contour above the streambed and encountered many side drainages with short stretches of willows. Often I thought it would have been easier to walk along the streambed. When you see a good route, head south toward the pass southeast of hill 4599.

Walk to the top of the pass southeast of hill 4599. Clear water and many camping spots are available in this pass. Exploring the strange rock formations of hill 4599 would be a fun dayhike from a camp in this pass. At the pass, walk along the slope on the southern side while maintaining the same elevation as the pass until you see the pond that marks where the route heads south. At the pond, take a break and enjoy the view of Stony valley from the saddle west of the pond. On a clear day look for the peaks of Mt. McKinley and the Alaska Range through the opening across the Stony valley *(photo 29D)*.

Walk south through the narrow valley until you reach the steep drainage at the base (north of) hill 4096. On a clear day, Mt. McKinley is visible from this point. Find a comfortable route down to the tundra below. Before descending, determine the route across the tundra that looks easiest to you. I selected the diagonal route shown rather than going straight to Sony Creek. The tundra I encountered was mostly knee high with areas of waist to head-high brush in the minor drainages.

At this point, the Stony Creek bed is full of willows but it is usually not difficult to thread your way between the willows following game trails, old stream channels, or gravel bars. I found the best routes were often next to the bluff at the edge of the tundra.

Walking solo in willows is scary for me, but I found it easier than walking in the tundra above the creek

Photo 29B. **Celebrating a great morning and view at my Bear Pass camp.**

bed. I made a lot of noise when walking in this area and walked slowly, continually looking ahead. Even with these precautions, I came within 100 yards of bears. While I stopped to eat blueberries and looked through the willows toward the creek, I saw the bears near the creek. Since the bears continued to eat soapberries, I concluded either they did not know I was there or, if they did know, they were not concerned. I quickly put on my pack and left quietly.

In about a mile the gravel creek bed becomes wider and more open and continues to be so until the Stony Creek canyon. The best route through this canyon is on the west bank. There are some cut banks and side ravines to negotiate but finding a route is not difficult. Once out of the canyon head for the road across the broad plane. Grizzlies frequent this plane so be alert, particularly if you see buses stopping.

Variations: Instead of climbing out of the Toklat River where I did, cross the Toklat River to avoid the steep bank. Walk north along the gravel bar and then cross the river again to reach Sheldon Creek. Walk up the Sheldon Creek gravel streambed until the junction with willow-clogged Bear Draw. At this junction climb the south bank toward hill 4066. Walk along the 3,800-foot contour to intersect the route described above. (Note: Crossing the Toklat River downstream from the bridge can be very difficult because there are fewer braids. When I did this hike, most of the Toklat River was flowing against the steep bank upstream from Sheldon Creek so I chose not to try crossing the river.)

Cautions

Make a lot of noise and be alert in the forest areas at the beginning of this hike and in the willows along Stony Creek. Route finding in the forest requires using a compass or, as I did, selecting a landmark that can be seen on the ridge above.

Photo 29C. **View of Bear Pass route from the Toklat side. The way to reach the pass is to contour along the slope well above the brush in the ravine below.**

Photo 29D. **Stony Creek valley from camp 2 on Hike 29. South peak of Mount McKinley (white) is visible at top right. Dark ridge at top left is Stony Hill.**

30

Toklat River Short Walk and Picnic

Location: Mile 53, Toklat Ranger Sta.
Time on bus (one way): 3 hours
Hike Length: 2.5 miles (4 km)
Hiking Time: 3 hours
Elevation Gain: none
Hiking Difficulty: Easy
Route Finding Difficulty: Easy
Backcountry Permit Area: 10
USGS Map: Mt. McKinley (C-1)

Highlights

This is one of the picnic hikes I have shared with Mom. It offers a view of Divide Mountain and the Toklat Drainage and opportunities to see caribou as they frequently wonder through. There are no streams to cross and the gravel bars are easy to negotiate. We found good picnic spots in the grassy areas along the low banks of the drainage that is the turnaround point for this hike. Kids can venture onto the gravel bars to look for rocks and animal tracks or play in the water *(photo 30A)*. Dall sheep are often visible on the mountains in this area.

Route description

Start this hike about 1/4 mile past the Toklat ranger station where the road runs near the river bar and it is easy to get onto the gravel bar. Walk up the gravel bar about one mile until you reach the drainage entering the Toklat from the right (west). Explore the grassy open areas along this drainage and stop to picnic. Remain in the area where visibility is good. Do not venture too far up this drainage due to the likelihood of encountering bears as the visibility along the drainage decreases. Return the way you came.

In 2004, this area was closed to hiking because wolves had established a den nearby. Check to see if this area is closed before doing this hike. If the area is closed continue to Highway Pass or Thorofare Pass to do a short hike. See Hikes 34 and 39.

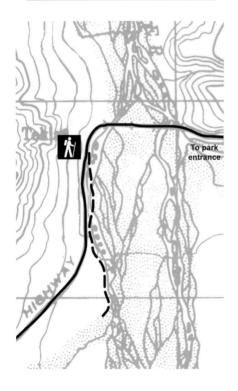

Hike 30
Contour interval 100 feet. Grid = 1 mile.

Photo 30A. **Jessica and Travers scouting for tracks and interesting rocks on Toklat River gravel bars.**

Photo 30B. **Mom enjoys the view and looks for sheep in the mountains along the Toklat River.**

Cautions

Visibility is generally good in this area. However bears frequent the area and often use the side drainage at the end of this hike as a travel route to Highway Pass. I recommend doing this hike on the return trip from Eielson so you will have two opportunities to view the area from the bus to determine if bears are present.

31

Toklat River to Eielson Visitor Center

Location: Mile 53, Toklat Ranger Sta.
Time on bus (one way): 3 hours
Hike Length: 20 miles (32 km)
Hiking Time: at least 3 days
Elevation Gain: 2,400 feet
Hiking Difficulty: Very Difficult
Route Finding Difficulty: Difficult
Backcountry Permit Areas: 10, 12
USGS Maps: Mt. McKinley (B-1), (C-1)

Highlights

This strenuous hike from the Toklat River Bridge to Eielson Visitor Center via a 5,100-foot pass between the Toklat River and Sunrise Creek offers a close-up view of the glaciers that have shaped the Denali region. In addition to the wide variety of landscapes, bears and caribou are common sights. Sheep are often seen on the surrounding ridges along the Toklat. Ptarmigan and other birds are found in the brush along the river gravel bars. Watch for wolves cruising the valley. The pass offers spectacular views of the Toklat valley, Mt. Eielson, Castle Rock and Mt. McKinley. It always amazes me that such a great wilderness trip is available so close to a park visitor center.

Route description

Start this hike about 1/4 mile past the Toklat ranger station where the road runs near the river bar. Walk up the river bar for about three miles to where the valley curves out of sight of the road and then pick up a trail on the grassy flats to the right of the river. Bears are very common in this lower part of the valley. Hiking is easy for the next three miles. Opposite a sizable though unnamed valley entering from the east (which offers an extremely interesting side trip into a seldom-visited area), the river flows by the first of a series of high bluffs on the east. It is possible to climb along the face of these bluffs, but if the river is low it might be advisable to cross over, keeping in mind that you'íll have to cross back over to the east side near the snout of the glacier two miles further on. Good camping spots are available near several clear streams entering from either side of the valley.

Note: In 2004, the starting place described above was closed because wolves established a den in the area. If this closure continues, then you will need to start this hike at the east end of the first Toklat River Bridge. (See start of Hike 28.) Walk along the bottom of Divide Mountain. Walking is easy at the base of the mountain. Walk upstream along the flat plane, selecting the easiest path through the occasional knee-high brush. Continue along the eastern edge of the western branch of the Toklat until you are past the closure area. Then you can cross the river or continue walking up the east side and cross later to continue the hike as described below.

Photo 31A. **Moraines at the head of Toklat valley. The route to Eielson (Hike 31) proceeds along the lateral moraine on the right side of the glacier, takes an abrupt right turn at the base of the mountains completely covered with snow, and then crosses a high pass to Sunrise Glacier.** Photo by Don Croner.

To continue to the pass, follow the lateral moraine on the right side of the glacier *(photo 31A)*. About 1/2 mile above the snout of the glacier a clear stream tumbles over a 100-foot waterfall on the right. This is the last clear water until the bottom of Sunrise Glacier on the other side of the pass. Beyond here the lateral moraine is extremely rough and rocky. Stay as high as possible to take advantage of somewhat easier going on the talus slopes along the upper edge of the moraine. Keep off the glacier unless you are equipped and trained for such travel.

About 1-1/2 miles past the last clear stream an arm of the glacier branches off to the right. The pass to Sunrise Glacier is visible at the head of this arm, just to the right of a huge hanging wall of ice. The main branch of the glacier continues on to an enormous amphitheater at the base of Scott Peak (8,828'). The upper part of the main branch of the glacier is heavily crevassed and should be avoided. Taking the arm trending to the right, climb up moraines and then a steep ravine to the 5,100-foot pass.

The spectacular view of the Toklat valley, Mt. Eielson, Castle Rock and Mt. McKinley looming in the distance makes the pass a tempting place to spend the night. There are flat camping spots on the ridge running north from the pass, but water must be packed up and winds can be daunting. Camping here should only be attempted in a quality mountaineering tent.

To continue to Eielson Visitor Center, descend a steep draw to Sunrise Glacier and proceed down

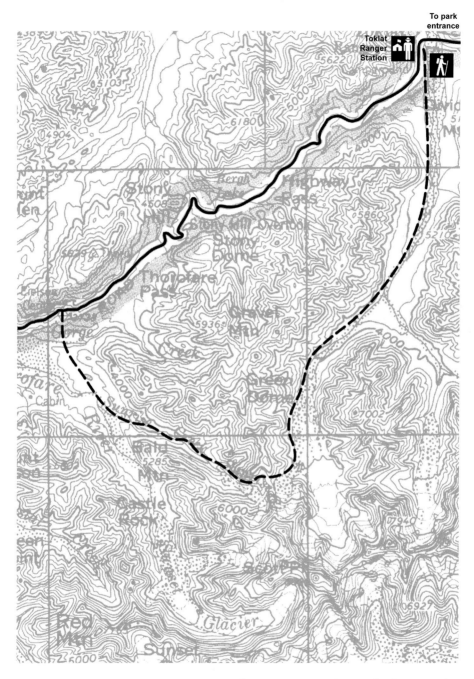

Hike 31
Contour interval 200'
Grid = 6 miles

the rocky moraines to the head of the Sunrise Creek canyon. At this point you have two choices. If you follow the floor of the canyon, you'll have to cross Sunrise Creek several dozen times where it flows against the canyon walls.

Photo 31B. **The end of Hike 31 viewed from Eielson. Sunrise Creek valley is the lighter-colored valley at top left. The plateau at right center (above the caribou) is the bench crossed after leaving Sunrise valley at the end of Hike 31.**

Do not choose this route if you feel the water is too high to make repeated crossings. The grassy bluffs to the right look inviting, but along this route you'll have to clamber in and out of numerous deep ravines that drop into the canyon. However most of these ravines contain clear creeks, and some of them have flat spots on the bottom for camping. Sheep are common on the surrounding ridges. Also watch for the rosy finch and snow buntings.

Right below where Sunrise Creek enters the Thorofare, climb a bluff to the right up onto a bench of grassy and low bush tundra and hike 2-1/2 miles north to Eielson Visitor Center. *(photo 31B).* As you cross the bench and after crossing Gorge Creek, search the slopes below the visitor center to find the trail up to the center. Watch for bears on this bench and in the brush along Gorge Creek. See Hike 48.)

Variations: If you do not want to tackle the trip down along the Sunrise Glacier and creek, plan a trip to explore the upper Toklat drainage. Since the Toklat and Sunrise Glacier drainages are in different backcountry permit areas, you will need to make this decision before obtaining permits.

Cautions

This hike is for those who are in excellent shape and have lots of experience finding routes and hiking in difficult terrain. Do not go alone! Do not venture onto any of the glaciers unless you are properly equipped and trained. Be prepared for wind and rain if the weather turns sour. River crossings may be required.

32

Highway Pass Perch

Location: Mile 57
GPS: N63°29.3′ W150°7.3
Time on bus (one way): 3.5 hours
Hike Length: 2.5 miles (4 km)
Hiking Time: 2.5 hours
Elevation Gain: 700 feet (235 m)
Hiking Difficulty: Easy
Route Finding Difficulty: Easy
Backcountry Permit Area: 33
USGS Map: Mt. McKinley (B-1)

Highlights

On a sunny day, I lingered five hours on this short hike to enjoy the view and photograph wildflowers. The high spots on this hike are perfect for watching for bears and caribou in the valley and for golden eagles soaring over the cliffs. In June and July, wildflowers abound in this area. In late August, Highway Pass is a patchwork of red and gold vegetation. The panoramic view stretches from the Toklat River to Stony Dome. On a clear day, Mount McKinley is visible along most of this hike. *(photo 32A)* In June and early July, long-tailed jaegers and American golden plovers are usually nesting in the flatter areas along the road at the pass summit. (Note: This route intentionally avoids areas near the road that are usually closed to hiking during nesting activity.) *(photo 32B)*

Route description

Ask the bus driver to let you off about one mile east of the Highway Pass summit. At this point the road is making a sharp loop. A good landmark is a ridgeline on the south side of the road that looks like a peninsula jutting east toward the Toklat River valley.

Walk northwest up the ridgeline until you reach the small plateau at the base of the steep mountainside. To minimize impact on the vegetation, walk on the rocky surfaces of the ridgeline. Select a route west that maintains your altitude while crossing the intervening drainages. The ridges in between drainages are good spots for picnics. Descend along the ridge that ends where the road crosses the first drainage that flows toward Stony Creek.

Variations: Extend this hike west and descend into the Stony Creek drainage before returning to the road. Walk up any of the ridgelines to the base of the mountain for a picnic and return without doing the traverse.

Cautions

Visibility is very good on this hike. However, if you see buses stopping on the road for more than a few minutes, then be alert for bears that may be out of your sight in ravines or behind ridgelines.

Photo 32A. **Mount McKinley from Hike 32 on a glorious June day.**

Photo 32B. **Look for long-tailed jaegers near the road and while hiking in Highway and Thorofare Pass.**

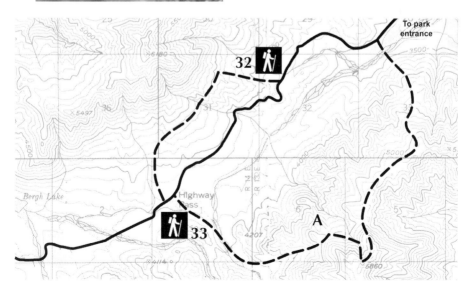

Hikes 32 and 33
Contour interval 100 feet. Grid = 1 mile.

149

33

Hill 5860 Traverse

Location: Mile 59
GPS: 63° 28.3′ W150° 9.4′
Time on bus (one way): 3.5 hours
Hike Length: 5 miles (8 km)
Hiking Time: 6 hours
Elevation Gain: 2,000 feet (600 m)
Hiking Difficulty: Moderate
Route Finding Difficulty: Moderate
Backcountry Permit Area: 11
USGS Map: Mt. McKinley (B-1)

Highlights

"The view must be great from up there," I thought while riding the bus through Highway Pass. The view was better than I imagined. From the first saddle my eyes were led southwest by a series of ridgelines to Mount McKinley. *(photo 33A)* To the north I saw the rolling green of Highway Pass contrasting with the gravel road and steep rocky slopes north of the road. From the summit, the Toklat River valley unfolded before my eyes. *(photo 33B)* In June, alpine wildflowers were a treat as I walked or took a break. Near the summit a herd of 29 caribou were headed for snowfields to find relief from heat and flies.

See hiking map, page 149.

Route descriptions

This hike starts where the westernmost drainage of the Toklat River comes out of the mountains. Ask the bus driver to let you off at the western end of Highway Pass just as the road begins to level out in the Stony Creek drainage. Bears are often seen in Highway Pass so examine the area before starting to hike. Visibility is good in this area.

Walk upstream along the westernmost drainage of the Toklat River until you reach the first major drainage from the west. Follow this side drainage east until you reach the saddle *(Point A on map, page 149)* at the headwaters. On a clear day, Mount McKinley is visible from this saddle.

At the saddle, there are two ways to reach the summit of hill 5860. I used the route described below. An alternate route is to continue up the ridge to the southeast of the saddle. I have descended this ridge encountering some steep scree that I could have climbed by zigzagging and following faint sheep trails in the scree.

From the saddle your goal is to continue east contouring around the bowl. In early June, the east side of the saddle contained a snowfield. The snow was soft enough that I could descend it by kicking steps. If the snow were too frozen, it would be best to detour to avoid the risk of sliding into the rocks about 100 feet below. Later in the summer, the snowfield will be gone or very small. Walk east in the bowl until you reach the main drainage from the summit ridge to the south *(photo 33C)*.

At this point I decided to reach the summit ridge of hill 5860 by climbing up this drainage. I chose to kick steps into soft snow in the

Photo 33A. **Taking a break at the first saddle on Hike 33. Mt. McKinley is visible at the top left. Photo taken from the saddle at point A on the map.**

middle of this drainage rather than to climb the adjacent scree. I regretted this decision when the snow became more frozen near the top and there was ice along the edges that made it risky to get off the snow. Most of the snow will be gone by mid-summer so this route to the summit will be a long climb on scree.

Continue the traverse by returning along the summit ridge to the east. After passing the saddle at the headwaters of the drainage described above, look for a game trail in the scree on the north side of the hill to the east. Follow this trail or make your own traverse across the scree to reach the ridge beyond the hill. The slope is steep but I found the scree stable along the sheep trail. Continue following this ridge until you descend to the wide ridge that continues east.

Walk east along the wide ridge until you reach the end of the ridge.

Look for the route down. *(photo 33D)* A good landmark is the abrupt curve to the north in the road. This curve is just out of sight to the left of Photo 33D. Descend along the ridge that looks easiest to walk. As you near the bottom, look closely for bears in the brush along the drainage between the bottom of the ridge and the road. Bears travel this area frequently. Also look for the best place to climb out of the drainage to the road. Descend to the drainage, cross it, and climb to the road.

Sometimes the drainage near the road at the east end of this hike is closed to hiking when wolves occupy a den in the area. If this situation occurs, you will need to return to the road by selecting a route down farther west or retrace your steps. As you ride the bus look for a good area to descend and mark it on your map.

Photo 33B. **View west of the Toklat River from the summit of Hill 5860.**

Photo 33C. **This is the bowl referenced in Hike 33. My route to the summit of hill 5860 followed the drainage that enters from the right before the distant saddle. My route down from the summit followed the ridgeline at top from right to left down to the distant saddle.**

Photo 33D. **I descended the ridgeline at left-center (with snow patches) to reach the road.**

Variations: Do this hike only as a traverse by continuing across the bowl instead of climbing hill 5860. Because of the numerous patches of snow, I think water would be available in this bowl for most of the summer. Another option is to only climb hill 5860.

Cautions

Wear good boots to climb and descend the steep scree slopes on hill 5860. The summit is wide and has few landmarks. If visibility is low, good map and compass skills will help find the alternate route down the northwest ridge to the saddle at point A on the map, page 149.

34

Highway Pass and Stony Creek

Location: From Mile 58 to 62
Time on bus (one way): 4 hours
Hike Length: Short walks
Hiking Time: About 1 hour per mile.
Elevation Gain: Varies
Hiking Difficulty: Easy
Route Finding Difficulty: Easy
Backcountry Permit Areas: 11, 33
USGS Map: Mt. McKinley (B-1)

Highlights

This area is great for a stroll 100 feet from the road or for dayhikes of a mile or two to enjoy the bird life and wildflowers. *(photo 34A)* Because visibility is good in this area, wildlife can easily be spotted from the road or when hiking along the flanks of the mountains. Bears and caribou are common throughout the summer. Also look for sheep in the mountains north of the road. Golden eagles are often seen soaring above the flanks of these mountains. Long-tailed jaegers and American golden plovers frequent the area near the highest road elevations of Highway Pass. Wildflowers are everywhere, particularly in the small, lush ravines. On a clear day, Mount McKinley is visible from the pass *(photo 34C)*.

Photo 34A. **Highway Pass seen from Stony Dome.**

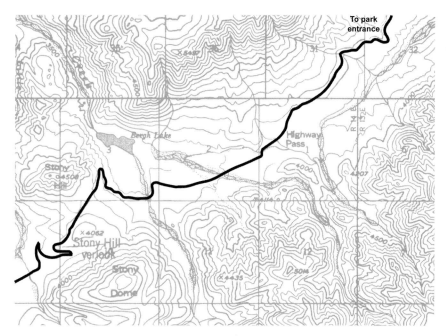

Hike 34. Areas on both sides of the road are good for picnic and flower hikes
Contour interval 100 feet. Grid = 1 mile.

Route Description

You can see everywhere so pick a destination that suits your ability and curiosity. During nesting periods, some areas along the road (particularly in Highway Pass) are temporarily closed to hiking. White cardboard signs along the road indicate closed areas.

If you want to climb, south of the road there are ridges located between the branches of Stony Creek that lead to hills 4435 and 5014 (shown on USGS map). From the road you can see routes onto these ridges.

An interesting trip is to the former sight of Bergh Lake on the big Stony Creek about 1/2 mile downstream (north) from the road. An earthquake on July 18, 1953 caused an enormous landslide that blocked the Stony Creek valley, creating a lake. Stony Creek has since cut through the rubble that swept across the narrow valley and the lake has drained, but the enormous scar left by the landslide remains clearly visible on the mountainside above the right side of the creek. Bergh Lake was named after Knute Bergh who piloted the plane carrying Lt. Gordon Scott of the U.S. Geodetic Survey that crashed near here in 1953, killing them both.

To explore downstream on Stony Creek, get off at the last (going west) bridge before the road climbs Stony Pass. Walk along the bench on the west side of Stony Creek. This is a popular area for bears so keep a good watch. When Stony Creek enters the narrow canyon where Bergh Lake used to be, look for a social trail on the bluff along the west side of Stony Creek. You can follow this trail to extend your day outing or to explore the area behind Stony Hill. *(See Hike 37.)*

Stony Area Wildflowers

At least 132 species occur in the immediate area.

The ubiquitous northern and narcissus-flowered anemones appear as early as late May at both high and low altitudes. At the same time, the dainty little yellow bog saxifrage bursts forth in lower areas while higher up the gorgeous purple mountain saxifrage can be found blooming right to the snow line among the rocks. Rocks absorb sunlight and then radiate heat, creating a thin layer of warmth even when the air above is near-freezing.

Sprinkled here and there are slender-stemmed rock jasmine, buttery villous cinquefoil, white eight-petaled dryas, and the tiny urn-shaped pink flowers of alpine blueberry. This is just the prelude.

The real show begins in late June and stars Indian paintbrushes, alpine and Lessing's arnica, whitish and glaucous gentians, shooting stars, three-toothed, spotted, red-stemmed and rusty saxifrages, lagoons, Macoun's poppy, both arctic and alpine forget-me-nots, moss campion, white mountain heather, dwarf arctic butterweed, harebells, bluebells and a host of others.

The season is short, but some players, particularly the various gentians, remain on stage through August. See them all by exploring from the creek beds to the top of Stony Dome. *(See Hike 38.)*

– Don Croner

(above) Photo 34C. **Mount McKinley from the Toklat side of Highway Pass.**

Variations: Because tents must be more than one-half mile from and out of sight of the road, camping options are limited in the open tundra between Highway Pass and Stony Dome. However, there are good out-of-sight camping spots south of the road along either branch of Stony Creek or the western most fork of the Toklat River. From these valleys it is easy to make dayhikes east toward Highway Pass or explore Stony Dome and Thorofare Pass.

(opposite page) Photo 34B.
Whorled-leaf lousewort.

Cautions

Watch for bears. The lower vegetation provides good visibility but there are many depressions and ravines that can hide bears so make noise when you approach these areas. Flowers will tempt you to look at the ground a lot; just remember to take time to look around for bears too. If you see buses stopping for more than a few minutes, determine the reason because by this time in the trip, longer bus stops usually mean bears have been spotted.

35

Hill 5014 Climb or Circumnavigation

Location: Mile 60, Stony Creek
Time on bus (one way): 4 hours
Hike Length: 5 to 6 miles (8-9.6 km)
Hiking Time: 5 to 6 hours
Elevation Gain: 1,200 (for circumnavigation) or 1,400 (to summit) feet
Hiking Difficulty: Moderate
Route Finding Difficulty: Moderate
Backcountry Permit Area: 11
USGS Map: Mt. McKinley (B-1)

Highlights

This route explores hidden valleys and follows a route used by animals to get through a pass. Tracks indicate caribou use this route. Look for caribou in June or July when they are moving through the area and often seek ridge breezes and snow patches for relief from insects and heat. Wildflowers will be a highlight during late June and through July because of the elevation and habitat variation. Choosing the circumnavigation alternative allows exploration of two valleys at stream level and provides more opportunity for wildlife encounters. The Stony Creek drainage is the area where I have seen wolves occasionally and bears often feeding on grass and bear flowers in June and July. Choosing to return to the road via a ridge walk from hill 5014 will provide a view of Highway Pass. While it was overcast when I was there, based on other hikes in the area I would expect to see Mount McKinley from the summit and along some of the ridge walk.

We had a surprising challenge when fog closed in while we were on the summit. It was so thick that we dared not get separated by more than 200 feet *(photo 35A)*. Selecting and finding the best ridge for descent to the road was difficult. Using the map, I chose the eastern-most and widest ridge to follow toward the road.

Route description

Ask the bus driver to let you off the Stony Creek Bridge where the Park Service road grader often parks. This is the western-most bridge on Stony Creek just before the westbound climb over Stony Pass. Check the area for bears, particularly if you see buses stopped in the area.

Begin hiking upstream along the western (right) side of Stony Creek. You can hike along the left (east) bank but it is not as easy. Follow the stream until it begins to flow along the

Photo 35A. **Heading toward the summit of Hill 5014 from the saddle referenced in Photo 35B.**

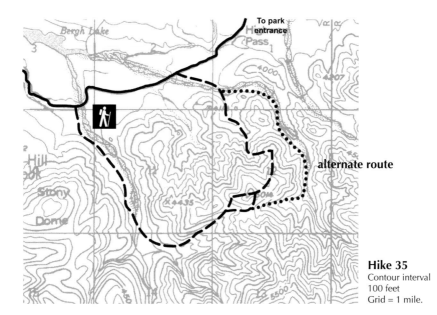

Hike 35
Contour interval
100 feet
Grid = 1 mile.

western bank blocking your progress or until you like the looks of hiking along the eastern side of the valley. Crossing Stony Creek via stepping-stones is possible but it might be necessary to wade calf deep water if you cannot find or create adequate stepping-stones.

When you reach the eastern-most branch of this creek, head east. The major portion of this branch soon turns south but you continue east along the smaller drainage. Shortly you will see a small (one foot wide and one inch deep) red stream which seems to start out of the southern hillside about 30 feet above. At this point, look north and you will see the cliffs of a steep ridge. Your route follows the foot of this ridge toward the saddle to the south of hill 5014.

Watching for a narrow (10 feet wide) drainage coming in from the north (your left). Follow this drainage upstream or hike along its right bank until you achieve a plateau in the valley below the ridgeline to the north. Walk along the plateau until you once again intersect the stream that continues on to the pass on the south side of hill 5014 that will now be visible. Continue along the stream toward the pass. *(photo 35B)*

To reach the summit of hill 5014, climb out of the creek and onto the ridgeline at the saddle between hill 5014 and the cliffs parallel to your route. You can also climb to the summit from the pass at the head of the valley.

For a ridge walk from the summit toward the road, walk north along the eastern-most ridge. When you reach the dog-bone-shaped promontory, follow the drainage to the valley floor either on the right or left of the ridge. (We went left as shown on the map.) You may also continue following the ridge, but the footing gets worse due to scree and rock outcrops along the ridgeline and the drainages off the ridge are harder to descend. Once you reach either valley, follow that drainage until you reach the road.

Variations: From the summit, walk down to the pass located at the head of the stream that you had been following earlier. Walk east from the pass down the drainage into the eastern-most branch of Stony Creek. Follow Stony Creek downstream (north) until it crosses the road (alternate route shown on Map 35).

If you are good at route finding and map reading, you may try walking other ridges from the summit toward the road. From below the other ridges looked more difficult than the route described above.

If you do not want to climb hill 5014, continue in the streambed to the pass at the head of the valley. Once you cross the pass, follow the drainage down to the major eastern branch of Stony Creek.

Another possibility is to cross into the Toklat River drainage through one of the saddles along the eastern branch of Stony Creek or walk the ridgeline between these two drainages.

Cautions

During June and July, bears frequently graze in this area and they travel through at other times. There are three places on this route to look extra carefully for bears. Before starting, search the area between the two branches of Stony Creek involved in this hike. Second, watch carefully as you walk along the main valley floors when there are blind corners and high bushes. Finally, take time to observe the area between the two branches of Stony Creek as you descend from the ridge or as you exit the valley and head toward the road. It may have been several hours since

Photo 35B. **Travers watches raindrops in a pond along Hike 35 route to Hill 5014 (top left). The route to the summit climbs the saddle (top center) near the snow patches. Note the game trail on the slope to the left, above the creek. (The pond usually is not there.)**

you last checked this area. If you see buses stopping, particularly if they remain stopped for several minutes, gain some elevation and find out why they are stopping before continuing to the road.

Scree along this route is easy to negotiate. However most scree spots are not visible from the road. If you are alone and are disabled, obtaining help with visual signals will be difficult.

36

Stony Hill Ridge Walk

Location: Mile 62, Stony Pass
Time on bus (one way): 4 hours
Hike Length: 2.5 miles (4 km)
Hiking Time: 3 hours
Elevation Gain: 600 feet
Hiking Difficulty: Moderate
Route Finding Difficulty: Easy
Backcountry Permit Area: 33
USGS Map: Mt. McKinley (B-1)

Highlights

Stony Hill provides an excellent view of Highway Pass and the valleys of both Stony creeks. A special treat is the view north of the meadow *(see Hike 37)* and canyon where the two Stony creeks join. It is a good perch to watch for caribou, bears, wolves, marmots, golden eagles and maybe a gyr-falcon. Mt. McKinley is visible (clouds permitting) during the initial climb from the road on the south side of Stony Hill *(photo 36A)*.

An arctic ground squirrel at the base of Stony Hill delayed my start on this hike. I could not resist stopping to watch and photograph as he stood on his front porch surrounded by grass and flowers. As I climbed toward the ridge, I noticed a gyrfalcon perched on the summit. (Later I found scat and feathers at the summit indicating frequent use of this perch.) Topping the first ridgeline, I discovered five caribou resting on the backside about 100 feet below the summit ridge. On the west end of Stony Hill Ridge, marmots whistled and ducked under rocks refusing to be easily photographed.

Route description

Get off the bus at Stony Overlook. Tell the driver to let you out at the place where tour buses turn around on Stony Pass. Enjoy the view; hopefully Mt. McKinley will be out for you. Check for bears that are common on both sides of the road toward the eastern side of the pass. Walk east along the road and chose a spot to cross the tundra saddle to the base of Stony Hill without losing much elevation. Walk

Photo 36A. **Pausing to enjoy Mt. McKinley on the way to the summit of Stony Hill (Hike 36).**

up the ridge at the southeast end of Stony Hill. (You can also begin this hike at the hairpin curve just before the road reaches the top of Stony Pass. From the curve you will see an easy ridge to follow to the top.) Once on the top it is an easy walk along the ridge to the summit. Continue to the west end of the ridge to check for marmots. Once at the west end, follow the south side of the ridge down to Little Stony Creek and walk along the creek to the road.

Variations: Once you get to the Stony Hill summit ridge you can see and choose several routes down to the tundra plateau on the north side of Stony Hill. I have walked west on the summit ridge until I reached the elevation of the plateau. Once on the plateau I walked east on the plateau toward Stony Creek.

There is a bluff of about 100 feet high along Stony Creek but there are several places to descend. I descended along the edge of the gully next to Stony Hill. On the bank immediately above the creek bed there is a path. Follow this path south to the wide vegetated plane of Stony Creek valley and then walk across this plane toward the road. If you see the busses stopping, look carefully for bears along your route *(see Hike 37)*.

Cautions

Bears frequent both Stony Creek valleys and the pass, particularly when they are eating grasses and bear flowers in late June and July.

Photo 36B. **Arctic lousewort**

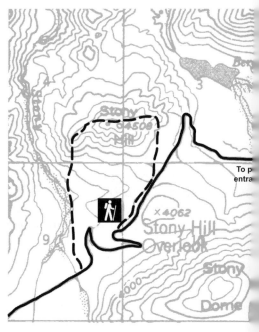

Hike 36
Contour interval 100 feet.
Grid = 1 mile.

37

Stony Hill Circumnavigation

Location: Mile 63
GPS Coordinate: N63° 27' W150° 14.2'
Time on bus (one way): 4 hours
Hike Length: 3 miles (4.8 km)
Hiking Time: 3 hours
Elevation Gain: 300 feet
Hiking Difficulty: Easy
Route Finding Difficulty: Easy
Backcountry Permit Area: 33
USGS Map: Mt. McKinley (B-1)

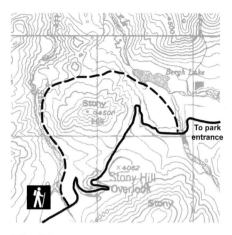

Hike 37
Contour interval 100 feet. Grid = 1 mile.

Highlights

My first view of this area was from Stony Hill (see Hike 36). Looking down, I was so delighted with the beauty and prospect of easy walking in the meadow below that I altered my planned ridgeline route and explored this meadow on my way back to the road. Walking on the plateau among the flowers and across the undulating green grasses and low tundra was as delightful as I had imagined when looking down on it. Hidden from the sight and sound of the road by Stony Hill, I felt I had discovered a secret meadow. The following year I returned to do this circumnavigation and share the area with a friend.

I photographed marmots and pikas in the rocks at the base of the north side of Stony Hill about a half-mile from Stony Creek at the end of this hike. During other trips I have seen bears and wolves in big and little Stony Creek valleys. The whole area is good for flower viewing. Even in mid-August, I found a variety of gentians including whitish gentian, my favorite. *(photo 29A)*

Route description

To circumnavigate Stony Hill, begin on the Little Stony Creek side so you get a chance to ride the bus over Stony Pass just in case Mt. McKinley is out. Get off the bus at the first place where the road crosses Little Stony Creek. Walk downstream until the stream narrows at the end of the western ridge of Stony Hill. From here one option is to climb northward onto the plateau behind Stony Hill by first climbing onto the lower end of Stony Hill ridge just before the Little Stony Creek valley narrows. Then follow the contour around behind Stony Hill to reach the plateau.

My preferred option (if the water is not too high) is to continue along the toe of the bank on the east side of Little Stony Creek *(photo 37)*. Eventually you will reach a spot where the canyon narrows and the creek drops substantially through boulders. Just before this spot, you will find an easy spot to climb out of the creek bed and begin the journey across the meadows behind Stony Hill. Walk east toward Big Stony Creek.

While there is a bluff about 100 feet high along Stony Creek, there are several places to descend. I descended along the edge of the gully next to Stony Hill. On the bank immediately above the creekbed there is a path. Follow this path south to the wide vegetated plane of Stony Creek valley and then walk across this plane toward the road. If you see the buses stopping, look carefully for bears along your route.

Variations: One alternative is to begin this hike by first climbing Stony Hill (Hike 36) and then descend to the meadow. Another variation is to explore further north along the meadow and low ridgeline between Big and Little Stony Creeks.

Cautions

This hike is technically easy. However, bears frequent both Stony Creek valleys and the meadow between, particularly when they are eating grasses and bear flowers in late June and July. Bears in the meadow have caused me to change my hiking plans. You can detour around a bear by climbing the north side of Stony Hill but this route will usually require some hard scree scrambling. The easiest alternative is to retrace your route to the road. As you walk along Stony Creek toward the road at the end of this hike, watch for bears. If buses, particularly those returning to the park entrance, are stopping for several minutes, alter your route to the road to avoid the area near where the buses are stopping unless you can clearly see that buses are stopping for something besides a bear.

Photo 37. **Travers hiking along Little Stony Creek at the first place where it flows against the base of Stony Hill (Hike 37). The hike route continues along the creek to the low bench in the background (where the canyon becomes too narrow to walk through without wading) and then climbs to the right to the meadow.**

38

Stony Dome Flower Walk and Climb

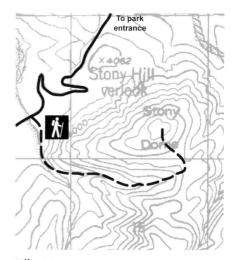

Hike 38
Contour interval 100 feet. Grid = 1 mile.

Location: Mile 63
GPS Coordinate:
N63° 27' W150° 14.2'
Time on bus (one way): 4 hours
Hike Length: 4 miles (6.4 km)
My Hiking Time: 4 hours
Elevation Gain: 1,000 feet
Hiking Difficulty:
Easy to Moderate on climb
Route Finding Difficulty: Easy
Backcountry Permit Area: 11
USGS Map: Mt. McKinley (B-1)

Highlights

Even after five hikes to the top of Stony Dome, I still have not had enough of this area! Along the route, my mom and friends enjoyed exploring the narrow valley containing a small stream bordered by flowers *(photo 38)*. Marmots monitored our progress and whistled from the slopes of Stony Dome. Views of Mount McKinley (when it is out) are spectacular from the dome and lower ridges. However I will climb Stony Dome just for the flowers or the pleasure of viewing the green valleys and red mountains of Highway Pass to the east. *(photo 34A)* This is a good flower hike because habitat includes dry tundra, stream meadows and rocky alpine slopes. Even late in the season the Little Stony Creek drainage has good flowers. I frequently see caribou and occasionally grizzlies in this area.

There are very few tundra tussocks on this hike! Whoopee! The beginning of this route is almost like walking in a pasture. Hiking from the road into the valley does not require any climbing and leads to areas for picnicking out of sight of the road.

Route description

Get off the bus at the first place the first Little Stony Creek crosses west of the Stony Overlook. Hike south on the right side of the creek to the notch where the creek emerges at the foot of the west ridge of Stony Dome. Enter the notch along the right side of the creek. As you enter the narrow valley of Little Stony Creek, make noise

Photo 38. **Lynn and Kathy on Hike 38.**

and watch for bears. Continue along the creek until you see the first valley coming in from the left (east). Cross Little Stony Creek and walk up the ridge on the south side of this small valley until you can easily drop down into this valley. Walk up the valley until you reach the saddle at the head of the stream. Once on the saddle, chose a route to reach the top of Stony Dome. (I zigzagged up the slope toward the left (west) side of the summit ridge bench.) Return the way you came.

Variations: To circumnavigate Stony Dome, descend into Stony Creek from the saddle south of Stony Dome.

Accomplished hikers and map-readers can descend (or climb) Stony Dome in several locations. Based on my observations, the west ridge of Stony Dome looks like a good route.

For a pleasant stream valley walk that is out of sight of the road and requires no climbing, continue to follow the east fork of Little Stony Creek toward its headwaters.

From this streambed, it is easy to climb onto the ridge north of the creek for a view of the valley toward the road. From this low ridge, you can hike across the flat tundra to the road.

Cautions

Look for bears between the road and Stony Dome while you are still on the bus. As you enter the narrow valley of Little Stony Creek, make noise and watch for bears. When you return, take advantage of your elevation to scout for bears in the brush along Little Stony Creek. Also look for bears that may be in the wide-open tundra between you and the road.

You can usually cross little Stony Creek by jumping about five feet or finding some stepping-stones. At worst, the crossing would require wading a narrow strip of water about six inches deep. Shoes with good traction are needed on the upper slopes of Stony Dome.

39

Thorofare Pass Stroll

Location: Mile 64
Time on bus (one way): 4 hours
Hike Length: 3 miles (4.8 km)
My Hiking Time: 3 hours
Elevation Gain: 400 feet
Hiking Difficulty: Easy
Route Finding Difficulty: Easy
Backcountry Permit Areas: 11, 12
USGS Map: Mt. McKinley (B-1)

Highlights

Birds, flowers, small streams and hidden valleys are reasons I have taken several friends on this quick hike even on rainy days. *(photo 39C)* Picnic spots along the way range from secluded valleys to vistas with a perfect view of Thorofare Pass where caribou or bear frequently roam. American golden plovers and long-tailed jaegers frequent the Thorofare Pass area at the beginning of this hike. Watch for golden eagles and gyrfalcons. If clouds permit, Mount McKinley is visible while crossing Thorofare Pass and while walking along the ridge at the end of this hike.

Photo 39A. **Emily crossing a typical stream encountered in Thorofare Pass at the beginning of Hikes 39, 40, 41, and 42.**

Route description

Leave the bus at or just before Thorofare Pass summit (mile 64.5), about two miles east of Eielson Visitor Center. Search the area south toward Gravel Mountain for bears before you get off the bus. Your goal is to walk up the headwaters of the westernmost branch of Little Stony Creek at the base of Gravel Mountain. This small drainage is west of the branch shown in blue on the USGS and *Trails Illustrated*® Map. *(photo 40B)*

Select a route across the tundra along the subtle divide between the Little Stony Creek and Gorge Creek drainages. Expect to encounter some wet tundra and small streams. *(photo 39A)* At the foot of Gravel Mountain follow the Little Stony Creek drainage to the base of the ridge. At the base of the ridge, follow the left branch of the drainage and climb toward the ridge that divides this creek from the

adjacent drainage to the east.

Once you are on the ridge that separates the two drainages cross over to the next ridge that runs toward Stony Dome. Follow this ridge till it ends at the foot of Stony Dome. As you near the end of the ridge, drop down to the left toward the flat land, do not go straight off the end or off to the right. Walk to the road across the firm tundra with few tussocks.

While walking on the ridge, watch for bears in the valley toward the road. If you see a bear, select a route to the road that maintains a safe distance from the bear. You can get off the ridge and head to the road just about anywhere. *See map in Hike 40.*

Variations: Instead of hiking along the ridge toward Stony Dome, you can drop into the creek valley to picnic or simply enjoy the area out of sight of the road. Follow the creek back to the road. At the foot of Stony Dome, the creek emerges from a canyon. Stop at this point and climb an adjacent bank to determine if there are bears between you and the road.

Cautions

Bears frequently graze in or cross Thorofare Pass. Visibility is good in the broad meadows of this pass. However the headwaters of the small drainages and the area behind the ridge at the end of this hike cannot be viewed from the road. Make noise and watch for bears in these areas.

Photo 39B. **Gyrfalcon photographed in the Thorofare Pass area.**

Photo 39C (right). **You can explore small streams like this at the foot of Gravel Mountain (top right) on Hike 39.**

40

Gravel Mountain

Location: Mile 64
Time on bus (one way): 4 hours
Hike Length: 5 miles (8 km)
My Hiking Time: 6 hours
Elevation Gain: 2,000 feet
Hiking Difficulty: Moderate
Route Finding Difficulty: Easy
Backcountry Permit Area(s): 11, 12
USGS Map: Mt. McKinley (B-1)

Highlights

Near the top I saw at least 20 caribou enjoying snow patches or crossing the ridge. Since I associate caribou with the tundra, I am always amazed to find caribou up high in rocky areas. *(photo 40A)* Based on the prominence of a trail continuing across the top of the mountain, I think caribou frequently use this ridgeline to cross between the Toklat and Thorofare drainages. On the early part of this hike, I paused frequently to enjoy a small creek, flower-studded alpine meadows, and views of Highway Pass, Thorofare Pass, Eielson Visitor Center and occasionally of Mt. McKinley poking through the clouds. Eventually the geology and hardy alpine flowers became the reasons for stops to photograph or marvel. Near the top an extensive field of river bottom gravel left me wondering when a river had been here and I delighted at discovering the reason for the mountain's name. Next came an area of purplish rock and then formations that reminded me a lot of Arizona.

American golden plovers, Lapland longspurs and long-tailed jaegers are often seen in the area between the road and the beginning of this climb. Golden eagles often soar along the ridges on both sides of the road.

Route description

Leave the bus at or just before Thorofare Pass summit (mile 64.5), about two miles east of Eielson Visitor Center. Search the area south toward Gravel Mountain for bears before you get off the bus. Your goal is to reach the top of the western ridge of Gravel Mountain about mid-way up from its western end. Examine the terrain looking for the least-steep route onto the ridge at the headwaters of the western-most branch of Little Stony Creek. *(photo 40B)*

Select a route across the tundra along the subtle divide between the Little Stony Creek and Gorge Creek drainages. Expect to encounter some wet tundra and small streams. (*See photo 39A.*) Once across the divide, follow the meadow of the western-most branch of the Little Stony Creek to the base of the ridge. (Note: this small drainage is west of the branch shown in blue on the USGS and *Trails Illustrated*® Map.) At the base of the ridge, follow the left branch of the drainage about 50 feet then begin climbing to the right at an angle zig-zagging up toward the ridge line. After reviewing my photos and the map, I concluded it is also possible to follow the

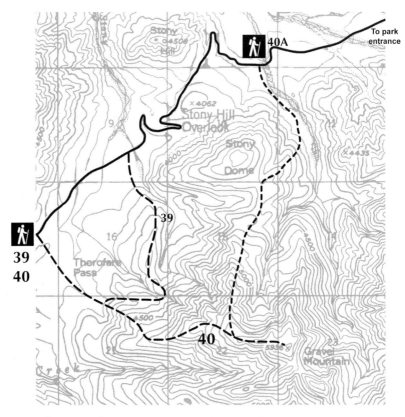

Hikes 39 and 40
Contour interval 100 feet. Grid = 1 mile.

Photo 40A. **Young caribou near Gravel Mountain summit (Hike 40).**

Photo 40B. **View of Gravel Mountain from the plains of Thorofare Pass. Hike 40 follows the ridge at right center to the main ridge along the skyline and then turns left to follow this ridge to the summit. Hike 39 explores the drainages at the foot of Gravel Mountain while heading east (left) toward Stony Dome.**

ridgeline. Going up the west end of the main ridge is also a good option.

After reaching the ridgeline, follow it to the summit. The ridge is wide and easy walking if you follow caribou trails through areas of loose gravel. For the last 100 feet or so of elevation to the summit, the ridge narrows and negotiating loose rock outcrops requires some exposure to steep drops. Return along the same route.

Variations: Rather than retrace my steps, I descended north toward Stony Dome along the <u>eastern</u> side of the ridge that divides Little and Big Stony Creeks. After reaching Stony Creek, I followed it to the road. However walking and route finding along this descent are more difficult due to loose rocks and jumbled terrain. This alternate return route is shown as 40A on the map for this hike.

Cautions

Watch for bears, particularly when crossing the tundra in Thorofare Pass at the beginning and end of this hike. Be prepared for wind and rain and carry water. There are few landmarks on the broad plain near the summit so make sure you remember where to begin your return. The final route to the summit follows a narrow trail with some exposure to steep drops when negotiating rock outcrops. Do not descend the alternate route toward Stony Dome unless you are good at map reading, route finding and walking on scree.

41

North Fork Gorge Creek Valley

Location: Mile 64, Thorofare Pass area
Time on bus (one way): 4 hours
Hike Length: 4 miles (6.4 km)
Hiking Time: 4.5 hours
Elevation Gain: 700 ft.
Hiking Difficulty: Easy
Route Finding Difficulty: Easy
Backcountry Permit Areas: 11, 12
USGS Map: Mt. McKinley (B-1)

Highlights

Low clouds added mystery and solitude on the day I hiked into this hidden valley. Muldrow Glacier, Thorofare River, Eielson Visitor Center, and the multi-colored side of Mt. Thoro are visible from the bench at the mouth of this valley. When clouds permit Mt. McKinley is visible from Thorofare Pass.

Because of the proximity to Eielson Visitor Center, I was surprised and delighted to see only one set of human tracks in this valley. I was alone to explore and absorb its beauty. (photo 41A)

American golden plovers, long-tailed jaegers and willow ptarmigan lured me away from their nests as I crossed the tundra meadows. Flowers fill the meadows of Thorofare Pass. In the Gorge Creek valley there are flowers that grow in rockier and dryer areas. Caribou and grizzly bear are frequently seen in Thorofare Pass.

Route description

Leave the bus near Thorofare Pass summit (mile 64.5), about two miles east of Eielson Visitor Center. Scout the area for bears before you get off the bus.

This route crosses the saddle between the Little Stony Creek and Gorge Creek drainages. From the road, study the drainages and veg-

Photo 41A. **Low clouds add mystery at the head of North Fork Gorge Creek valley.**

Photo 41B. **North Fork Gorge Creek valley viewed from near Eielson.** Hike 41 heads into this valley from the level of the next bench (left center, A) above the wide plain below. Hike 42 follows the lower plain and crosses the North Fork of Gorge Creek where the valley walls form the point of a "V" as the drainage begins to cross the lower plain (B). Hill 4851 is the flat-topped hill (center) that forms the far side of North Fork valley.

etation patterns to the south. Your goal is to pick the driest route across meadows and small creeks to reach the highest level of the bench at the west end of the ridge coming down from Gravel Mountain *(photo 41B)*. Select a route that follows higher ground to reduce the stretches of marshy tundra. (I managed to select a route with only about 25 feet of tussock-hopping through wet areas and with places to step or hop across the small (three feet wide) streams (see *photo 39A*)).

After reaching the bench at the foot of the west ridge of Gravel Mountain, continue walking along the contour maintaining your elevation. Your goal is to reach the northern fork of Gorge Creek at the toe of the ridge at the highest level of the bench. When you reach the hidden valley, turn east and walk into the valley along the hillside about 100 feet above the creek bed. Look for faint game trails for easiest crossing of small (50 feet wide) scree patches. Eventually the valley widens. After passing a small waterfall you can drop into the creek bed. Continue into the valley as far as you wish. If you drop into the creek at any point, retrace your side-hill route back up to the bench for your return as it becomes difficult to get out of the creek further down stream.

Once out of the valley and back on the bench, return to the road.

Variations: For a longer return hike, turn right (east) along the foot of Gravel Mountain ridge and explore the meadows and small valleys that form the headwaters of Little Stony Creek. (See Hike 39.)

From the North Fork valley, it

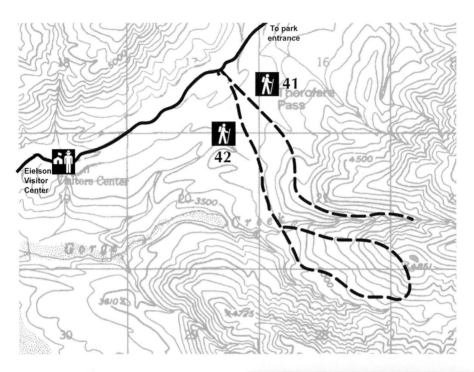

Hikes 41 and 42
Contour interval 100 feet. Grid = 1 mile.

looked possible to scramble up the scree slopes on the north side to reach the ridgeline of Gravel Mountain. Once on this ridge, you could follow the route described in Hike 40.

Cautions

The route in Gorge Creek valley requires side hill walking and crossing stretches of scree. I found the scree crossings easy if I stayed on faint animal trails and there is no exposure to cliffs or steep slopes along this route. Visibility is generally good for spotting bears but there are swales and small drainages that could hide a bear.

Photo 41C. **Arctic ground squirrel.**

42

Hill 4851

Location: Mile 64, Thorofare Pass
Time on bus (one way): 4 hours
Hike Length: 5 miles (8 km)
Hiking Time: 5.5 hours
Elevation Gain: 1,000 feet
Hiking Difficulty: Moderate
Route Finding Difficulty: Easy
Backcountry Permit Area: 12
USGS Map: Mt. McKinley (B-1)

Highlights

This is a valley of contrasts. Steep, rock walls streaked with silver streams falling from high snow patches are interspersed with green tundra strips struggling to reach the peaks on the south side of upper Gorge Creek valley. *(photo 42B)* The north side of the valley is a wide, gently-rising carpet of tundra and flowers that promises an easy route up the valley. None of my rainy-day photographs captured the rapture I felt and beauty I saw from Hill 4851. Gorge Creek breaks free of its inner canyon constraints at the foot of Hill 4851 and becomes an inviting gravel path leading farther up the valley. I shared the beauty (and the rain) with about 25 caribou cows and calves. The rain did not stop long-tailed jaegers, American golden plovers and ptarmigans from venturing out to lure me away from their nests as I crossed the Thorofare Pass saddle. The slopes up to Hill 4581 are good for seeing alpine flowers that like rocky, exposed environments.

Route description

Leave the bus near Thorofare Pass summit (mile 64.5), about two miles east of Eielson Visitor Center. This route crosses the saddle between the Little Stony Creek and Gorge Creek drainages. Scout the area for bears before you get off the bus.

From the road, study the drainages and vegetation patterns to the south. Select a route that follows higher ground across Thorofare Pass to reduce the stretches of marshy tundra. I managed to select a route with only about 25 feet of tussock-hopping through wet areas and with places to step or hop across the small (three feet wide) streams. *(photo 39A)* Also avoid crossing any of the minor ravines draining west into the main Gorge Creek Canyon.

Your goal is to cross the north fork of Gorge Creek where the west end of the ridge from Gravel Mountain begins to rise from the broad bench above the main canyon of Gorge Creek. *(photo 41B)* At this point, you can cross the north fork ravine where it is about 30 feet deep. It looked more difficult or impossible to cross further downstream toward the main Gorge Creek canyon. *(photo 42A)*

Before starting to cross the north fork of Gorge Creek ravine, select some options for climbing out the other side. Make sure the water is low enough for you to cross and walk along the stream to the point where you have selected to climb out of the ravine. *(photo 42A)*

To cross the ravine, I followed caribou tracks that angled down a soft dirt bank to bottom. The water level was low enough to leave plenty of room for walking along the stream. Walking downstream about 50 yards past a rock outcrop that constricts the ravine a little, I found a faint animal route that angled up a grassy bank out of the ravine. No rock scrambling was required.

Note the location where you cross so you can find it on the way back. Continue up the ridge that parallels the creek and leads to hill 4851.

The return route I used begins at the saddle to the south of the small lake just below the summit of hill 4851. For the shortest and quickest return, stay high enough as you contour along the side of Hill 4851 to stay about the same elevation as the North Fork Gorge Creek crossing point while avoiding side-hill walking that is too steep to be comfortable.

Variations: To allow more time to explore further up the Gorge Creek valley, walk around the foot of hill 4851 and follow the bench further into the valley. In the valley, there are plenty of spots to camp and spend a few days exploring. Another option is to continue on up the ridge past hill 4851 toward Gravel Mountain.

It is possible, but difficult, to reach the main Gorge Creek valley from the Stony Creek valley (mile 60). The upper Stony Creek canyon provides some formidable obstacles. After entering the upper canyon, you will have to clamber over mammoth boulders for 1/2 mile until a 10-foot waterfall halts travel along the creek. At this point, climb out of the canyon up a very steep ravine on the left to a high, grassy bench. Following this bench it is still necessary to climb in and out of some deep ravines that drop down into the canyon. Above the canyon is a large rocky bowl, perhaps the cirque from an old glacier, vegetated with only the very hardiest of alpine flowers: Macoun's poppy, dwarf hawk's beard, dwarf arctic butterweed, etc. The pass to Gorge Creek is to the right, south of Gravel Mountain. From the pass, drop down a canyon to the alpine meadow on upper Gorge Creek. Caribou like to hang out in this meadow and on the surrounding ridges throughout the summer. Near where Gorge Creek enters its gorge (about even with hill 4851), remain on the bench above the gorge and follow the return route described above.

Photo 42A. **North Fork of Gorge Creek crossing point described in Hike 42.**

Photo 42B. **Waterfalls and steep slopes are features of the western side of the main Gorge Creek valley.**

Cautions

I did not get close enough to the main Gorge Creek canyon to see if it is possible to walk along the creek through the canyon as a hiking route. Unless a ranger confirms you can walk through this canyon or climb out of the canyon at other spots, <u>do not risk following the bed of Gorge Creek as an alternate route.</u>

Crossing the north fork of Gorge Creek ravine near the toe of the Gravel Mountain ridge requires finding a spot to descend and ascend a 25-to 50- foot deep ravine with loose sides. Crossing this ravine further downstream looked more difficult.

Visibility is generally good but ravines and blind spots can hide bears.

43

Thorofare Pass Bench Walk

Location: Eielson Visitor Center
Time on bus (one way): 4 hours
Hike Length: 2 miles (3.2 km)
Hiking Time: 2 hours
Elevation Gain: 500 feet
Hiking Difficulty: Easy
Route Finding Difficulty: Easy
Backcountry Permit Area: 33
USGS Map: Mt. McKinley (B-1)

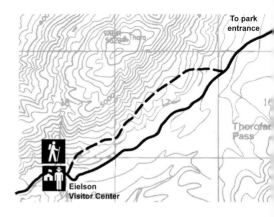

Hike 43
Contour interval 100 feet. Grid = 1 mile.

Highlights

The tumbling stream and banks of flowers near the beginning of this hike made it hard for me to continue hiking. I was tempted to spend the day photographing many kinds of flowers along this stream. My notes contain a specific reference to the fragrance of this area. After a few minutes of hiking, there are great lunch spots among the flowers and out of sight of the road. On one occasion Mom and I enjoyed doing about the first 30 minutes of this hike to get away from the bustle of Eielson. We ate our picnic lunch, spent time enjoying the flowers and occasionally walked a few yards to a small ridge to see if Mt. McKinley was peaking out of the clouds. On our way back to Eielson, Mom had her first bear detour to add excitement to the trip.

Dall sheep are sometimes visible on the slopes of Mount Thoro. This bench offers a good vantage point to spot and watch bears and caribou that frequent Thorofare Pass. When caribou travel this bench, it is a good place to try for a photograph of a caribou silhouetted against Mount McKinley or at least the Alaska Range. To try for a caribou silhouette in the morning, it is best to travel the route east to west rather than west to east as described below.

Route Description

Get off the bus at Eielson Visitor Center. Walk back (east) along the road past the large stream in the ravine at the first curve. Continue on the road past the small stream cascading down from above the road. This stream is about 2 feet wide in a narrow ravine filled with flowers and grass. When the road curves away from the ravine or just beyond, select a route up the slope north of the road. Continue to the top of the bench and enjoy the view. The bench is wide enough that you can find places to picnic where you cannot see the road.

Once on top of the plateau you can either walk along the edge where you can see the road and valley below or walk back away from the edge for a more isolated experience. You will cross several drainages running off the bench. These are easier to cross on the uphill side of the bench at the foot of Mount Thoro rather than along the outer edge.

Continue as far as you want to go. I decided to go down when I reached a point were the bench narrowed and turned away from the road. This spot is easy to find since there is a wide drainage dropping down to the road. I contoured across the top of this drainage and followed the left (east) side down to the road. See "My Thanks to The Unknown Ranger" for an account of my descent.

Variations: The main variations on this route are to return to Eielson by retracing your steps or to walk along the road rather than waiting for a bus. After you reach the road, you can also walk to Little Stony Creek and maybe spot some grayling in the pools by the culvert, one of the few spots where graying can be found along the park road.

Another option is to do the hike in reverse. When Mt. McKinley is out, you will be walking toward it.

Cautions

The main caution is to watch for bears. If buses are stopping on the road for five to ten minutes anywhere near where you plan to return to the road, be extra cautious until you are sure there are no bears near the road. Stops of this length so near Eielson are most likely for bears.

Photo 43A. **Follow the road past this stream to reach the ridge to start Hike 43.**

My Thanks to the Unknown Ranger

While riding the bus toward Eielson Visitor Center, I saw bears grazing near the road in Thorofare Pass. I was planning to do the Thorofare Bench Hike 31 that ends along the road in this pass. So I made a mental note to be extra careful when I selected a spot to descend to the road at the end of this hike.

From past trips, I knew bears liked to eat the lush grass in the ravines of this area. Bears also often take naps in the warm afternoon sun. Sleeping bears are hard to spot if they lie in a ravine or low spot. Their blond coats make them look like hummocks of dry grass.

At the end of my hike, I examined a wide swale that looked like an easy route to the road about 500 feet below and half-mile away from me. I noticed buses were stopping on the road for long periods of time. This made me think a bear was near the road. With my binoculars I checked the valley and roadside where the buses were stopping. The only animal I saw was a small caribou.

I was surprised the buses were stopping for a caribou. It is unusual for a bus to stop for a small caribou at this point in the trip because passengers have usually already seen much bigger caribou. I thought; "Those people are having a bad wildlife viewing day if they are spending this much time on a single, young caribou."

Seeing no bears near where the busses were stopping, I decided the route to the road below was safe.

"Oops!" I stopped quickly. I noticed a light brown hummock in a ravine about 20 feet from the road near where the buses were stopping. With binoculars, I watched the hummock for about 15 minutes before concluding the light brown spot was grass and that I was suffering from "bearanoia." After all the young caribou had just walked near the blond spot and did not seem to be in a hurry.

While waiting to see if the light brown hummock moved, I noticed the route to the road looked easier on the far side of the swale, about 200 yards further away. Rather than continue to descend where I had started down, I crossed to the far edge of the swale before continuing toward the road. The young caribou had now reached a point directly below along my route to the road. The buses kept stopping.

Then a ranger stopped and waited.

"Why does a ranger care about me walking toward this caribou?" I wondered. People walk by caribou every day in the park. To avoid any possibility of being chided by an over-zealous ranger, I stopped about a quarter a mile from the road and snacked while I waited for the caribou to move out of my way. When the caribou moved, I continued my walk

Photo 43B. **Grizzly grazing on blueberries in Highway Pass.**

toward the road. While I was walking the ranger drove up and down the road below me before leaving. I concluded the ranger left after seeing my route to the road was not going to disturb the caribou.

After reaching the road, I waited for the next bus from Eielson. About 300 yards before the bus reached me, it stopped for a long time. When I got on the bus, the person I sat beside asked; "Did you see that bear sleeping in the ditch by the road?"

Suddenly I understood the ranger had remained to make sure I was not walking toward the sleeping bear that I did not see. Feeling sheepish for my earlier, unfounded annoyance at the ranger, I silently thanked the unknown ranger for watching out for my safety.

44

Exploring Around Eielson Visitor Center

Location: Eielson Visitor Center
Time on bus (one way): 4 hours
Hike Length: 1/2 to 3 miles (5 km)
Hiking Time: 1/2 to 4 hours
Elevation Gain: 0 to 700 feet
Hiking Difficulty: Easy to Moderate
Route Finding Difficulty: Easy
Backcountry Permit Areas: 12, 13
USGS Map: Mt. McKinley (B-1)

Photo 44A. **Travers and Lynn on the trail to the Thorofare River from Eielson Visitor Center.**

Highlights

Eielson is a busy place but it does not take much walking to get away from the crowds and noise of the Eielson Visitor Center for a picnic, to examine tundra flowers, and, if clouds permit, view Mount McKinley in the peace and quiet. Just follow the developed trail leading toward the river valley below or walk along the road to reach prime picnic and flower-viewing spots. The area around Eielson receives heavy use, so please stay on the designated trails to minimize impact on the area.

Routes

There is a trail from the visitor center down to the Thorofare River gravel bars. (*photo 44A*) Allow plenty of time for the return climb (700 feet) up to the visitor center and take plenty of water and snacks with you! If you are up for a longer hike, instead of returning directly to Eielson, hike up the left-most branch of Gorge Creek for a ways. Find an easy place to climb out of the drainage onto the tundra bench and then return to the road. The location of this route is shown on the Hike 44 map. This area is visible from Eielson, so you can decide if this route looks like something you can do and select a tentative route before you start downhill.

Any hike to the river requires a strenuous climb back to the visitor center. Returning to the road via Gorge Creek involves a less steep climb but you will have to select the route out of the creek valley and walk across tundra to reach the road. The terrain and tundra are easy walking for most people with sturdy walking shoes that have good traction.

You can walk west along the road to stretch your legs without any climbing and on sure footing. Traffic on the road west of Eielson is generally lighter than on the road east of the center.

By walking east along the road about half a mile (.8 km), you can reach the tundra area of Thorofare Pass. This area is a great place to picnic or to look for flowers and birds, particularly the long-tailed jeager and American golden plover. Foxes and caribou are often seen in this area. Walking in the tundra here is easy so you can get far enough away from the road to get out of the dust. Visibility is also good so you should be able to see bears a long way away.

Photo 44B. **The motley coat of this bull caribou indicates this animal is still shedding winter fur. Photo taken near Eielson.**

Cautions

The trail down to the river requires good traction and can be slippery when it is wet.

Bears sometimes come right to the visitor center door or stroll through the parking lot sending everyone into the building or onto the buses. So be alert anytime you are walking around this area. Fortunately the visibility is good, particularly when you are on the road or in the tundra area of Thorofare Pass to the east.

Make noise and watch for bears in the brush near and along the Gorge Creek gravel bars. As you descend to the gravel bars, stop frequently to watch the brush below for a few minutes before you continue your descent.

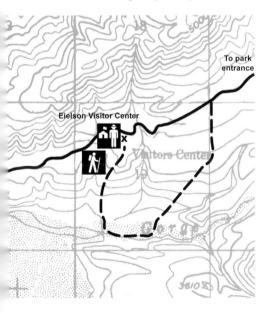

Hikes 44
Contour interval 100 feet. Grid = 1 mile.

45

Thoro Ridge #1

Location: Eielson Visitor Center
Time on bus (one way): 4 hours
Hike Length: 4.5 miles (7.2 km)
Hiking Time: 5 hours
Elevation Gain: 1,100 feet
Hiking Difficulty: Moderate
Route Finding Difficulty: Moderate
Backcountry Permit Areas: 33, 34
USGS Map: Mt. McKinley (B-1)

Highlights

Flowers and views!! While the views of Muldrow Glacier and Mount McKinley (when it is out) get better as you climb above Eielson, the unexpected reward for your effort is the view north from the top. Multicolored Mount Galen and the distant hills and valleys show the vastness and beauty of the wilderness never seen by most of the travelers along road *(photo 45A)*. Alpine flowers were everywhere on the ridge and in the drainage you follow to the top. Even in early July, there were still north-facing areas just beginning to bloom.

A low-flying golden eagle looked me over and marmots whistled encouragement as I climbed. On the way down, I saw a marmot so big I thought it was a bear until I checked with binoculars. I have frequently seen caribou and grizzly bears near the visitor center and Dall sheep on the mountain. Mount McKinley came out as I left Eielson after my hike. I hope you get a similar reward for your efforts.

Route Description

A trail has been constructed up the face of Thoro Ridge. It starts on the bench across the road from the Eielson Visitor Center. It took me about 40 minutes, pausing only to catch my breath, to reach the top on this trail.

Walk west along the ridge until you reach the first gentle ridge leading down to the road along the east side of the bowl (Point A on map). Descend along the western edge of the bench close enough to the edge of bowl to see the bottom most of the time. The final route to the road is along the edge of the drainage and will be visible if you have been walking where you can see into the bowl while descending the ridge. As you get near the road, your goal is to find and walk down the ridge that follows the edge of the drainage to the road. If you miss the route near the road, walk west till you hit the drainage and this route.

Follow the road back to Eielson. (This distance is included in the Hike Length and Time above.) You may be able to catch a bus from Wonder Lake.

Variations: Instead of heading west along the ridge, hike east to Thoro Peak (5,629'). It is a long walk uphill to the summit. *(photo 45B)* For a shorter (2.5 hour) hike and easier route finding, return to Eielson the way you came.

Photo 45A. **View north toward Mount Galen (top left) showing the multi-colored rock and soil. Hike 50 follows the valley below.**

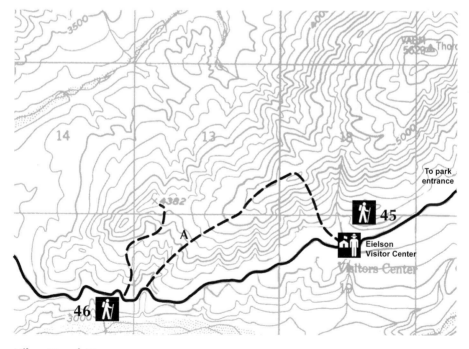

Hikes 45 and 46
Contour interval 100 feet. Grid = 1 mile.

Photo 45B. **View of the ridge leading to the summit of Mount Thoro from near where the Hike 45 route reaches the Thoro ridgeline.**

Another option is to end this hike by dropping down the north sie and following the route for Hike 50 to Little Stony Creek.

Cautions

While you can always see Eielson, route-finding difficulty is rated moderate because correct map and terrain coordination are required to find a safe route down unless you retrace your steps. Be sure to note where you came up in case you decide to return the same way. A mistake selecting a route down may result in an encounter with steep, loose scree and exposure to cliffs. While visibility is good for spotting bears along most of the route, brush or drainages can hide a bear just before you reach the road.

Photo 45C. **Hoary marmot on Thoro Ridge.**

46

Thoro Ridge #2

Location: Mile 67.7
Time on bus (one way): 4 hours
Hike Length: 5 miles (8 km)
Hiking Time: 5 hours
Elevation Gain: 800 feet
Hiking Difficulty: Moderate
Route Finding Difficulty: Easy
Backcountry Permit Areas: 33, 34
USGS Map: Mt. McKinley (B-1)

Highlights

The view north from the top features multi-colored Mount Galen and the distant hills and valleys that most people never see *(photo 45A)*. Views of Muldrow Glacier and Mount McKinley (when it is out) are superb. From mid-June to late July, alpine flowers are everywhere. While the rewards of this hike are similar to those of Hike 45, fewer people use this route and the hustle and bustle of Eielson Visitor Center is not visible along most of this route.

Golden eagles often soar above this area. You might see an eagle nest in the cliff above the road at mile 67.5. Marmots and pikas live in the rocks along this hike *(photo 45C)*. I have seen caribou and grizzly bears on this ridge, along the road, and near the visitor center. Tracks and scat indicate Dall sheep frequent this ridge.

Route description

Walk west along the road. Watch for milepost 67. In 2000, the letters were barely visible on this milepost. About mile 67.5, the road makes a distinct, sharp bend as it crosses a major drainage. *(photo 46A)* After the road leaves this drainage, along the north side of the road you will begin to see slopes that are easy to follow up to the ridge line. *(photo 46B)* Choose a place to leave the road and head for the summit ridgeline for hill 4382. (Note: you can also continue on the road to Grassy Pass and then walk east up the spine of the ridge leading to hill 4382. Along the way watch for marmots and enjoy the wildflowers and view on top. If you plan to retrace your route to the road rather than do one of the variations, then take note of some landmarks so you can retrace your steps.

If space is available, you can catch

Photo 46A. **This shows the bend in the road used to help locate the beginning of Hike 46 which traverses the ridgeline above the ravine. Golden eagles often nest on the cliff at left center.**

Photo 46B. **Start Hike 46 on this slope. The route continues behind the hill at top left.**

a bus returning from Wonder Lake rather than walk back to Eielson. The hike length noted above includes the walk back to Eielson.

Variations: You can follow the ridgeline west to Grassy Pass (mile 68.5). This route will require some good route finding to negotiate steep scree slopes on the west end of hill 4382.

Instead of heading west along the ridge, hike east until you are above the Eielson Visitor Center and follow the route described at the beginning of Hike 45 to descend to the center.

Cautions

Be sure to note where you came up so you can return the same way. Choosing another route back to the road requires good map-reading and route-selection skills to avoid steep slopes, loose scree and exposure to cliffs.

47

Around Mt. Eielson

Location: Eielson Visitor Center
Time on bus (one way): 4 hours
Hike Length: 14 miles (22.4 km)
Hiking Time: Two days
Elevation Gain: 1,600 feet
Hiking Difficulty: Difficult
Route Finding Difficulty: Moderate
Backcountry Permit Area(s): 12,13
USGS Map: Mt. McKinley (B-1)

Highlights

The route crosses varied terrain; braided river bars, low brush, and alpine tundra and includes an option of climbing Mount Eielson. There are great views of Mount McKinley and the Muldrow Glacier from the pass behind Mount Eielson. Northern harriers and sheep are often seen. Watch also for northern wheatears. Caribou and grizzlies frequent the Thorofare River gravel bars and adjacent tundra. The geology along this hike is fascinating. However, backcountry permits are hard to get for this popular area. *(photo 47C)*

Photo 47A. **View up the Thorofare River valley. Hike 47 traverses the tundra plain (center). The edge of Mount Eielson is at top right. Sunrise Creek joins the Thorofare from top left center.**

Route description

Take the trail that starts just to the right of Eielson Visitor Center and descends a sharp ridge to Gorge Creek. Cross Gorge Creek and pick up a trail on the other side that climbs a 50-foot bluff to a broad, rolling bench of low bush and grassy tundra. Hike two miles south across this bench and past a small lake *(photo 47A)*. The country is open and visibility is good, but bears use this area heavily so keep alert for them in gullies and depressions.

Drop down off the bench near where Sunrise Creek enters the Thorofare River. Cross Sunrise Creek, usually no problem. Then cross the Thorofare, picking a place where the river is broken into numerous channels. A clearwater stream, Contact Creek, enters the Thorofare on the right, below a steep alluvial fan of light gray, granitic rubble. Follow Contact Creek up a steep canyon that climbs about 1,300 feet in a little more than a mile. Contact Creek probably got its name from the fact that its canyon runs directly through a contact between the light gray granite of Mt. Eielson and the tan Paleozoic slates of Castle Rock to the south.

The pass at the head of the canyon has some excellent camping spots if it isn't too windy. Mount McKinley soars to the southwest and Scott Peak (elev. 8,828 ft.) lies to the southeast.

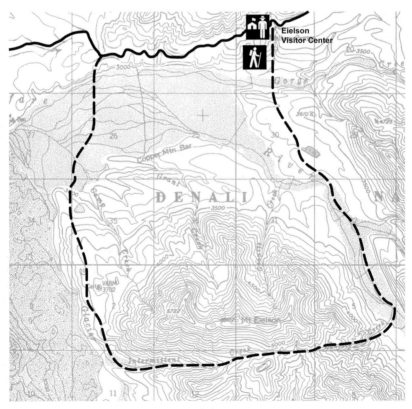

Hike 47
Contour interval 100 feet. Grid = 1 mile.

Photo 47B. **Multiple braids of the Thorofare River in the area usually crossed at the end of Hike 47 and on Hike 49**

Water is available a few hundred yards down the other side of the pass at the headwaters of Wolverine Creek.

To climb Mount Eielson, follow sheep trails up a ridge that runs directly north from the pass. It is a fairly easy climb up granitic rock and talus slopes to a ridgeline and then on to a point about 5,600-feet high. To reach the true 5,802-foot summit about 1/4 mile further on requires some tricky rock scrambling.

From the pass continue along the southern flank of Mount Eielson to a gap in the mountains leading to Intermittent Creek. On the top of this gap, notice the extremely sharp contact line between the light granites and the darker slates. You can put one foot on the granite and the other on slate, right where they came together 38 million years ago.

Drop down Intermittent Creek to its confluence with Glacier Creek. Then climb the bluffs to the high bench overlooking Glacier Creek and pick up a trail leading north.

Cross Camp Creek (watch for bears) and the Thorofare River *(photo 47B)*. Climb a steep, brush ravine leading up the bluffs to the road, or walk up Gorge Creek to the trail up to Eielson Visitor Center.

Variations: Combine with the Anderson Pass trip for a longer outing or make this a long dayhike to the pass or Eielson summit ridge and return along the same route.

Cautions

Thorofare River crossings are required. Remember the river will usually be higher in the evening than it is in the morning. Be cautious with a late crossing, particularly at the end of a long, tiring day and when you are anxious to get back to the road. Bears are common in the Thorofare valley and near the visitor center. The ability to select a good route and to hike in steep and rocky terrain is required as is good stamina.

Mount Eielson

Mount Eielson was probably formed about 38 million years ago when the Kula tectonic plate, advancing north, was being shoved under the North American Plate. Pushed down into the hot lower mantle of the earth, the leading edge of the Kula Plate melted and the molten material rose up into huge pockets in the overriding plate where it slowly cooled and solidified into granite. The surrounding softer rock was later eroded away, leaving Mount Eielson.

Granitic intrusives are often mineralized, and Mount. Eielson was once considered a hot prospect for copper and zinc. Its original name was, in fact, Copper Mountain. Joe Quigley, one of the men who started the 1905 Kantishna stampede, staked a number of claims on the mountain along a vein of copper-zinc deposits several miles long. An abandoned mining tunnel can still be seen on the upper slopes of the mountain from the Thorofare River bar, but there was never any large-scale development of the claims.

Much to the amazement of local prospectors, pioneer Alaskan bush pilot Ben Eielson landed a plane on the Thorofare gravel bar in 1924. After Eielson was killed in a plane crash in Siberia in 1929, the mountain was named after him.

– Don Croner

Photo 47C. **Mount Eielson viewed from Thorofare Pass.**

48

Grassy Pass to Eielson Loop

Location: Mile 66
Time on bus (one way): 4 hours
Hike Length: 5 miles (8 km)
Hiking Time: 5 hours
Elevation Gain: 700 feet
Hiking Difficulty: Moderate
Route Finding Difficulty: Moderate
Backcountry Permit Area: 13
USGS Map: Mt. McKinley (B-1)

Highlights

The road leg of this hike has great views of the Thorofare River valley, Muldrow Glacier and the Alaska Range. The rest of this hike offers an intimate view of the Thorofare riverbed with opportunities to see ptarmigan and wildflowers. In 2004, I was surprised and delighted to see two bull moose in the willows along the bottom of the bluff. For several years, golden eagles have occupied a nest on a ravine bluff above the road near mile 67.7, so watch for them soaring overhead. Grassy Pass, where this hike descends to the river, is known for its wildflower display in late June and early July. Walking this stretch of the road, I have also seen bear, caribou and fox. The spots of mud and sand in the riverbed are great places to look for wolf and bear tracks, as are the edges of the road when it is muddy.

Route description

See map page 201.

Before leaving Eielson Visitor Center, walk around it on the west side and locate the trail down the ridge. This is the trail that you will use when climbing up to Eielson at the end of this hike.

Walk west along the road from Eielson Visitor Center until you reach Grassy Pass, the local name for the place where the road turns away from the Thorofare River bluff and heads north into the tundra. While standing on the road at Grassy Pass, you will see a ravine that descends to the riverbed. *(photo 48A)* Follow the ravine to reach the riverbed. As you descend the brush gets higher but it is easy to get through. Make noise. There are some muddy spots, particularly if it has been raining. Smile and remember mud is a great place to see animal tracks!

Once on the riverbed, walk upstream on the gravel at the bottom of the bluff. I was able to walk on the north side of the main stream and jump the side streams. However if the water is higher, you may encounter more streams to jump or have to splash across ankle-deep water to walk on gravel a bit further out from the bottom of the bluff. Look for tracks in spots of mud and sand and for ptarmigan along the edge of the brush at the foot of the bluff.

Walk on the gravel until you are almost due south of Eielson. At this point, your goal is to be at the north edge of the riverbed gravel bordering

Photo 48A. **Ravine at the beginning of Hikes 48 and 49. Mount Eielson at top left.**

the brushy plane at the bottom of the bluff. If you are at the north edge of the gravel, Eielson will not be visible. The main ridge that leads down from Eielson is green on the west side and bare, light brown dirt on the east side. *(photo 48B)* There is a similar but smaller ridge about 100 yards (meters) east. The trail to Eielson goes up this smaller ridge. Look for the trail or look for hikers on the trail in order to see where you want to reach the bottom of the ridge.

People that come down from Eielson frequently follow the same path from the bottom of the ridge through the brush to reach the gravel bar along Gorge Creek. Look for this faint path through the brush and follow it to the bluff at the bottom of the small ridge. If you do not find the faint path, just select the best route through the vegetation to reach the bluff and begin climbing the smaller ridge to find the path. The vegetation between the riverbed and bottom of the small ridge is sparse enough to easily get through. GPS coordinates for the base of the bottom of the trail are N 63° 25.4', W 150° 18.9' based on the NAD 1927 datum for Alaska.

Variations: Upon reaching Grassy Pass explore a ridge on the east or west side of the road and return to Eielson along the road. You can climb east along Mt. Thoro ridge and descend to Eielson via the trail leading down to Eielson. (See Hike 45.)

Cautions

Bears frequent this area. So make noise whenever you cannot see, particularly on the descent to the riverbed and when walking through the brush at the end of this hike. The lower part of the trail up to Eielson may be slippery when wet so wear shoes with good traction.

Photo 48B. **Path through brush from Gorge Creek to the bottom of the trail up to Eielson Visitor Center. The trail to Eielson follows the ridge with a small bare spot to reach the larger bare ridge at the top right.**

49

Anderson Pass

Location: Eielson Visitor Center.
Time on bus (one way): 4 hours
Hike Length: 26 miles (41.6 km)
Hiking Time: Allow at least 3 days
Elevation Gain: 2,300 feet
Hiking Difficulty: Difficult.
Route Finding Difficulty: Moderate
Backcountry Permit Areas: 13, 18
USGS Map: Mt. McKinley (B-1)

Highlights

This strenuous hike to the first pass through the Alaska Range east of the Mount McKinley massif offers spectacular mountain scenery and excellent chances to see bears, caribou and sheep along the way. The McKinley strand of the Denali fault system, one of the major geological features of the North American continent, runs right through Anderson Pass. This is probably the best place in the park to witness the awesome tectonic forces that have shaped the Denali region and to see the right-angle bend of the Muldrow Glacier *(photo 49)*.

The view from the pass is panoramic. To the west Muldrow Glacier extends 25 miles to its source high on Mount McKinley. The glacier is flanked on the right by a sheer 1,000- to 2,000- foot wall of granite that stretches off 20 miles to Gunsight Pass (6,400') at the base of Pioneer Ridge.

About five miles east of Gunsight Pass is a notch in the wall—McGonagall Pass —used by mountain climbers to gain access to upper Muldrow Glacier *(see Hike 57)*. To the left rises a row of giants: Mount Mather (12,123'), named after Stephan T. Mather, head of the National Park Service, 1917-29; Wedge Peak (10,240'); Ragged Peak (9,160'); Mount Brooks (11,940'), named for Alfred H. Brooks, the first man known to have set foot on Mount McKinley; and Mount Tatum (11,140'), named after the Reverend Robert Tatum, one of the four men who first climbed the true summit of Mount McKinley in 1913. To the southeast is a clear view down West Fork Glacier and the valley of the West Fork of the Chulitna River 30 miles to the Parks Highway at Broad Pass.

Snow buntings are often seen flitting about and that Pan American migrant, the surfbird, has been known to put in appearances along Glacier Creek.

Route description

Walk or ride the camper bus about two miles west of Eielson Visitor Center to where the road abruptly swings to the right, away from the bluffs overlooking the Thorofare River. This area is called Grassy Pass. While standing on the road at Grassy Pass, you will see a ravine that descends to the riverbed. *(photo 48A)* Follow the ravine to the riverbed. As you descend the brush gets higher but it is easy to get through. Make noise. There are some muddy spots, particularly if it has been raining. Smile and remember mud is a great place to see animal tracks. *(photo 47B)*

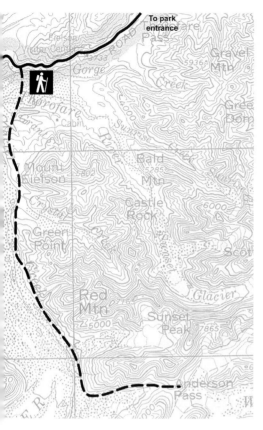

Hike 49
Contour interval 200 feet. Grid = 6 miles.

Wade the Thorofare River. Hike south across Camp Creek (note that the lake indicated on the map at the confluence of Camp Creek and Grant Creek is now dry) and climb the 200' bluffs to the left of Glacier Creek. This bluff and the Muldrow Glacier moraine are visible at the top right of *photo 48A*. Watch for bears as you hike along bench above Glacier Creek.

Hike south along the edge of the high bench overlooking Glacier Creek about 2-1/2 miles past Mount Eielson to where Intermittent Creek enters from the left. This bench is great blueberry-picking country in the fall. The blueberries also attract bears. The jumbled, grassy hillocks of lower Muldrow Glacier stretch out to the right across Glacier Creek. At first glance, this surface may not appear to be a glacier, but the glacial ice that lies beneath the vegetated surface can be seen at various places. *(photo 49)*

Drop down the bluffs, cross Intermittent and Crystal Creeks (both clear water creeks; good places to stop for tea), then ford Glacier Creek right above its confluence with Crystal Creek where it's broken up into numerous channels. Glacier Creek is usually pretty easy to cross at this point, although it can get rambunctious after heavy rains. Above here Glacier Creek runs through a canyon formed by a granite ridge on the left and the lateral moraines of Muldrow Glacier on the right; the left (east) side is impassable.

After hiking south for about five miles through the canyon and across an expanse of river bars, a valley partially filled with the moraines of an unnamed glacier descending from Sunset Peak enters from the left. There are a number of grassy camping spots with clear water on either side of this valley. Notice that Glacier Creek now starts at the snout of this glacier, not further south as indicated on the map.

Continue south up the now dry streambed of old Glacier Creek through a lush, grassy, boulder-strewn valley. This idyllic little meadow has what must be one of the highest concentrations of marmots in the park. The clearwater creek that flows out of the mountains where the beginning of Glacier Creek is indicated on the map is the last good water until half way up Anderson Pass. This is the last place to camp on grass before the pass. About 1/2 mile further on, the unnamed glacier dropping down from

Anderson Pass enters from the left, opposite the great right-angle turn of Muldrow Glacier where it heads west toward Mount McKinley.

Although not indicated on the map, a sizable river gushes out of the snout of the Anderson Pass glacier, flows about a mile, and then plunges into a huge hole under Muldrow Glacier. This river reappears miles later at the terminus of Muldrow Glacier to the northwest as part of the McKinley River.

To reach Anderson Pass, keep to the lateral moraines along the left side of the glacier. The climb is over increasingly rugged glacial rubble. Clear streams flow out of the mountains to the left at two different points. As you approach the top, keep hard to the left and come out on a ridge a few hundred feet above the pass (5,300'). The ravine leading to the pass itself is very steep.

There are flat places to camp on top but the pass is windy and water must be carried up from below. Return the way you came.

Variations: If you have the energy and time, combine this trip with Hike 47.

Cautions

Ability to select a good route in steep and rocky terrain is required. Thorofare River crossings are required. The river will be higher in the evening than in the morning. Be cautious with a late crossing; particularly if it comes at the end of a long tiring day. Bears are common in the Thorofare valley, along lower Glacier Creek and near the visitor center.

Photo 49. **The bumpy, vegetated area (foreground) is the terminal moraine of Muldrow Glacier. The darker band of material in the center is gravel over the glacier beneath. Ice shows from underneath gravel near the center of the picture. Hike 49 to Anderson Pass goes along the foot of the mountains to the left of Muldrow Glacier and turns left at the foot of the glacier at the top-center below the clouds.**

Discovery and Use of Anderson Pass

None of the earliest explorers of the Denali region were aware of Anderson Pass. In 1898, a U.S.G.S. survey party led by George Eldridge and Robert Muldrow (for whom the glacier is named) crossed the Alaska Range in the Broad Pass area to the east, and in 1899 a U.S. Army reconnaissance party under Lt. Joseph Herron crossed Simpson Pass west of Mount McKinley, but the 160 miles in between remained a mystery. In 1902, Alfred H. Brooks of the U.S.G.S. explored the northern foothills from west of Mount McKinley to the Nenana River for the first time and passed right by the terminus of Muldrow Glacier, but he made no attempt to follow it south.

In 1903, explorer and mountaineer Dr. Frederick Cook also traveled along the northern foothills after an unsuccessful attempt to climb Mount McKinley. Frantically searching for a route back through the Alaska Range before winter snows trapped him on the north side, he passed right by the mouth of Glacier Creek without realizing that there was a pass at its head (where Cook finally did cross the range is somewhat of a mystery; apparently over a glacier at the head of the main branch of the East Fork of the Toklat).

Shortly after 1906, Pete Anderson, a Kantishna gold miner, discovered the pass while he was prospecting up Glacier Creek. He soon realized that the pass was the shortest way from the south through the Alaska Range to the Kantishna Hills. Miners described the trip over the pass as being 18 miles "from willows to willows." The pass was later named after him.

Tom Lloyd, the miner who organized the first successful ascent of the North Peak of Mount McKinley in 1910, took horses over the pass, and Belmore Browne's 1912 mountain climbing expedition crossed it from the south, calling it Muckluck Pass. John and Paula Anderson (apparently no relation to Pete), who ran a roadhouse at Wonder Lake during the early days of the park, crossed the pass in winter by dog sled, an accomplishment that testifies to the stamina of these early pioneers.

– Don Croner

50

Around Mount Thoro

Location: Mile 68.5
GPS: N63° 25.9' W150° 22.9'
Time on bus (one way): 5 hours from Park entrance, 45 min from Wonder Lake
Hike Length: 6 miles (9.6 km)
Hiking Time: 7 hours
Elevation Gain: 1,100 feet
Hiking Difficulty: Moderate
Route Finding Difficulty: Moderate
Backcountry Permit Areas: 33, 34
U.S.G.S. Map: Mt. McKinley (B-1)

Highlights

Caribou frequent this wide green valley. I enjoyed the multi-colored soil and rocks on the slopes of Mount Galen and Mount Thoro and in the banks of Moose Creek. This route crosses several small streams lined with flowers and tumbling over rocks. Golden eagles often soar over Mount Thoro and northern harriers patrol the valley. Watch for ptarmigan along this route. *(photo 50B)* Mount McKinley and the lower end of Muldrow Glacier are visible form the starting point of this hike. At the end of this hike, Arctic grayling are often seen in the clear waters of Little Stony Creek. The valley is easy walking.

Route description

Because of bus schedules this dayhike is easiest to do while camped at Wonder Lake. Take one of the camper buses that leave the campground early in the morning and return on one of the late camper buses going to Wonder Lake. Backpackers coming from either direction can easily reach the starting point on the camper bus. If you are coming from the park entrance on a shuttle bus, do this route as a dayhike by starting at Hike 45 and dropping down the north side of Thoro Ridge to intersect this route about mid-way.

When approaching from Wonder Lake, ask the bus driver to stop just before reaching the final sharp bend in the road before Grassy Pass. A good landmark is the "slippery when wet" sign just before (west) of this curve. When approaching from the park entrance ask the driver to let you off at the first sharp curve after Grassy Pass. (Note: Grassy Pass is the name that bus drivers use for the saddle where the road leaves the bluffs above the Thorofare River.)

Look for an easy way to scramble up the bluff northwest of the sharp curve. Once on top of the bluff, select a route east that looks good to you. The valley is wide and easy hiking. *(photo 45A)*

Any route will involve crossing ravines flowing from Mount Thoro. It is possible to hike along the Moose Creek gravel bars but this option will increase the distance and time. I selected a route east across the first drainage where the willows were thinnest. After crossing the first drainage, I chose to hike east along the 3700-foot contour at the base

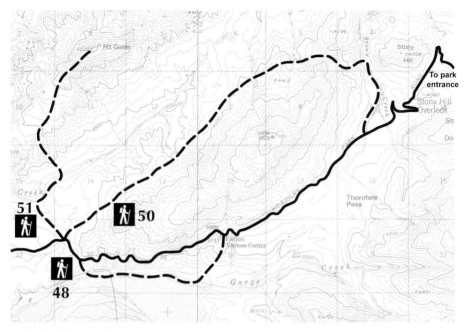

Hikes 48, 50, and 51
Contour interval 100 feet. Grid = 1 mile.

of the Thoro Ridge to maintain the approximate elevation of the pass to Little Stony Creek.

At the pass above Little Stony Creek, I followed caribou trails in the scree slope south to maintain my elevation through the canyon rather than immediately dropping into the narrow canyon bottom. When I encountered a major ravine and saw the Little Stony creek valley below was also wider and easier walking, I descended along the edge of this ravine to the creek. After exiting the canyon the creek was too wide to jump so I walked parallel to the western most branch of the creek until I reached the road.

Variations: Doing this hike as a backpack will allow time to climb Mount Galen or explore Moose Creek or Little Stony Creeks. For a longer backpack combine it with Hike 37, Stony Hill Circumnavigation or an exploration of the Stony Creek drainage north of Stony Hill.

Cautions

Visibility is good on most of this hike. When there are ravines with willows that can hide a bear, make noise and check out the ravine before crossing.

Photo 50A. **Stream along Hike 50.**

Photo 50B. **White-tailed ptarmigan**

Mount McKinley Geology

The McKinley strand of the Denali fault system runs right through Anderson Pass. This fault system is the northern extension of a line of faults, including the well-known San Andreas Fault in California that separates the North American Plate, which underlies much of the North American continent, and the Pacific Plate, which underlies much of the Pacific Ocean. The fault enters the park near Cantwell, runs west through Easy and Foggy passes, across Anderson Pass, and up the middle of Muldrow Glacier to Gunsight Pass and beyond.

For the past 30 million years the Pacific Plate has been sliding northwest along the edge of the North American Plate. During this time all of Alaska south of the fault has moved perhaps 150 miles west of the rest of Alaska north of the fault. The fault is active today and the Pacific Plate is moving west at the rate of about eight feet a century.

One visible manifestation of this lateral, or "strike-slip" faulting, is offset drainages, of which Muldrow Glacier is a classic example. The right angle turn of the glacier is a result of its source, Mount McKinley, moving west 25 miles in relationship to its outlet north of the fault.

The Pacific Plate is, at least in the Denali region, rising vertically. This is illustrated by the row of giant peaks to the left of Muldrow Glacier, just south of the fault. Beyond Gunsight Pass, the north face of Mount McKinley—the awesome Wickersham Wall—indicates that the Pacific Plate has risen some 10,000 feet above the North American Plate.

Photo 50C. **North face of Mount McKinley.**

51

Mount Galen

Location: Mile 68.5
GPS: N63° 25.9' W150° 22.9'
Time on bus (one way): 5 hours from park entrance, 45 min. from Wonder Lake
Hike Length: 6.6 miles (10.6 km)
Hiking Time: 6.5 hours
Elevation Gain: 1,800 feet
Hiking Difficulty: Moderate
Route Finding Difficulty: Easy
Backcountry Permit Area: 34
USGS Map: Mt. McKinley (B-1)

Highlights

I climbed Mount Galen for the views. On a clear day, Mount McKinley is visible throughout this hike. *(photo 51)* Even on cloudy days, much of the Alaska Range, the Muldrow Glacier and McKinley River valley will be visible. Moose Creek valley (green in the summer and golden in fall) is a delight to view and is frequented by caribou. The summit provides a great view north of the rolling hills and east into the Stony Creek drainage. The range of habitat presents a variety of wildflowers. In late August whitish gentian, my favorite, was still blooming on the slopes of Mount Galen.

See map, page 201.

Route description

Because of bus schedules, this day hike is best to do while camped at Wonder Lake. Take one of the camper buses that leave the campground early in the morning and return on a late camper bus going to Wonder Lake. Backpackers with a permit for the area can reach the starting point on the camper bus from the park entrance.

When approaching from Wonder Lake, ask the bus driver to stop just before reaching the final sharp bend in the road before Grassy Pass. A good landmark is "slippery when wet" sign just before (west) of this curve. When approaching from the park entrance ask the driver to let you off at the first sharp curve after Grassy Pass. (Note: Grassy Pass is the name that bus drivers call the saddle where the road leaves the bluffs above the Thorofare River.)

Look for an easy way to scramble up the tundra bank west of the sharp curve. Once on top of the bank, look east for the first small drainage that flows toward Moose Creek. Walk north on the ridge above this drainage until you reach where this drainage enters Moose Creek.

Before descending to Moose Creek, study the slope of Mount Galen to find the ridgeline up that looks easiest to climb. The ridge route that I used is about one-half mile upstream. After looking for bears, descend to the Moose Creek gravel bars and walk upstream on the south side of the creek about one-half mile (0.8 km). The goal is to pass most of the higher brush on the lower slope of Mount Galen and reach a spot where the vegetation will be easier walking

Photo 51. **View of Mount McKinley from lower slope of Mount Galen.**

when starting up the ridge to Mount Galen.

When you are at the base of the ridge leading up Mount Galen, cross Moose Creek. This clear creek is usually too wide to jump but it is shallow. Wearing gaiters, I was able to wade quickly across without getting water in my boots.

Look for the best route through the vegetation and start up the ridge leading onto Mount Galen. The vegetation becomes thinner and the walking easier at the first bench. When possible minimize impact on the ridge vegetation by walking on the rocky surfaces. Upon reaching the wide plane of the summit ridgeline, determine some landmarks that will allow you to easily find the route down to Moose Creek. When returning along the wide summit ridge, it is easy to get confused about the way down. As you continue to the summit, occasionally look back to locate landmarks that will help you retrace this route. A rock cairn marks the summit. Enjoy the view from the summit and return to the road along the same route.

Variations: Based on my review of the map and field observations, I am sure there are other routes for this hike. Pick one that looks good to you.

Cautions

I did not find any water on top. Be prepared to wade Moose Creek. Make noise and watch carefully for bears when hiking through willows in ravines or along Moose Creek.

52

Moose Creek Dayhike or Backpack

Location: Mile 74.
GPS Coordinate:
N63° 26.5' W150° 33.5'
Time on bus (one way): 4.5 hours
Hike Length: dayhike 7 miles, backpack 13 miles (21 km)
Hiking Time: dayhike 7 hours, backpack 3 days
Elevation Gain: 300 ft. on dayhike
Hiking Difficulty: Moderate dayhike; Difficult backpack
Route Finding Difficulty: Easy dayhike; Moderate backpack.
Backcountry Permit Areas: 35, 41, 42
USGS Maps: Mt. McKinley (B-2), (C-2)

Highlights

This hike follows the valley of Moose Creek through the relatively low hills in the western end of the park beyond Eielson Visitor Center. Scattered stands of spruce along the creek offer a change of scenery from the surrounding tundra. Moose Creek is one of the park's few sizable clearwater streams and supports a population of grayling, making this hike of particular interest to die-hard fishermen. There are many beaver ponds near the old mining road at the end of this hike.

During the 1905 Kantishna stampede, gold was found on Moose Creek and a number of its tributaries and many of the river bottoms remain staked. This area was famous for its large coarse nuggets.

The best grayling fishing is in some deep holes the first mile or two below the confluence of Moose Creek and the North Fork. These fish are generally small and most easily caught on tiny wet flies and nymphs. Very small spinning lures will also work. Since this area is in the northern addition to the park, outside the wilderness area, a state fishing license is required. A surprising amount of grayling can be found in little Jumbo Creek, which enters Moose Creek from the south.

Route description

A faint, unmarked, 3-1/2 mile trail to the Moose Creek ranger cabin starts at a gravel pit on the right side of the road near mile 75, directly across from the terminus of Muldrow

Photo 52A. **Watch for moose along the road or when hiking in the area between Eielson and Wonder Lake.**

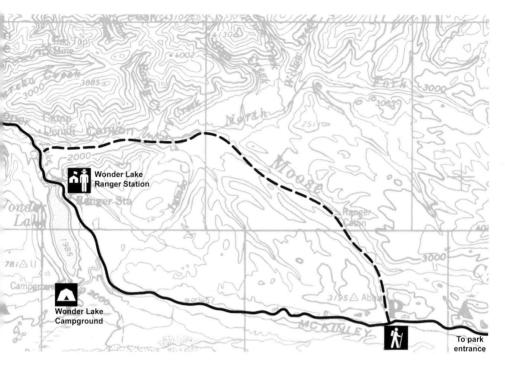

Hike 52
Contour interval 100 feet. Grid = 6 miles.

cabin is shown as a dotted line on the U.S.G.S. map beginning in Section 14, Township 17 South, Range 16 West. It is located in the valley east of the survey monument labeled "3195 Abba" shown on both the USGS and *Trails Illustrated*® in backcountry permit area 35. The ranger cabin but not the trail is shown on the *Trails Illustrated*® map. Most bus drivers will know where the Moose Creek trail starts. If not, tell them it is at an old gravel pit on the north side of the road.

The trail starts at the top of the road bank to the west of the old gravel pit entrance. Climb to the top of the road bank and look northwest toward a low divide. You will see a trail through the brush *(photo 52B)*. Also walk about 50 feet north of the road until you can see into a tundra depression about 100 yards away. On the far side of this depression you will see the trail climbing out of this depression.

Follow the trail across a low divide to the Moose Creek valley. Brush is waist-high along much of early part of the trail, so if it is wet, wear rain pants. Once Moose Creek is visible, the trail becomes difficult to follow. The trail is overgrown with chest-high brush were it crosses drainages. It is usually possible to spot a route through this brush or to detour toward Moose Creek to find lower vegetation. Even in the knee-high tundra vegetation, it becomes difficult to find the trail. Just pick the best route to walk through the tundra as you work toward a large grove of spruce trees where the ranger cabin is located. This cabin is locked and not available for public use, but the

Photo 52B. **The start of Moose Creek trail (Hike 52) is shown in the lower right corner. The trail continues through the small valley in the background.**

spruce forest itself is a pleasant place to camp. Bears are often in the tundra area. This part of the route makes a good dayhike.

From here, hike 4-1/2 miles along Moose Creek northwest to its confluence with the North Fork. There is no real trail through this area. Follow game trails and river bars. At times it's helpful to wade down the creek to avoid thickets of willows and alders. Where Moose Creek meets the North Fork find the old mining road that runs from the road near the Moose Creek bridge to mining claims on Glen Creek, Spruce Creek, and Willow Creek.

From the confluence of Moose Creek and the North Fork, it is about a five-mile hike on the old mining road to the park road. There are some excellent camping spots on the bluffs overlooking Moose Creek. Expect to see moose and bears in this area. To return, you can catch one of the park shuttle buses that provides service to Kantishna. Only a few of the Wonder Lake buses go to Kantishna, so check the schedule before you start.

Variation: Start this hike along the old mining road near the Moose Creek Bridge to explore this end of the valley without doing the full traverse.

Cautions

Watch for bears. While visibility is good along the initial part of the route, there are patches of brush, small hills and low areas that can easily hide a bear, so make noise. Hiking through the brush along Moose Creek until you hit the old mining road will be a challenge, hence the difficult rating as a backpack. Make a lot of noise when you are in this brush.

53

Xerxes Ridge

Location: Mile 85; junction with Wonder Lake Campground road
Time on bus (one way): 6 hours
Hike Length:
3 miles (5 km) from road;
6.5 miles (10.4 km) from campground
Hiking Time: 3 hours from road
Elevation Gain: 500 feet from the road; 800 feet from campground
Hiking Difficulty: Easy
Route Finding Difficulty: Easy
Backcountry Permit Area: 36
USGS Map: Mt. McKinley (B-2)

Highlights

My initial reason for considering this hike was to see the upper Moose Creek drainage that I could not see from the road. After reviewing the map, I became obsessed with finding the XERXES survey monument (bench mark) with such a strange name. (We found it.)

Expect to see caribou in this area in July and August. Caribou seek refuge near the ponds along the route during hot, August days *(photo 53B)*. In the fall, moose may be found on the slopes between the ridge and road. In late August, fall colors include many crimson patches of alpine bearberry. Wildflowers would be good in June and early July. One of the best reasons to hike on this ridge is to find a breeze to keep the mosquitoes away in June or July when they are thick by Wonder Lake. On a clear day, full views of Mt. McKinley will add pleasure to this hike. Views of Wonder Lake and the McKinley River valley are also rewarding *(photo 53A)*. It is great hike for a wet day because the route avoids wet brush more than knee high.

Route description

Begin this hike from the main road about 200 yards before (south of) the turn-off to Wonder Lake Campground. The road in this area has a bank that is about four feet high and you can see the tundra just beyond the brush at the side of the road. Another way to identify where to begin this hike is to start at a gap through the brush about 70 feet north of the 30 mph speed limit sign which is on the west side of the road (right hand side of the road as you go toward the park entrance). Start hiking at a spot where you can get off the road and into the tundra without bushwhacking through taller brush.

Once you climb the bank above the road, select a route that avoids the higher brush and work your way south and east to the top of the ridge. Follow the ridge until you find the survey monument. In 1995, the remains of an old wood tower marker were lying on the ground near the monument and were visible in binoculars from nearby highpoints. The ponds shown on the map provide good landmarks to help locate the monument. Return to the road the way you came or chose an alternate route.

Hikes in the Wonder Lake Area

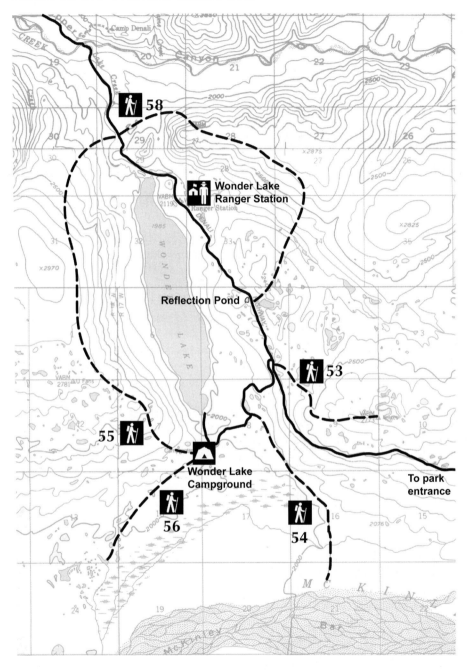

Hikes 53, 54, 55, 56 and 58
Contour interval 100 feet. Grid = 1 mile.

Photo 53A. **Lynn enjoys a sunny day on Hike 53. Wonder Lake is in the valley below and the campground is located just beyond the left edge of the photograph. Hike 55 explores the ridge beyond Wonder Lake.**

Variations: Main variations on this hike involve selecting different return routes or extending the ridge walk in either direction. You can explore the area with many ponds by walking further along the ridge and then dropping down to the road near the ponds. Busy beavers are seen in many of these ponds. For a shorter hike, you can head down to the road from the Xerxes point to catch a bus back to Wonder Lake.

Cautions

Watch for bears in areas where visibility is poor.

Photo 53B. **This bull caribou eventually bedded down near this pond.**

211

54

McKinley River Bar Trail

Location: 1/2 mile before Wonder Lake Campground
Time on bus (one way): 6 hours
Hike Length: 7 miles (11 km)
Hiking Time: 6 hours
Elevation Gain: 50 feet
Hiking Difficulty: Easy but wet in spots
Route Finding Difficulty: Easy
Backcountry Permit Area: None.
USGS Map: Mt. McKinley (B-2)

Highlights

I like this trail through the taiga forest as a pleasant change from tundra hiking. *(photo 54B)* Historically climbers used this trail to begin an ascent of Mount McKinley from the north. Nowadays few climbers begin from this side of the mountain.

While this trail has been improved, you may still encounter muddy spots after periods of rain. All of the stream crossings now have bridges so you no longer test your broad-jump skills or ability to balance on a log. *(photo 54A)* The real water hazard is the McKinley River at the end of this hike. Seeing this river bar and its many channels will give you a lot of respect for people who do cross this river with heavy packs.

Watch for caribou on the McKinley River gravel bar and also in the tundra areas at the beginning of the trail. Bear and moose are often in this area. I've seen recent bear scat or tracks each time I've done this hike. Also watch for spruce grouse.

Route Description

See map in Hike 53.

To reach the trailhead, walk from the Wonder Lake Campground about 1/2 mile toward the main park road. A sign marks the beginning of this trail. Follow the well-defined trail through the tundra and forest. When you get through the forest and reach the McKinley River Bar, identify some landmarks to help you find the forest trail when you are ready to return.

Cautions

You cannot see very far ahead or on either side of the trail when you are in the forest. Watch for bear sign and make some noise and when possible hike with a companion. Usually there is someone in Wonder Lake Campground who wants to do this hike.

Do not cross the braided streams on the McKinley River Bar unless you are skilled in river crossings.

Photo 54A. **Lynn crossing a stream on the McKinley Bar Trail, before trail improvements.**

Photo 54B. **McKinley Bar Trail emerges from the taiga forest.**

55

Wonder Lake Ridge

Location: Wonder Lake Campground
Time on bus (one way): 6 hours
Hike Length: 3 miles (4.8 km)
Hiking Time: 4 hours
Elevation Gain: 600 feet
Hiking Difficulty: Easy
Route Finding Difficulty: Moderate
Backcountry Permit Areas: 15, 43
USGS Maps: Mt. McKinley (B-2), (C-2)

Highlights

On a clear morning or evening there are spectacular places along this route to experience and photograph Mount McKinley. In fact there are great views from the service road less than one-quarter mile into this hike. We were lucky. Mount McKinley was completely visible when we started and Wonder Lake was calm with exciting reflections of the sky and surrounding hills *(photo 55B)*. We started a little late on a clear morning so the sun was already too high and too far in the south to allow good photos of Mount McKinley's north face. Next time I will try to get my companions to start earlier or wait till the evening when the sun is once again shining on Mount McKinley's north face. From the ridge, we could see almost back to Eielson Visitor Center. In the fall, blueberries are a great treat near the top.

Route description

See map in Hike 53.

Walk west along the service road that runs through the Wonder Lake Campground. When you are able to see the turn around loop at the end of this road, look left (north) toward the ridge and you will see a trail going up the ridge. *(photo 55A)* Find where the trail leaves the road and goes through the alders and brush. Hikers using the route created this un-marked trail. The route climbs a series of benches. Follow the route past an old wood stave water tank. Near the wood tank, a pond appears to block your progress but you will see the trail climbing the bench across the pond. Go to the right of the pond. Work your way around the edge and through the brush on the driest route you can find until you get to the route up the bench that you saw from the other side of the pond.

Once you get past the alders to the top, make careful note of where the trail is located for your return. On top you will see other trails in the tundra so it is important to remember the route you used to get through the brush on the way up. From past experience, I know that missing the route down leads to a lot of bush whacking through alders. A good landmark is the old wood stave water tank. The trail goes past the east side of this tank. Do not descend into the brush until you can see this tank. When you are above the tank, the trail down will be nearby.

On the ridge, the vegetation turns

Photo 55A. **The social trail at the start of Hike 55 can be seen on the bluff at top center of this photograph taken at the end of the service road described in the text.**

into tundra and walking becomes easier. Once you are in the tundra, follow the ridgeline as far as you want to go or continue on the traverse described under variations below. Walking to the west along ridgelines will lead to tundra ponds that reflect Mount McKinley.

Variations: One option is to follow the ridge until it is possible to descend to the road north of Wonder Lake. This traverse will take at least six hours. We traversed the ridge from south to north. We started late and had to rush to complete the traverse in order to catch the last bus from Kantishna to Wonder Lake Campground.

To avoid rushing to catch the bus at the end of the hike, do the traverse from north to south ending at the campground. Traversing from north to south also means you may be reaching the south end of the ridge when the evening sun is shining beautifully on Mount McKinley.

Begin the north-to-south hike across from a small cabin on a hill (called the Hawks Nest) about 1/2 mile past the north end of Wonder Lake. (The bus driver will know this cabin.) Cross the creek on a small bridge or jump across and head up the ridge above the creek. Once you are on the first bench, you will be able to select a route up the ridge. Try to find people and animal trails to make walking through the tussocks easier as you head to the ridgeline.

Allow a long day for a traverse because of the tussock walking and to allow time to enjoy the views instead of walking constantly. The easiest walking route is to quickly get to the top of the ridge and walk along the highest part of the ridge that has the fewest tussocks. If you chose to contour on the Wonder Lake side of the ridge, walk beside a line of brush about eight feet tall about two thirds the way up the ridge which looks like an overgrown road or ditch. The walking along the side of this feature seemed to have fewer tussocks. Unfortunately this line of vegetation and easier walking does not go the entire length of the ridge.

If you traverse from north to south, finding the social trail down through the alders requires some good trail-finding skills. Go as far as you can on the tundra paralleling Wonder Lake. Once you reach the alders at the south end of the ridge, walk along edge of the alders away (west) from Wonder Lake until you find a social trail heading down. There are several trails so look below on the second bench for the old wooden water tank near a pond. If you cannot see the tank, continue walking west until you find another social trail that is above the tank. The best trail through the alders begins to descend toward the tank below. The trail down passes on the east of this tank and nearby pond.

For a backpack trip into permit area 43 or to climb Busia Mountain, begin near the cabin as described above for the beginning of the north to south traverse of Wonder Lake Ridge. The mountain is named after Johnny Busia, an old-time resident of Kantishna. From the top of Busia Mountain drop down one of the ridges to the road along Eldorado Creek and follow it across Moose Creek to the road near the mouth of Eureka Creek. There is no bridge across Moose Creek in Kantishna so be prepared to wade water that may be more than two feet deep and moving fast at the ford.

Cautions

Good route-finding skills are required to find your way off the ridge with minimum bushwhacking if you do not go down the way you came up. Make a lot of noise when you are going through brush. Carry plenty of water, as it is difficult to find water when you are on the ridge if you do the traverse. There are tundra ponds at the southwest end of the ridge if you explore this area.

If you do the traverse variation of this hike from south to north, do not be tempted to descend to the road from the last bench until you are across from the Hawks Nest Cabin, otherwise you may find difficult hiking and bushwhacking to reach the road once you are off the ridge. Also check the bus schedule to make sure you know when the last bus runs from Kantishna toward Wonder Lake Campground.

Photo 55B. **Lynn enoys the view of the north end of Wonder Lake (Hike 55).**

56

Tundra Pond Exploration

Location: Wonder Lake Campground
Time on bus (one way): 6 hours
Hike Length: 4 miles (6.4 km)
Hiking Time: 4 hours
Elevation Gain: 50 feet
Hiking Difficulty: Easy
Route Finding Difficulty: Easy
Backcountry Permit Area: 15
USGS Map: Mt. McKinley (B-2)

Highlights

This hike follows a series of seemingly-random ridges separated by shallow draws stretching from the Wonder Lake Campground to these ponds and beyond *(photo 56B)*. These ridges can be combined for a fun hike to explore or to backpack in the area. Walking is easy with a minimum of bushwhacking and no wet areas to cross. The location of Wonder Lake Campground is always visible so it is impossible to get lost. I selected a route along these ridges to reach some ponds where I had observed (with binoculars) a pair of trumpeter swans from the ridge above Wonder Lake Campground (see Hike 55). The swans were there along with other ducks. While hiking, I saw several northern harriers and what may have been a pair of hawk-owls.

I also wanted to check out the possibility of these ponds as foreground for a Mount McKinley photograph. *(photo 56A)* On a still day, Mt. McKinley reflections would be great. Even when the mountain is not clear the views of the McKinley River and to the west offer fine scenery for a picnic. *(photo 56B)*

Route description

See map in Hike 53.

Walk west through the Wonder Lake Campground along the service road for about seven minutes from the restroom. Beyond the last campsite, the road is lined with alders. Watch for a gap in the alders about 15 feet wide that has a social trail following a ridgeline descending from the road. The social trail eventually ends on a small knoll. From this point you will be selecting the route. Before starting down this trail, study the terrain and select a route that looks good to you and remember what the ridges look like and general direction that you want to go.

At the end of the social trail, look for a route to reach the next ridgeline with minimum elevation loss and through the shortest vegetation in the intervening draw. (I managed to find game trails across most draws by finding where the walking looked easiest to reach the next ridge.) Once on the next ridge, follow it as long as it is going the way you want to go. Look for a good place to reach the next ridgeline. Most of the ridgelines have game trails that lead to the best place to cross to the next ridge. Continue this approach until you reach the ponds.

Wonder Lake

Grant Pearson, an early park ranger and later park superintendent, tells the story of the naming of Wonder Lake in his book *My Life of High Adventure:* "A party of miners was systematically prospecting the country during the Kantishna stampede, when a couple of them suddenly came on a four-mile stretch of water from the north. One miner said, 'I wonder how we missed this before.' With frontier humor, the lake came to be called 'I Wonder Lake' by prospectors. When maps of the region were drawn up, the name apparently looked like a typographical error to the cartographer, who cut out the 'I'."

During previous ice ages, glaciers swept out of the Alaska Range and marched across the valley of the McKinley River to this ridge. Tongues of these glacial advances crossed the gaps in the hills east and west of Wonder Lake and extended into the valley of Moose Creek to the north. One glacial advance left the terminal moraine that dammed water, forming Wonder Lake.

Photo 56A. **Mount McKinley viewed from Hike 56 near Wonder Lake.**

Photo 56B. **View of the seemingly-random ridges used to reach the tundra ponds (mid-center) on Hike 56. Mount McKinley is shrouded in clouds at top-left.**

Most of the ridges offer at least one high point so you can look ahead and plan your route. Each time you stop to look ahead also look back to identify landmarks for your return. However, the system ridges offer several route options so you may want to try a different route home. Because the campground elevation is slightly higher, it is easier to see the ridgeline patterns on the return trip.

Variations: The system of ridges separated by shallow draws offers many possibilities for exploring the area. For a long dayhike, continue until reaching the McKinley River gravel bar and return along the same route. Another option for returning is to follow the gravel bar to the McKinley Bar trail. However the beginning of the McKinley Bar trail, which is at the edge of a spruce forest, may be hard to find if you have not been there before.

For a loop hike, begin by following the Wonder Lake Ridge Hike to reach the ridge above Wonder Lake. Walk west about 1.5 miles along this ridge until you see a route down to the tundra ponds at the end of this hike. Head to the ponds and then return along the route described above.

Cautions

While the vegetation on this route is low, the terrain is rolling and can easily hide a bear. Make noise as you approach areas where you cannot see ahead. Study the brush in draws before you cross them to reach the next ridge.

Around the ponds, you will encounter the same insects that are found near Wonder Lake so be prepared if you plan to spend time near the ponds.

57

McGonagall Pass Backpack

Location: Mile 86, Wonder Lake Campground
Time on bus (one way): 6 hours
Hike Length: 38 miles (61 km)
Hiking Time: 5 plus days
Elevation Gain: 3,800 feet
Hiking Difficulty: Difficult (see Caution)
Route Finding Difficulty: Moderate
Backcountry Permit Areas: 20
USGS Map: Mt. McKinley (A-2), (B-2)

Highlights

At its closest point to the road, Mount McKinley is still 27 miles away. This hike takes the route used by mountain climbers to historic McGonagall Pass, which overlooks Muldrow Glacier and provides a mind-boggling, close-up look at Mount McKinley (*photo 57*). No special mountaineering equipment or skills are necessary to reach the pass itself. The most difficult part of the hike is crossing the formidable McKinley River, 2.5 miles from the trailhead.

Caribou, moose and bear are frequently seen along the way. The rolling tundra hills between the McKinley River and Clearwater Creek are an important caribou summer area, especially during years when deep or late snows hinder migration to calving areas south of the Alaska Range. Calving usually occurs around the beginning of June. Moose and bears are also common in this area. Also watch for Northern harriers and whimbrels around the small ponds beyond Turtle Hill.

Route description

The trail to McGonagall Pass starts about 1/2 mile before the Wonder Lake Campground (mile 85) at the "McKinley Bar Trail" sign on the left side of the road. Take this trail 2.3 miles through tundra and a spruce forest to the edge of the mile-wide McKinley bar. Before crossing the river, look around for a wading staff left behind by previous hikers if you did not bring one.

The best time to cross a glacial river like the McKinley is in the morning. After the day warms up and glacial ice begins to melt, the river can rise appreciably.

After heavy rains the McKinley may be impossible to cross. If it rains after you have crossed the river, you may not be able to cross back over immediately when you return. Keep this in mind when planning for food and fuel. The river usually goes down quickly after its stops raining.

The best places to ford the river are upstream for a mile or so from where the McKinley Bar trail comes out of the woods. Look for a place where the river is broken up into numerous channels. After crossing the river, look for a grove of seven cottonwood trees about 1/2 mile south of the river bar. These are the

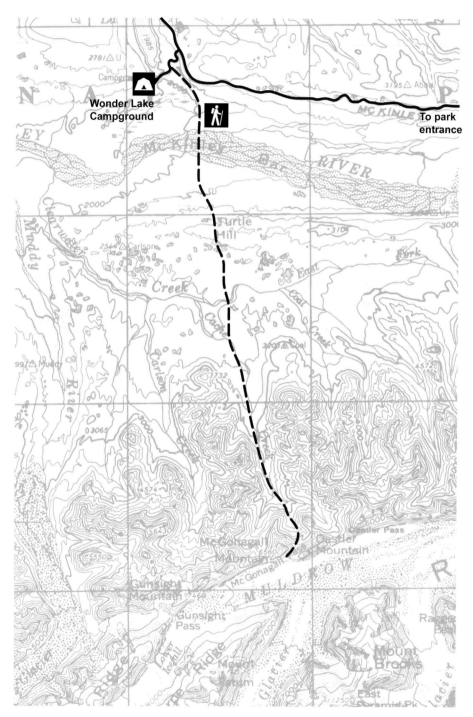

Hike 57
Contour interval 200 feet. Grid = 6 miles.

McGonagall Pass: A Window into the Early Climbing History of Mount McKinley

McGonagall Pass is a notch in a wall of granite that rises up to 2,000 feet above the north side of Muldrow Glacier from Gunsight Pass east 20 miles to where the glacier takes a right angle turn at the foot of Anderson Pass. The south side of Muldrow Glacier is lined by a row of 9,000-foot to 12,000-foot peaks separated by Traleika and Brooks glaciers, each more than a mile wide. To the west, soaring above it all, is Mount McKinley (20,320').

Alfred H. Brooks of the U.S. Geological Survey first explored the foothills north of Mount McKinley in 1902. Although involved primarily in geological research, Brooks climbed to the 7,500-foot level on the northwest face of Mount McKinley, making him the first man known to have set foot on the mountain. The first real attempt to reach the summit was made the following year by Judge James Wickersham of Fairbanks. This group reached the 8,100-foot level of the imposing 14,000-foot north face of Mount McKinley, which now bears Wickersham's name, before being forced to turn back. By now it was clear that the north face—the Wickersham Wall—was a no-go. It remained unclimbed until 1963.

—Don Croner

Photo 57. **Looking up Muldrow Glacier from McGonagall Pass. The notch to the right of center is Gunsight Pass with Pioneer Ridge extending to the left toward the North Peak of Denali.** Photo by Don Croner.

only sizable deciduous trees in the area and should be conspicuous. The trail through the tundra passes directly to the left of them and continues past Turtle Hill to Clearwater Creek. (*Note:* This trail was visible in the 1980s when Don Croner did this hike. It may be overgrown and difficult to locate or follow if it has not been used frequently. In any case you can find your way across the tundra toward the pass if you can navigate with a map.)

Clearwater Creek is the halfway point of the hike to the pass. From here it's about 9-1/2 miles either way. Cross the creek and swing right through a brushy area (watch for bears) and then around a low bluff before heading south again up the valley of Cache Creek. Although it may not be obvious at first glance, the bank to the left where the trail crosses Cache Creek for the first time is the moraine of an ancient glacier that swept down from McGonagall Pass. About 1-1/2 miles further on, the trail climbs up onto the right arm of a very conspicuous U-shaped moraine left by a later glacial advance. Flocks of ptarmigan numbering in the hundreds are often seen in this area toward the end of the summer.

After crossing Cache Creek one more time, the trail begins to climb to the pass. Right below McGonagall Mountain, Cache Creek splits into two branches, one branch heading to the right of the mountain and the other to the left. Take the left branch. After about 1/4 mile, the creek splits again. The right branch goes to McGonagall Pass. Here you will find the last good camping spots on grass. (Archdeacon Hudson Stuck set up his base camp here for the first ascent of the south peak in 1913.) The valley quickly narrows into a steep boulder-strewn ravine leading to McGonagall Pass (5732′).

It is possible to camp on the pass, but it can get extremely windy and snow can fall at any time. The pass is sparsely vegetated with fragile mats of moss and purple mountain saxifrage sprinkled here and there with golden saxifrage. Do not camp on these vegetated areas. Sometimes there are fresh water seepages in the area of the pass; at other times water must be carried up from Cache Creek. Do not go out on the glacier itself unless you are properly equipped and have experience in glacier travel. Return to the road the way you came.

Cautions

This hike is rated difficult due to the McKinley River crossing. Because of this river crossing, I think this hike is the most dangerous one described in this book. Be sure and plan extra days of food and fuel in case the river is too high to cross on your return due to rains. I recommend you do not attempt this crossing alone.

Route finding difficulty is rated moderate because of the long tundra crossing without real obvious terrain features to mark the route. You will need good map-reading skills to clearly identify your destination as you cross the tundra to the foothills of the Alaska Range where the route becomes more obvious. Good stamina and boots as well as a staff for crossing the river are essential.

58

Bound Point

Location: Mile 88
GPS: N63° 30.1' W150° 53.4'
Time on bus (one way): 30 min. from Wonder Lake Campground
Hike Length: 3.5 miles (5.6 km)
Hiking Time: 4 hours
Elevation Gain: 800 feet (264 m)
Hiking Difficulty: Moderate
Route Finding Difficulty: Easy
Backcountry Permit Areas: 26, 42
USGS Maps: Mt. McKinley (B-2), (C-2)

Highlights

Bound Point provides a unique overview of the Wonder Lake area and Moose Creek valley to the north. *(photo 58A)* I always plan for a picnic or long rest stop at this point. On a still day I heard a loon on Wonder Lake. In the fall I snacked on blueberries and lingonberries as I climbed to the ridge at the north end of this hike. On a clear fall day, red alpine bearberry leaves provide a good foreground for pictures of Wonder Lake. The south end of the hike crosses a wide valley with a stream that has beaver ponds. Caribou frequent the kettle pond area at the south end of this hike. *(photo 58C)*

"Ansel Adams' Point" is what some bus drivers and lodge workers call Bound Point. I hoped to see if the view and angle matched Ansel Adams' famous picture of Mount McKinley. Because Mount McKinley was not visible during all three of my hikes to this ridge, I did not get photographs to compare with Adamsí print. However, I think the angle of view from this point is not the same as in Adams print. I do know that Adams was in great shape if he carried his 8x10 camera gear up to this point!

Route description

Do this hike while camped at Wonder Lake or on a backpacking trip in the area. From the campground take one of the buses that goes to Kantishna. Ask the driver to let you off at the parking area at the old boundary of Mount McKinley National Park. The old boundary crosses the road about 1/2 mile (800 meters) north of the place where the road is at the edge of Wonder Lake. If you are planning to photograph at a specific time of day and are in shape, allow 1.5 hours to get to the top from this point.

You will see that the northwestern end of the Bound Point ridge is covered with head-high alders, the darker green vegetation. I have threaded my way through the alders to reach the top. However I found it easier to reach the top along the route described because there are fewer alders. *(photo 58B)*

From the parking area, begin hiking east through the notch in the small hill. Once at the notch you will see a small drainage. Select an easy route through the willows to cross

Photo 58A. **View of Wonder Lake on a foggy day from Bound Point.**

this drainage. Your goal is to walk east below the alders on the north slope of Bound Ridge. The tundra vegetation along this traverse and on the climb is knee-high and soft, like walking on foam rubber. The walking conditions in this part of the hike are the reason for the moderate hiking difficulty rating.

As the alders thin, begin climbing east at an angle. There is a line of alders and willows about half way to the top. Head for the thinnest part of this brush where you can see that the vegetation beyond is lower all the way to a fringe of alders at the top. It is easy to get through the top alders by following a small, shallow drainage that descends from the top. Look east for this very small drainage after you get through the middle line of alders and willows. GPS coordinates at the top of this drainage are: N63° 30.1' W150° 53.3'. When in doubt, the easiest way to find a good route to the top is to just head for the top by zig-zagging to find the least steep and least vegetated way.

Hike southeast along Bound Ridge while maintaining your elevation and remaining above the alders. Walk until you are about even with the large tundra ponds on the ridge across the valley. Look for a route down that is mostly free of alders. Cross the creek near the small ponds about 100 yards (100 meters) downstream from the larger pond with the beaver house. These small ponds are a little north of and below the bigger tundra ponds on the ridge above. I was able to jump the creek near these small ponds.

After crossing the creek, walk up slope toward the large tundra ponds. Choose a route that goes on either side of the large ponds and then follow the easy walking along ridgelines toward the road. A narrow strip of alders borders the road. Look for one of the frequent game trails through the alders. Hike length and time does not include returning along the road to the

Photo 58B. **Western end of Bound Point. Route for Hike 58 is on the back side of this ridge to the left (out of view).**

campground, about 2.3 miles from Reflection Pond. *(photo 58C)*

If you do this hike from south to north, start the hike near Reflection Pond (mile 85.4) or north of the buildings that are about one mile north of the campground road junction. When you reach the Bound Point area, find the route down by walking west from the Bound survey monument. Look for the start of a small, shallow drainage dropping north off the ridge. A good distant landmark is the distinct bow in Moose Creek to the north.

Variations: Do either end of this hike for a shorter day hike. The south end of this hike, with its ponds and easy walking terrain, is a good place for a day of exploring.

Cautions

Make noise in the few areas where the vegetation and terrain could hide a bear.

Photo 58C. **Valley crossed at the end of Hike 58.**

Photo 58D. **Look for wolf tracks in sand or mud on all hikes.**

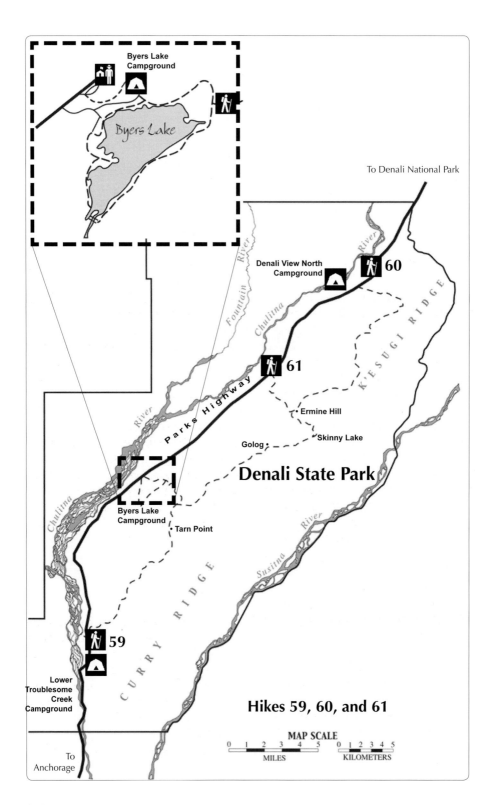

Chapter 5

Denali State Park

Overview

Containing 325,240 acres (131,722 hectares), Denali State Park offers a wide range of opportunities to explore true wilderness. Its western boundary is shared with Denali National Park and Preserve. The park is about 133 miles (212 km) north of Anchorage via the George Parks Highway, the major road link between Anchorage and Fairbanks. This highway provides access to the Kesugi Ridge trails described in this book.

Kesugi Ridge, a 35 mile-long north/south alpine ridge, borders the Parks Highway. *Kesugi*, a Tanaina Indian dialect word meaning "The Ancient One," is an appropriate description for this granite alpine ridge that dominates the eastern half of the park. On a clear day Kesugi Ridge hikers have an unencumbered view of Mount McKinley and the Alaska Range to the west. A hike up (1,500 feet, 456 meters) any of the four (4) hiking trails provides access to a trail along Kesugi Ridge for hikes ranging from 15 to 36 miles (24-58 km). The ridge trail follows a broad alpine tundra plane past ponds, across creeks and around granite boulders. *(photo 60B)*

Weather

Be prepared for a wide range of weather. Summer temperatures are usually near 60° F (15° C) with occasional highs over 80° F (27° C). On rainy days expect temperatures nearer 50°F (10° C). There is little shelter from wind on this ridge. In mid-summer, nearly 21 hours of daylight allow plenty of time to hike and explore. Weather on my hikes included thick fog, rain and sunshine.

Hikers should be prepared for bad weather that can last several days. There are only four places to get off Kesugi Ridge, so bring good quality rain gear, clothing that insulates when wet, and durable tents. Bring a sun hat and sunscreen for the great days!

Camping

Developed campgrounds are located near three trailheads: Byers Lake (74 spaces), Troublesome Creek (20 spaces) and Denali Viewpoint North (6 for tents spaces). Spaces are available on a first come, first served basis. See map at left.

Backcountry camping is allowed anywhere along the ridge trail. In order to reduce camping impact near popular Skinny Lake, a designated camping area is being established. Elsewhere please camp away from the trail and avoid spots where others have camped. This will minimize damage to the alpine tundra. Bring a stove because campfires are not permitted on Kesugi Ridge.

Transportation / Logistics

Alaska/Yukon Trails provides daily bus service between Anchorage and Fairbanks. The bus will drop hikers at Byers Lake and other Denali State Park trailheads. However the bus does not stop at the trailheads unless there is someone to drop off or unless you flag the bus down at the end of your hike. If you plan to catch the bus after your hike, please let them know when you plan to catch the bus so they can be looking for you. For more information and reservations contact:

Alaska/Yukon Trails
P. O. Box 99708
Fairbanks, Alaska 99711
Phone: 1-888-600-6001 from U.S. and Canada
FAX: 1-907-456-5135
Internet: www.alaskashuttle.com
E-mail: Info@AlaskaShuttle.com

Guided hikes

Alaska Nature Guides offers guided hikes in Denali State Park. They are based at Byers Lake. Hikes include 5.5 hour hikes on portions of the routes described in this book as well as longer custom trips. Nature hikes in the vicinity of Byers Lake are also offered. They offer shuttle service from the near-by McKinley Princess Hotel for clients.

Alaska Nature Guides
P. O. Box 170
Talkeetna, AK 99676
Phone: 1-907-733-1237
Email: info@alaskanatureguides.com
Website: www.alaskanatureguides.com

Hiking conditions

Four trails provide access to Kesugi Ridge and are easy to follow. Little Coal Creek and Ermine Hill trails are the best designed and maintained. Footing is occasionally difficult on the Troublesome Creek Trail due to creek bank erosion. The Byers Lake trail up the ridge is steep and poorly maintained and is slippery when dry and worse when wet.

Ridgeline hiking is easy. At the Little Coal Creek end of the ridge, the route crosses short boulder fields that require walking across uneven boulders that may be slippery when wet. A slip into a crack with a full pack may result in injury. Short stretches of the trail descending into the lowest valleys along the ridge route are slippery when dry or wet. *(photo 61B)*

Kesugi Ridge Hiking Routes

Trail	Starting Point	Ending Point	Distance
Troublesome Creek Trail (Hike 59)	Troublesome Creek Trailhead	Byers Lake Campground	15.2 mi (24.3 km)
Kesugi Ridge Trail (Hike 60)	Little Coal Creek Trailhead	Byers Lake Campground	27.4 mi (43.8 km)
Kesugi Ridge Trail (Hike 61)	Ermine Hill Trailhead	Little Coal Creek Trailhead	16.7 mi (27.5 km)
Troublesome Creek/ Kesugi Ridge Trail (Hikes 59 & 60 combined)	Troublesome Creek Trailhead	Little Coal Creek Trailhead	36.2 mi (58 km)

Source: Alaska Department of Natural Resources, Division of State Parks and Outdoor Recreation website www.dnr.state.ak.us/parks/.

Navigating

Along most of the route, a well-worn trail is clearly visible in the alpine tundra. However the path is not visible in some long rocky areas. Fortunately in rocky areas the route is marked by cairns about 75 feet (14 meters) apart. I was able to follow these cairns in fog so dense that I could not see the next cairn while standing at a cairn. I kept the known cairn in sight until I could spot the next cairn in the fog. *(photo 59A)*

If your map does not show the route, take the time to copy it from the maps on display at the trailhead. Also note the magnetic declination is about 27° east, significant enough to cause a navigation error. *For those using a GPS, set the datum to 1927 North American datum, frequently called NAD 27. Otherwise your GPS reading may be off up to 200 meters in the longitude reading.*

The waterproof *Trails Illustrated* map for Denali National Park also shows the Kesugi Ridge hiking routes. This is a good map for trip planning and identifying distant landmarks. For navigation I prefer the USGS maps referenced for each hike. You will need to draw the route on the USGS maps. The Alaska Natural History Association also publishes a contour map of Denali State Park with the hiking routes shown but no navigation information such as magnetic declination or location coordinates. See Appendices A and B for more details on these maps and where to obtain them.

Bring a compass. I camped about one mile from the trail and awoke the next morning to fog reducing visibility to 100 feet (30 meters). Since

I had located my camp on the map the day before, I used my compass to determine and walk the correct direction back to the trail.

Food storage in bear country

Park rangers and I encourage you to use bear proof containers to help prevent bears from becoming habituated to humans as a source of food. Bear proof food containers are available at the Byers Lake Visitor Center near the Veterans Memorial (mile 147.1 on the George Parks Highway). There is no cost to use the containers but a $25 refundable deposit is required. Usually the Visitor Center has containers, but in peak season the supply may be exhausted when you need one.

Approved bear proof food containers are sold at the Anchorage REI Store at (1200 West Northern Lights Blvd., phone 1-907- 272-4565) and other Anchorage and Fairbanks sporting goods stores. The REI price is about $70. This is a good investment in your and future hiker safety. If you are traveling and do not want to take the container home, consider donating it to the visitor center for others to use.

At camp, store your food and garbage at least 100 yards (100 meters) downwind from your tent. Also cook in a different spot that is 100 yards from your food storage location and downwind 100 yards from your tent. *There are no trees suitable for hanging food along the Kesugi Ridge.* Please pack out all garbage to keep bears from getting it and to keep the area clean for others. Thanks!

More park information

Check the Denali State Park website for more park information: www.dnr.state.ak.us/parks/. Select "Jewels of the ASP System" and then select "Mat-Su and Copper River Valleys."

During the summer, stop at the visitor contact station at the Alaska Veterans Memorial, at mile 147.1 on the George Parks Highway. For additional information, contact the Denali Ranger through the Mat-Su/CB Area Headquarters at: Alaska State Parks - Mat-Su/CB Area, HC 32, Box 6706, Wasilla, AK 99654-9719. Telephone: 1-907-745-3975, and fax 1-907-745-0938.

Photo 59A. **A cairn looms in the fog marking the Kesugi Ridge route—a welcome sight.**

Photo 59B. **Trail to the Troublesome Creek Valley on Hike 59. Note cairn on the boulder.**

Emergencies

The trail between Little Coal Creek and Byers Lake is used frequently in the summer. The ridge and upper forest portions of the trail between Byers Lake and Upper Troublesome Creek are used less frequently. Fishermen often use the south end of the Upper Troublesome Creek trail, particularly on weekends.

Cell phone reception along the ridge trail is not reliable. Since there are only 4 trails off the ridge, it may take several hours to reach the highway. When you get to the highway, try to get someone to stop. Most likely they will have a cell phone or be willing to take you to a phone. Most trucks on the road will also have a CB radio or cell phone.

In case of an emergency, contact the Alaska State Troopers at:

- Talkeetna Post, mile 12.5 Talkeetna Rd. Call 911 or (907) 733-2256
- Cantwell, mile 209.6 Parks Highway (907) 768-2202

Summer emergency telephone locations:

- Mt. McKinley Princess Lodge, mile 132.5 Parks Highway;
- Denali View North Campground Host, mile 162.7 Parks Highway;
- Alaska Veterans Memorial, Visitor Contact Station, mile 147.1 Parks Highway; and
- Byers Lake Campground Host, mile 147.0 Parks Highway.

59

Troublesome Creek to Byers Lake

Location: Mile 137.6
Bus time from Anchorage: 4 hours
Hike Length: 15.2 miles (24 km)
Hiking Time: 2 days
Elevation Gain: 2,200 feet (667 m)
Hiking Difficulty: Moderate
Route Finding Difficulty: Easy
USGS Map(s): Talkeetna (C-1)

Highlights

I enjoyed the two worlds of this hike. First is a 7-mile trail through a spruce and birch forest along clear, boulder-strewn Troublesome Creek. On a late June weekend, smiling fishermen waded the creek or were returning along the trail. Ferns and wildflowers sprinkled the forest floor. *(photo 59C)* My special treat was a mother spruce grouse and her chick in the trail. Merganser chicks cruised small rapids while their parents kept watch from a deep pool. I plan to return and photograph the granite boulders that push the creek around.

As the trail climbs above tree line, the world changes to the wide-open alpine tundra. Granite boulders still dot the landscape and occasionally become the platforms for cairns that mark the trail. *(photos 59A, 59B)* As I neared Tarn Peak, the high point of this hike, the granite boulders became soft shapes in the fog. I camped near Tarn Peak for an extra day hoping to get clear weather to photograph. All day the fog rolled in and out and floated like ghosts through draws and around stunted trees. The next day brought thicker fog reducing visibility to about 100 feet.

Since I camped about one mile off the trail, I needed my compass to determine the correct direction to regain the trail. On a clear day I plan to return to Tarn Peak.

Route description

Note: In 2009, the trail along Troublesome Creek remained closed due to flood damage. Contact the state park at 1-907-745-3975 to determine current conditions,

This route begins at the Upper Troublesome Creek trailhead. With a full pack I prefer to start at this trailhead because the trail at Byers Lake is very steep and not as well maintained. I also prefer leaving my vehicle at Byers Lake where there is more activity and monitoring. Byers Lake is about 10 miles (16 km) via the highway from the Troublesome Creek trailhead.

See the *Denali State Park Overview* for information on shuttle service from Byers Lake to trailheads.

The disadvantage of starting at the Troublesome Creek end is the long hike before reaching the better camping areas above tree line. With a full backpack I did not hike as fast as planned and had to camp on the lumpy, spongy forest floor. Tree roots across the trail and short eroded sections of the trail along the creek bank slowed my hiking. The moderate hiking difficulty rating is due to these conditions and to the steep, poorly maintained trail off the ridge at Byers Lake.

The forest trail is easy to follow. Once above tree line, the trail is visible in the alpine tundra and well marked with cairns in the few rocky areas. *(photos 59A, 59B)*

If you are hiking from Byers Lake, finding where the trail enters the Troublesome Creek Valley forest may require some searching to find the route through the fringe of alders. However, it did not look difficult to find the right spot to search. The trail through the alders is distinct when you are close so do not get fooled by faint trails.

Variation: A dayhike along Troublesome Creek is a delightful opportunity to experience a boreal forest of white spruce and birch while listening to the sounds of a creek. For a shorter but steeper hike to get above tree line, do an overnight or dayhike from Byers Lake.

Cautions

In the past, the trail along Troublesome Creek has been closed from mid-July to September due to bears using the drainage as a travel corridor. To determine trail closure status, contact the park at 1-907-745-3975. The most important way to avoid any incidents is to make noise as you travel along the creek and make sure bears never get any of your food or garbage. Please use bear proof food containers when you are camping in Denali State Park. Bearproof food containers are available at the Byers Lake Visitor Center. See the Denali State Park Overview chapter.

Photo 59C. **Delightful forest at the beginning of the Troublesome Creek Trail, Hike 59.**

Photo 60A. **The Ermine Hill Trail (Hike 61) joins with the Kesugi Ridge Trail (Hike 60) in this valley.**

60

Kesugi Ridge

Location: Mile 163.9 Parks Highway
Time on bus (one way): 4 hours
Hike Length: 27.4 miles (43.8 km)
Hiking Time: 4 days
Elevation Gain: 2,000 feet (630 m)
Hiking Difficulty: Moderate
Route Finding Difficulty: Easy to Difficult
USGS Maps: Talkeetna Mountains (C-6), (D-6); Talkeetna (C-1)

Highlights

I hiked this trail in the fog and again when I could see the foothills and top of Mount McKinley. *(photo 61A)* The potential view is motivating me to plan a photography trip when I am more certain to get a totally clear view of Mount McKinley.

In any condition, hiking along Kesugi Ridge is a treat. The trip begins with a forest stroll and then climbs up a well-maintained trail to reach alpine tundra. The trail continues along the ridgeline with occasional ravine and saddle crossing and one forested valley crossing involving a 1,000 feet (304 meters) elevation change. Along the way I enjoyed streams lined with wildflowers, unique granite boulder formations and views of the Chulitna and Susitna River valleys. The alpine tundra reminded me a little of the *Sound of Music* movie. Music I heard included streams flowing over granite rocks, American golden plovers calling, marmots whistling, and unseen coyotes yipping in the fog.

Route description

This route follows the Kesugi Ridge from Little Coal Creek to Byers Lake. With a full pack I prefer to start at the Little Coal Creek trailhead because the trail at Byers Lake is very steep and not as well maintained. I also prefer leaving my vehicle at Byers Lake where there is more activity and monitoring. Byers Lake is about 17 miles (27 km) via the highway from the Little Coal Creek trailhead. See the *Denali State Park Overview* for information on shuttle service from Byers Lake to other trailheads.

Before leaving the trailhead, study the route on the posted map. If your maps do not show the route, draw the route on your maps. After leaving the Little Coal Creek trailhead, there is a short walk through forest before the trail begins climbing. The trail is well designed and easy to negotiate. After about 2 hours, the trail reaches the first rocky ridgeline and the beginning of a series of rock cairns that mark the route above tree line. Along most of the route, it is easy to follow the well-worn footpath in the tundra. However, cairns are needed in areas where the route crosses rocky terrain. I was glad the cairns are about 75 feet (23 meters) apart in rocky areas. I encountered fog so dense that I could not see the next cairn until I was about 25 feet from the previous cairn. *(photo 59A)*

After crossing the headwaters of Little Coal Creek, the trail climbs to a saddle that is the highpoint (3,400 feet (1,033 km)) of this route. Good camping spots abound along the route to the Ermine Hill Trail junction at mile 13.5 (21.6 km). *(photo 60A)* Shortly after Ermine Hill junction, the trail crosses a forested valley where the trail is often bordered by waist high grass. I would not chose to camp in this valley. From Ermine Hill junction it is about 4 miles (6.4 km) to Skinny Lake where there are a few camping spots along the trail ridge above the lake. A designated camping area is being developed at Skinny Lake. Beyond (south of) Skinny Lake camping areas are plentiful. South of Skinny Lake is Golog Hill, the highest point (2,970 feet) (902 meters) on this part of the trail.

My last campsite was near Whimbrel Hill. From this camp I reached the junction with the Troublesome Creek trail in one hour. From there it took two hours of non-stop hiking to cover the remaining 3.5 miles (5.6 km) to the Byers Lake parking area. If it has been raining, allow more time to hike down because the steep, poorly maintained trail will be slick.

Variations: On a clear day try a dayhike from either trailhead to get above timberline and enjoy the view. Do a round trip backpack from either of the trailheads, set up camp and do some exploring without a pack.

Cautions

Some of this route crosses short fields of boulders that can be slick when wet. A slip on these boulders

Photo 60B. **Hiking along the Kesugi Ridge.**

while carrying a heavy pack could result in an injury.

Weather can change quickly on this ridge. Be prepared for strong wind and heavy rain. If the weather becomes severe, the Ermine Hill Trail (Hike 61) is the only place to easily get off the ridge in mid-hike. Route finding rapidly becomes difficult when fog or low clouds make it hard to see the cairns that mark the trail in the rocky areas of this route.

The valley between Ermine Hill Trail and Skinny Lake is forested and the trail goes through high grass. I saw fresh bear scat in this area so I made a lot of noise. When camping on Kesugi Ridge, please use a bearproof food container and always store it at least 100 yards (100 meters) from your camp. These containers are available free at the Byers Lake visitor information center. See the *Denali State Park Overview* section.

61

Ermine Hill to Little Coal Creek

Location: Mile 156.5
Time on bus (one way): 4 hours
Hike Length: 16.7 miles (26.7 km)
Hiking Time: 2 to 3 days
Elevation Gain: 1,400 feet (426 m)
Hiking Difficulty: Moderate
Route Finding Difficulty:
Easy to difficult
USGS Map:
Talkeetna Mountains (D-6)

Highlights

One of my favorite spots is the valley where the Ermine Hill trail joins the Kesugi Ridge trail. This valley has a small lake surrounded by granite hills. *(photo 60A)* The power of weathering is clearly visible on the crumbling surface of granite boulders at the east end of the valley and south along the Kesugi Ridge trail. Marble-sized pebbles cover the ground around these boulders.

A short climb north along the ridge trail leads to an overlook with a spectacular view of the Ermine Hill area and Chulitna River valley. On a clear day Mount McKinley is visible from this overlook. On a foggy day loons calling from the lake gave me goose bumps.

Route description

The Ermine Hill trailhead is a parking area along the edge of the George Parks Highway about 7.5 miles (11.8 km) south of the Little Coal Creek trailhead.

If you have only one vehicle, hide your packs at the Ermine Hill trailhead and then park at the Little Coal Creek trailhead. Then walk, bike or hitchhike back to the Ermine Hill trailhead. I rode my bicycle from the Little Coal Creek trailhead and then stashed it in the woods at the Ermine Hill trailhead.

While at the Little Coal Creek trailhead study the route on the posted map. If your maps do not show the route, draw the route on your maps.

The first mile (1.6 km) of the trail is forested. Next is a steep climb on a well-maintained switchback trail to get above tree line. The remaining hike to the Kesugi Ridge trail junction is a gradual climb on a good trail with great views. From the junction, follow the Kesugi Ridge trail north to the Little Coal Creek trailhead. See hike 60. Good campsites abound from the Ermine Hill trail junction north to Little Coal Creek.

Variations: From the Ermine Hill trail junction, hike south to Byers Lake. If you hike toward Byers Lake, then it is 4 miles (6.4 km) after the junction to some camping spots on the trail ridge adjacent to Skinny Lake. Camping spots are easier to find be-

Photo 61A. **Typical section of the trail along Kesugi Ridge. Note the twin summit peaks of Mount McKinley rising above the clouds. On a clear day, the views of the Alaska Range are outstanding.**

yond Skinny Lake. See Hike 60.

If you are hiking to Byers Lake, leave your vehicle at Byers Lake and get a ride, bike or walk the 9.5 miles (15.2 km) to the Ermine Hill trailhead.

Cautions

Some of this route crosses short fields of boulders that can be slick when wet. A slip on these boulders while carrying a heavy pack could result in an injury.

Weather can change quickly on this ridge. Be prepared for strong wind and heavy rain. Route finding rapidly becomes difficult when fog or low clouds make it hard to see the cairns that mark the trail in the rocky areas of this route.

Photo 61B. **Climbing out of a valley along the Kesugi Ridge trail.**

Appendices

Appendix A: Information and Reservations

1. Information for advance planning

Denali National Park and Preserve Headquarters
P. O. Box 9
Denali National Park, AK 99755
Phone: 907-683-2294
Internet: www.nps.gov/dena

Headquarters staff provide information about backcountry and road permits, travel conditions, and rules. It does not handle the campground and bus reservations. See next listing for reservation and permits.

Alaska Public Lands Information Center
605 West 4th Avenue
Anchorage, AK 99501
Internet: www.alaskacenters.gov

This is the place to obtain information on Denali and other parks while in Anchorage. Located in downtown Anchorage in the white fortress-style building between F and G Streets.

Alaska Geographic
810 E. 9th Ave.
Anchorage, AK 99501
Phone: (907) 274-8440
866-257-2757
Internet: www.alaskageographic.org
(Source of books and some Denali maps)

This organization operates a mail order service and has a bookstore located in the Denali National Park Visitor Center complex near the park entrance. Most of the in-print books listed in the Books and Maps Appendix can be obtained from them. The store usually has all the Denali national and state park-specific books and maps and many of the Alaska natural history books.

U. S. Geological Survey
4210 University Dr., Room 208
Anchorage, AK 99508
Phone: (907) 786-7011

(Source of USGS maps referenced in hike descriptions.)

The Anchorage office stocks all USGS maps of Alaska. Credit card orders by phone and mail are accepted. Shipping fee is $5.00 per order. Map prices in 2009 are: $8.00 for 1:63,360

(1 inch per mile) scale; and $9.00 for 1:250,000 (1 inch per 4 miles) scale. All hikes in this book are covered on the following 1:63,360 scale maps:

Denali National Park Maps
Healy B-6, C-4, C-5, C-6, D-5
Mt. McKinley B-1, B-2, C-1, C-2

Denali State Park Maps
Talkeetna Mountains C-6 & D-6
Talkeetna C-1

REI (Recreational Equipment Inc.)
1200 W. Northern Lights Blvd.
Anchorage, AK 99503
Phone: 1-907-272-4565
Website: www.REI.com

This store is a popular spot for people to obtain camping gear and food. The store also sells books and maps for exploring Alaska. They carry the *Trails Illustrated*™ Denali National Park map. The store also has a machine for printing custom USGS maps for Alaska on waterproof paper.

Title Wave Books
1360 W. Northern Lights Blvd. (near REI) *or* 415 W 5th Ave. (downtown)
Anchorage, AK 99503
Phone: (907) 278-9283
Website: www.wavebooks.com

I look here for used and out-of-print copies of books listed in Appendix B: Books and Maps.

2. Campground and park bus reservations

Doyon / ARAMARK
Joint Venture
241 West Ship Creek Ave.
Anchorage, AK 99501
Website: www.reservedenali.com
Phone: 1-907-272-7275
Toll Free U.S. only: 1-800-622-7275.

Reservations by internet, mail or fax are accepted beginning December 1, for the next summer. When using the Internet, be sure to select the Shuttle Bus and Campground Reservationî service. Phone reservation lines open in mid-February for the next summer. Callers from the United States can use the toll free number. Callers from Anchorage or a foreign country must call 907-272-7275. Hours of operation are 7 a.m.-5 p.m. Alaska Time. Reservations are handled by a private business so if these numbers do not work in the future, contact the Denali National Park Headquarters (1-907-683-2294) or at www.nps.gov/dena to obtain the current numbers.

3. Transportation to Denali National Park

Alaska Railroad Corporation
P. O. Box 107500
Anchorage, Alaska 99510-7500
Train station: 411 W. 1st Avenue.
Passenger Reservations in
Anchorage and international:
1-907-265-2620.
US toll free: 1-800-544-0552.
Website:www.akrr.com

The following companies offered bus service to Denali National Park during the 2009 season.

Alaska Park Connection
In US, 1-800-266-8625
Website: www.alaskacoach.com

Alaska/Yukon Trails
From US and Canada:
1-800-770-7275
Website: www.alaskashuttle.com

4. Rental cars at the park entrance

There is at least one company near the park entrance that will rent cars. If you are not a U.S. resident, contract them about insurance requirements.

Denali Dome Home
Bed and Breakfast and Car Rental
P.O. Box 262
Healy, AK 99743
Rental Car Phone: 1-907-683-5397
Toll Free: 1-800-683-1239
Email: keys@denalidomehome.com
Website: www.denalidomehome.com

5. Denali National Park entrance complex

There are two places you must visit at the park entrance area. The Visitor Center has exhibits and a large bookstore. The Wilderness Access Center is where you obtain reservations and permits for campgrounds, backcountry camping, and shuttle buses. It is also the primary place in the park to obtain information. It also has interpretative displays and programs, and the backcountry travel interactive video. Hours of operation usually are 7 a.m.-8 p.m. during the summer.

6. Park entrance area lodges, commercial campgrounds and showers

Showers area available at the Riley Creek Mercantile located adjacent to the Riley Creek Campground inside the park. Some commercial campgrounds near the park entrance also have showers for their campers.

There are many lodges at, or within 20 miles of, the park entrance area. Lodges are often full in the peak times so make a reservation. I use the listed lodges because of their quality, location or price. For other entrance area lodges check out the information sources listed under *Other Lodging* below.

Denali Cabins
Location:
8 miles south of national park entrance.
Toll Free from U.S.:
1-888-560-2489
International and Anchorage:
1-907-644-9980
Website: www.denalilodges.com
Shuttle Service to the park entrance available.

Denali Grizzly Bear Cabins and Campground
About 50 tent sites.
Location:
6 miles south of Park entrance
P.O. Box 303
Healy, Alaska 99743
Toll free from U.S.: 1-866-583-2696
Phone: 1-907-374-8796 (Oct. 1-May 15)
1-907-683-2696 (May 16-Sept. 30)

Website:
www.denaligrizzlybear.com

7. Wonder Lake area lodges

The following lodges are located in the Kantishna area beyond Wonder Lake. Each of these lodges provides round trip bus transportation through the park. Each offers rides to the Wonder Lake area and guided hikes near Wonder Lake and in the Kantishna area.

Denali Backcountry Lodge
1-888-560-2489
International and Anchorage:
1-907-644-9980
Website: www.denalilodges.com

Camp Denali and North Face Lodges
Post Office Box 67
Denali National Park, AK 99755
Phone: 1-907-683-2290
Website: www.campdenali.com

Kantishna Roadhouse
1 Doyon Place #300
Fairbanks, Alaska 99701
Phone: 1-800 942-7420
Email: roadhouse@doyon.com
Website: www.kantishnaroadhouse.com

8. Other lodging information

I often use these the publications to find the very latest information on lodging and campgrounds near the park.

Denali Summer Times: An annual newspaper published each season that contains articles on what to do and many advertisements for businesses in the vicinity of Denali National Park. It is widely distributed at places near the park entrance.

The MILEPOST. Published annually since 1949, this guide describes what to see mile-by-mile along every road in and to Alaska. It also contains advertisements for businesses located along the road including a specific section for the Denali National Park area.

Website: www.themilepost.com

9. How to contact me

While I travel often, I will do my best to respond to questions regarding Denali or other areas of Alaska.

Ike Waits
P. O. Box 100200
Anchorage, Alaska 99510-0200
U.S.A.
Phone: 1-907-274-0471
Cell: 602-616-2545
Email:
 ikewaits@denaliguidebook.com
Website: denaliguidebook.com

Appendix B:
Publications and Maps—an Annotated Bibliography

This appendix contains five sections. Books and maps that are primarily about Denali National Park are annotated in the first two sections. These are the books that I use to obtain information and inspiration for planning trips and to understand the Denali environment and history. The third section contains other Alaska books that also include useful information about Denali. Books covering techniques for hiking in bear country or that contain other information about bears are listed in the last section.

Contact the book and map sources noted in Appendix A concerning the publications listed in this chapter.

1. Denali maps

Denali National Park and Preserve, Alaska. Trails Illustrated™ Map is a two-sided, color topographic map published by National Geographic. One side is a map (scale: one inch=5 miles) of the entire Denali National Park and Preserve and some of Denali State Park including the area of the hikes in this book. The other side shows boundaries of Denali National Park backcountry permit areas (scale: one inch = about 3 miles) and also contains information on backcountry rules, access and bears. I use this map for initial hike ideas and carry it with me to show the big picture and location of backcountry permit boundaries. I do not use this map for navigation. Waterproof material, 1999, 37"x25" folded to 4"x 9". Available at the Anchorage REI sporting goods store and the bookstores noted in Appendix A.

Denali National Park Map and Photo. Published by U. S. Geological Survey, Department of Interior. One side of this map covers the park and adjacent areas (about 20,450 square miles) at a scale of 1:250,000 (about 1"= 4 miles) showing vegetation shading and contour intervals of 200' with supplements of 100'. The reverse side has a false color satellite image map of the same area. This double-sided map is printed on waterproof and tear resistant paper. 41"x43".

U. S. Geological Survey Quadrangle Maps. These are 1:63,360 scale (1 inch = 1 mile) topographic maps. Contour intervals are 100 feet. I use these maps for detailed route planning and navigating. Each map is referenced by a name followed by a number. See Information Sources for sources of these maps. All hikes in this book are covered on the following quadrangle maps:

Denali National Park maps
Healy B-6, C-4, C-5, C-6, D-5
Mt. McKinley B-1, B-2, C-1, C-2

Denali State Park maps
Talkeetna Mountains C-6 & D-6
Talkeetna C-1

Map of Mt. McKinley. Published by University of Alaska, Fairbanks. This is Bradford Washburns's classic

245

map of Mt. McKinley. It also covers Mounts Hunter, Huntington, Silverthrone, and Brooks as well as the Ruth Amphitheater and The Moose's Tooth. Washburn did the surveying for this map from 1947 through 1959. It is a historic map and work of cartographic art which is finally available again! Full color, polyconic projection, 100' contour interval, 1:50,000 scale, and 30"x32". Specify folded on unfolded version.

2. Denali books

Backcountry Companion for Denali National Park. By Jon Nierenberg. This book explains the backcountry permit system and shows the boundaries of the backcountry permit areas **but does not suggest specific hikes.** Information on each backcountry permit area includes: brief area location description, vegetation and terrain, wildlife, rivers and streams and difficulty of crossing, glaciers and mountaineering, and specific USGS maps for the area. There is also a sketch map of the permit area boundaries and usually a color photo from the area. General information also includes the rules, how to get to the permit areas, weather, equipment recommendations, river crossing techniques, bear safety, and answers to the most frequent questions asked of Backcountry Permit Rangers. 1989, 94 pages, 27 photos.

Denali Journal — A Thoughtful Look at Wildlife in Alaska's Majestic National Park. By Tom Walker. While the journal entries express some personal feelings, they are packed with natural history information, ideas

Photo Z. **Blueberries are present on many trails in the Denali area.**

about places to visit and other historic and contemporary information. This journal condenses 20 years of exploration by Walker who divides his time between Denali and Homer. Armed with a camera and notebook, this Alaskan naturalist observes Denali's wildlife and describes in vivid detail their daily lives. Stunning scenes such as a bear defending her cubs against hungry wolves are recounted with a keen eye and sober respect. Contemporary issues such as park development, bear-human conflict, and wolf control are considered in their historical perspective. 1992, 208 pages, B&W photos.

Denali National Park Entrance Area Trail Guide. By Sheri Forbes. Most maintained trails in Denali are all within three miles of the park entrance. This guide covers these trails, provides brief bear country safety tips, and includes checklists of the animals, birds and plants you can expect to encounter along these trails. 1998, 42 pages, maps, illustrations.

The Denali Road Guide — A Roadside Natural History of Denali National Park. By Kim Heacox. This book explains what to look for and the "whys" of what you see along the park road. The mileposts described are keyed to important points of interest. This book also tells where you will most likely see some of the park animals. Revised 1999, 52 pages with color photos.

Denali Wildlife and Wilderness Calendar. Published by Greatland Graphics, Anchorage, AK (907-337-1234 or www.alaskacalendars.com). Features outstanding photos of Denali wildlife and landscapes by some of Alaska's top photographers. Bonus: Denali Nature Notes in each month tell what the park animals and plants are doing; also includes significant dates in park history. Hanging size: 13.5x20 in.

The Geology of Denali National Park. By Michael Collier. This first-person account of Denali geology is based on Collier's research and his wanderings in the park to see, feel, marvel and understand the geology that he read about in the writings of pioneer and modern geologist. He explains how the rocks were formed and subsequent tectonic movement, faulting, folding, glaciations and erosion that produced the park you see today. History and stories of the exploration and gold rushes in the area are included. Color pictures will help you match his descriptions with places in the park. Maps show how the geology of Denali fits with the geology of Alaska. 1989, 48 pages, 8x8, color photos.

A Geologic Guide to Mount McKinley National Park. By Wyatt G. Gilbert. I like this book because it contains both a description of the geology of the park and presents 10 annotated hikes to explore the geology. Each hike contains directions and notes on the geologic features along the route. There is also a colorful geologic map of the park road corridor. While this book is out of print, I occasionally see copies at the Title Wave Bookstore listed under information sources. 1979, 52 pages, illustrations, map and B&W photos.

High Alaska — A Historical Guide to Denali, Mt. Foraker and Mt. Hunter. By Jonathan Waterman. This book is destined to join the work of Bradford Washburn as a classic source of information for climbing Mt. McKinley (Denali) and nearby Alaska Range peaks. Significant routes (including unclimbed ones) are described and previously unpublished climber anecdotes are included. Guides to 42 routes and information for planning an expedition are given. It is well illustrated with 74 Bradford Washburn photographs, maps, and other unpublished color and black and white photographs. 1989, 400 pages, 7x10, maps, photos (32 color).

Field Guide to Mammals of Denali. By Adolph Murie. The author spent 25 summers studying Denali wildlife. This book is the latest edition of Murie's original publication *Mammals of Mount McKinley National Park, Alaska* with slight changes. It contains a separate chapter and black and white photographs for each of the 27 mammals found in the park.

Photo AA. **Caribou**

Each chapter has a narrative account of Murie's observations and conclusions about the animal's life in Denali. This book is light and easily fits in your pack or travel bag. 80 pages.

Mount McKinley — The History of North America's Highest Mountain. By Fred Beckey. This biography of Mt. McKinley begins with geology and covers early human history, early efforts to conquer the summit, and most notable summit attempts including those of the author. Also covers the challenges, logistics, planning, permits and suggested routes. Personal anecdotes and previously unpublished photographs make this volume unique. 1993, 320 pages, color and black and white photos.

Wildflowers of Denali National Park. By Verna E. Pratt & Frank G. Pratt. "Wow!" I said when I saw this book. With color coding, 410 color photos and a superbly-easy to understand glossary of illustrated plant characteristics, it is easy even for a layman to identify every flower. In addition, the book suggests several locations to visit and has a checklist of flowers you will find there. Other common shrubs, trees and mushrooms are covered. Yes, there are even shots of bears, caribou, and the smaller critters who enjoy Denali plants. Guaranteed to make you want to pack a lunch and enjoy the flowers. 1993, 170 pages, 6x9 in., maps, illustrations, and color photos.

The Wolves of Mount McKinley. By Adolph Murie. Between 1939 and 1941, Adolph Murie made a field study of the relationship between wolves and Dall sheep in Denali National Park (Formerly Mount McKinley National Park). His findings, first published in 1944, are reprinted in this book. It includes some wonderful sketches of wolves.

Murie described the life cycle of Alaskan wolves in greater detail than had ever been done. He also discovered a great deal about the entire ecological network of predator and prey. Wolf behavior, food, home life, and pack life are revealed. Four chapters reveal the relationships between wolves and Dall sheep, caribou, moose, grizzly bears, and foxes. As a bonus many relationships of these animals among each other are also described. 1944, 238 pages, black and white photos, 6x9 in.

3. Publications containing some information relevant to Denali

Alaska Weather Calendar. Published by Williwaw Publishing Co. Haines, Alaska (1-800-490-4950 or www.williwaw.com). In addition to spectacular pictures related to weather, there are graphs and charts for each month showing sunrise and sunset, temperatures and precipitation by region, and related weather statistics to help plan your trip. Hanging size is 13x21 in.

Alaska Wildlife Viewing Guide. By Michelle Sydeman and Annabel Lund. Provides a description, access information, and a contact number for 68 state and federal parks or refuges noted for their wildlife viewing opportunities. 1996, 96 pages, color photos.

Alaskan Wildflowers Commonly Seen Along Highways and Byways. By Verna E. Pratt. Verna's experience giving local classes and wildflower hikes shows. Flowers arranged by color and a chapter describing and illustrating plant family characteristics and flower parts to help difficult identifications help amateurs. Includes a blooming time chart, where to find flowers along Alaska roads, information on edible plants and color photos of 209 plants and information on 132 more. 1990, 136 pages, 6x9 in., color photos, illustrations.

Animal Tracks of Alaska. By Chris Stall. This pocket-size guide covers the tracks of more than 40 of the most common animals and some birds found in Alaska. Check the track size with the ruler on the edge the back cover and compare them to life-size tracks in the book. (Grizzly and moose tracks are shown half life-size). Text covers size, sounds, habitat, diet and key features and habits. 1993, 112 pages, 4x6 in., illustrations.

Gathering Paradise: Alaska Wilderness Journeys. By Larry Rice. He shares the joy of traversing ten of Alaskas most remote wilderness areas by kayak, rubber raft, on foot or by plane. Contains vivid accounts of encounters with bears, whitewater, stormy Bering Sea, splendid views and most of Alaskas wildlife. Based on Rice's summer explorations as a wildlife biologist since 1970 including hikes in Arctic National Wildlife Refuge, and Denali National Park plus dayhikes on other paddling trips in Glacier Bay and Katmai national parks, Killik River in Gates of the Arctic, Togiak National Wildlife Refuge, Becharof Lake, Misty Fjords National Monument, Aniakchak National Monument, and Unimak Island. 1990, 303 pages, photos, sketch maps.

Guide to Birds of Alaska. By Robert H. Armstrong. Information on identification, status, distribution and habitat is detailed for 437 species. Birds shown in color photographs. Also includes a list of accidental sightings of 50 species not common to Alaska and where they were seen. An Alaska bird checklist is provided for your records. 1995 edition, 322 pages, 6x9 in., color photos.

Moose. By Michio Noshino. Moose look ungainly and some say ugly. Yet a moose can speed through water, snow and tundra tussocks leaving pursuers behind. Photographs in this book capture this fleetness, the beauty and even delicateness of a moose, a remarkable achievement. Text gives insights into the life cycle of the moose as well as into the special place the animal holds in the traditional culture of Alaska's Athapaskan Indians. There is at least one breathtaking color picture on every page and many photographs are full page or two-page spreads. 1988, 91 pages, 8.5x11 in., color photos. *Out of print* but try Title Wave Books listed under information sources.

Mountain Bike Alaska 49 Trails in the 49th State. By Richard Larson. Describes 49 trails suitable for adventures ranging from family outings to expert rides. A summary table for each ride provides basic information including trailhead location, distance from Anchorage, trail length, riding time, difficulty, low and high points, elevation gain, and USGS maps needed. The author is an experienced mountain bike trip leader and has helped organized many of the mountain bike races and festivals in Alaska. Area covered includes Anchorage, Denali National Park and adjacent area, Wrangell-Saint Elias National Park, Kenai Peninsula, Matanuska Valley, and many trailheads along the road system connecting these areas. 1991, 121 pages, 6x9 in., maps.

On Location with Art Wolfe Outdoor Adventure Photography Travel side-by-side with world-renowned nature photographer Art Wolfe as he photographs Alaskas magnificent wildlife and landscapes. Learn from his expert instruction as he explains techniques that have made him one of the worlds best nature photographers. Through the miracle of video, you stalk Alaska wildlife and grandeur at Art's side as he explains what he is doing and how he is planning the shot then you see the results. Topics range from selecting the appropriate lens to framing intimate wildlife portraits to handling low-light macro photography. The video photographer also did a great job capturing the scenery, wildlife and adventure of the Wolfe's hikes and stalks. AREA: Denali, Katmai and other favorite nature photography areas.VHS, color, 50 min.

Roadside Geology of Alaska. By Cathy Connor and Daniel O'Haire. If there is a road (or a ferry), this book covers the geology along the route; even for dead-end roads out of Nome or Southeast towns. It is written for the road traveler who is also interested in some geologic time travel. Maps, photos and road logs guide the way. You will learn why there is gold on the Nome beaches, about the old and active volcanoes, what happened during the Good Friday Earthquake (1964) and about the faults that have created the mountains and valleys along your route. Area covered includes all roads and

Photo BB. **Caribou antlers**

ferry routes including Denali Park plus Katmai National Park. 1988, 250 pages, 6x9, photos.

Wager with the Wind: The Don Sheldon Story. By James Greiner. Sheldon is a bush pilot legend most famous for pioneering glacier landings on Mt. McKinley. However he was even more to those who lived, worked or played in remote Alaska. Those people depended on him for transportation, supplies and rescues. He operated from Talkeetna, Alaska, which is now the base of operation for several air charter companies flying climbers to the Kahiltna Glacier to begin Mt. McKinley climbs.

While accounts of pioneer high altitude glacier landings are exciting, to me the most exciting story is about Sheldon floating Susitna River Canyon rapids backward in a floatplane in order to rescue stranded rafters. There are many accounts of Mt. McKinley triumphs and tragedies which Don witnessed including his efforts to find the Wilcox party that lost seven climbers in a 1967 storm. 1982 ed., 258 pages, black and white photos.

4. Bears: natural history and hiking with them

Books listed in this section cover hiking with bears and provide natural history and photography information.

Backcountry Bear Basics: The Definitive Guide to Avoiding Unpleasant Encounters. By David Smith. The author debunks popular myths such as menstruation being a cause of bear attacks and bear bells being an effective way to ward off bears. He presents consequences and alternatives to the often-harmful ways backcountry visitors protect themselves from bears. All aspects of backcountry travel are covered including tips on cooking, food storage, and campsites. Accurate information on bear behavior and biology are provided to help you understand, rather than fear, the bears. 1997, 112 pages, illustrations and photos.

Bear Attacks: Their Causes and Avoidance. By Stephen Herrero. You will learn how to avoid encounters, how common they are, what many others have done during encounters and conclusions the author has drawn from studying both injury and non-injury producing bear encounters. You can best avoid encounters if you learn how bears act, what they eat, bear signs and proper hiking and camping techniques covered in this book.

Human behavior in and management of wilderness will determine the frequency of bear encounters and ultimately the fate of bears. Of particular importance is how we protect our food and dispose of garbage in the wilderness. Once a bear associates humans with easy food, then chances of encounters increase. Please, leave no treats for the bears; it could result in injury for the next hiker and ultimately death for the bear. 1985, 287 pages, 6x9, illustrations and photos.

Grizzly Country. By Andy Russell. Russell gave up outfitting hunters to photograph and study wildlife, particularly bears. His greatest adventures occur in the presence of grizzlies when he is carrying nothing more lethal than a camera. From Russell, you will learn the attitude and philosophy to make your travels in grizzly country safer and enjoyable.

I first read this book in 1967 during a summer of hiking in Denali National Park. I was looking for some reassurance about hiking alone and unarmed in grizzly country. Russell's respect and affection for the grizzly and his experiences in grizzly country became the foundation for my comfort with and approach to hiking in the grizzly's backyard.

Russell said he wrote this book because; *"It is high time some popular beliefs are revealed for what the are —untruths—before it is too late (for the grizzly)."* The grizzly's habitat and range, habits, antics, food, life cycle, temperament and personality are covered. *"One of the best first-hand studies of the big bears ever written."— The New York Times.* Areas covered include Alaska, Canada and Lower 48 states where grizzlies are found. 1967, 220 pages, 5.5x8 in., black and white photos.

Grizzly. By Michio Hoshino. Spend a year with grizzlies in Alaska through the spectacular, award-winning photography in this book. Includes scenic views and even the northern lights. But the grizzly photographs and author's brief narratives about his experiences obtaining them are the real pleasure in this book. If you have tried to get some good bear pictures you will appreciate the long and often cold or wet hours it took to get these photos and marvel at the quality and composition Hoshino achieves under these conditions.

This book won the 1986 Anima Award, the prize given to the most distinguished wildlife photography. Covers Denali and Katmai national parks and other Alaska locations. 1986, 88 pages, Color photos with limited text. 8.5x11 in.

The Grizzlies of Mount McKinley. By Adolph Murie. Contains descriptions of the daily routines and behavior of Denali National Park grizzlies based on observations Murie made over the 25 summers he spent in the park. A classic nature study written so everyone can enjoy and share his observations. He describes how families were formed, how they find food, and where they sleep at night. Relationships are revealed between the grizzlies and sheep, moose, caribou, rodents, wolves, foxes, wolverines, birds, and insects. The last two chapters are devoted to relationships with man and keeping the grizzlies wild. 1981 edition, 251 pages, 6x9 in., photos.

Appendix C

Denali National Park Backpack Summary Table

Backpack Number/Name	Road (MP)	Hike (mi)	Hike (km)	Hike (days)	Climb (feet)	Diff. (hike)	Diff. (route)	Permit area	Day hike*
8 Sanctuary to Savage	23	15	24	3	1,100	M	E	4,5	Yes
13 Teklanika to Sanctuary	38	35	56	5	2,300	D	D	5,6	Yes
14 Calico Creek	38	9	14	3	-500	D	M	6	Yes
18 Polychrome Basin	43	12	19	3	1,000	M	E	8	Yes
26 Toklat East Branch	51	20	32	3	800	E	E	9	Yes
27 Toklat to Polychrome	51	10	16	2	1,500	D	M	8,9	Yes
29 Toklat to Stony	53	15	24	3	700	M	M	32,33 & 39	Yes
31 Toklat to Eielson	53	20	32	3	2,400	D	D	10,12	Yes
47 Around Mt. Eielson	66	14	22	2	1,600	D	M	12,13	Yes
49 Anderson Pass	66	26	42	3	2,300	D	M	13,18	Yes
52 Moose Creek	74	13	21	3	300	D	M	35,41 & 42	Yes
57 McGonagall Pass	86	38	61	5	3,800	D	M	20	No

See page 41 for complete definitions for hiking times, hiking difficulty (Diff. hike), and route-finding difficulty (Diff.route). Key: E=Easy, M=Moderate, D=Difficult

*The beginning or end of these trips could be shortened to a dayhike.
** The route or destination is suitable for extending to backpack trip.

Photo CC. **Cathedral Mountain viewed from Hike 16.**

Denali National Park Dayhike Summary Table

Dayhike Number/Name	Road (MP)	Hike (mi)	Hike (km)	Hike (hrs)	Climb (feet)	Diff. (hike)	Diff. (route)	Back-pack**
1 Horseshoe Lake	1.2	1.5	2.4	2.0	200	E	E	No
2 Mount Healy Overlook	1.5	4.0	6.4	4.0	1,700	M	E	No
3 Triple Lakes	1.5	5.0	8.0	4.0	600	E	E	Yes
4 Savage Riv. Viewpoint	12.8	7.0	11.2	8.0	1,600	M	M	Yes
5 Savage Drainage Stroll	14.8	3.0	4.8	3.0	100	E	E	No
6 Savage River Canyon	14.8	2.0	3.2	1.5	50	E	E	Yes
7 Primrose Ridge	16.5	7.0	11.2	6.5	1,900	E	E	Yes
9 Teklanika Campgound	29.0	.5-4	.8-6.4	1-4	100	E	E	No
10 Teklanika Foothills	30.3	4.0	6.4	4.5	1,200	M	M	Yes
11 Igloo Mt. East	34.0	3.0	4.8	4.0	1,700	E	M	Yes
12 Igloo Mt. West	36.0	3.0	4,8	5.0	1,500	M	M	Yes
15 Cathedral Mountain	38.0	3.0	4,8	3-5	1,200	M	M	Yes
16 Sable Pass Ridge	38.0	7.0	11.2	5-7	1,300	E	E	Yes
17 Tattler Creek/Sable Mt.	38.0	5.0	8.0	6-8	2,500	M	E	Yes
19 Polychrome #1	46.0	2.5	4.0	2.5	500	E	E	Yes
20 Polychrome #2	46.0	4.5	7.2	5.0	600	M	M	Yes
21 Polychrome Bluffs	47.5	4.0	6.4	3-4	200	M	E	No

Photo DD. **Headwaters of the eastern branch of the Toklat River (Hike 26)**

Dayhike Number/Name	Road (MP)	Hike (mi)	Hike (km)	Hike (hrs)	Climb (feet)	Diff. (hike)	Diff. (route)	Back-pack**
22 Polychrome Picnic	47.5	2.0	3.2	2.0	200	E	E	No
23 Polychrome East #1	47.5	4.0	6.4	4.0	1,500	M	M	Yes
24 Polychrome East #2	47.5	4.5	7.2	5.0	1,500	M	E	Yes
25 Geode Mountain	47.5	6.5	10.4	7.0	1,700	E	M	Yes
28 Around Divide Mtn.	53.0	7.5	12	8.0	1,000	M	E	Yes
30 Toklat Walk & Picnic	53.0	2.5	4.0	3.0	0	E	E	Yes
32 Highway Pass Perch	57.0	2.5	4	2.5	700	E	E	No
33 Hill 5860 Traverse	59.0	5.0	8.0	6.0	2,000	M	M	Yes
34 Highway Pass and Stony Walks	58-62	.5-4	.8-6.4	1-4	varies	E	E	No
35 Hill 5014 Climb	60.0	5-6	8-10	5-6	1,400	M	M	Yes
36 Stony Hill Ridge Walk	62.0	2.5	4.0	3.0	600	M	E	No
37 Stony Hill Circumnav.	63.0	3.0	4.8	3.0	300	E	E	Yes
38 Stony Dome	63.0	4.0	6.4	4.0	1,000	E	E	No
39 Thorofare Pass Stroll	64.0	3.0	4.8	3.0	400	E	E	No
40 Gravel Mountain	64.0	5.0	8.0	6.0	2,000	M	E	No
41 N. Gorge Creek Valley	64.0	4.0	6.4	4.5	700	E	E	Yes
42 Hill 4851	64.0	5.0	8.0	5.5	1,000	M	E	Yes
43 Thorofare Bench Walk	66.0	2.0	3.2	2.0	500	E	E	No
44 Eielson Area Walks	66.0	.5-3	.8-5	.5-4	varies	E	E	No
45 Thoro Ridge #1	66.0	4.5	7.2	5.0	1,100	M	M	No
46 Thoro Ridge #2	67.7	5.0	8.0	5.0	800	M	E	No
48 Grassy Pass-Eielson	66.0	5.0	8.0	5.0	700	M	M	Yes
50 Around Mount Thero	68.5	6	9.6	7.0	1,100	M	M	Yes
51 Mount Galen	68.5	6.6	10.6	6.5	1,800	M	E	Yes
53 Xerxes Ridge	86.0	6.5	10.4	6.5	800	E	E	Yes
54 McKinley Bar Trail	86.0	7.0	11.0	6.0	50	E	E	Yes
55 Wonder Lake Ridge	86.0	3.0	4.8	4.0	600	E	M	Yes
56 Tundra Ponds	86.0	4.0	6.4	4.0	50	E	E	Yes
58 Bound Point	88.0	3.5	5.6	4.0	800	M	E	Yes

See page 41 for complete definitions for hiking times, hiking difficulty (Diff. hike), and route-finding difficulty (Diff.route).

Key: E=Easy, M=Moderate, D=Difficult

Bibliography

Brooks, Alfred H. *The Mount Mckinley Region, Alaska.* Washington: United States Government Printing Office, 1914.

Browne, Belmore. *The Conquest of Mount McKinley.* Boston: Houghton Mifflin, 1956.

Cole, Terrence. *The Sourdough Expedition.* Anchorage: Alaska Northwest Publishing Co., 1985.

Cook, Frederick A. *The Top of the Continent.* New York: Doubleday, Page, and Company, 1908.

Dunn, Robert. *The Shameless Diary of an Explorer.* New York: The Outing Publishing Company, 1907.

Gilbert, Wyatt G. *A Geologic Guide to Mount McKinley National Park.* Anchorage: The Alaska Natural History Association, 1975.

Moore, Terris. *Mount McKinley: The Pioneer Climbs.* Fairbanks: The University of Alaska Press, 1967.

Murie, Adolph. *The Wolves of Denali.* Washington: United States Government Printing Office, 1944.

Pearson, Grant. *My Life of High Adventure.* Englewood Cliffs, New Jersey, 1962.

Sheldon, Charles. *The Wilderness of Denali.* New York: Charles Scribner's Sons, 1930.

Stuck, Hudson. *The Ascent of Denali.* New York: Charles Scribner's Sons, 1930.

United States Adjutant General's Office. *Explorations in Alaska, 1899.* Washington: United States Government Printing Office, 1909.

United States Geological Survey. *Explorations in Alaska, 1898.* Washington: United States Government Printing Office, 1900.

West, Frederick Hadleigh, *The Archeology of Beringia.* New York: Cloumbia University Press, 1981.

Wickersham, James. *Old Yukon: Tales,Trails, and Trials.* Washington: Washington Law Book Company, 1938.

Photo EE. **Mount McKinley from Stony Pass overlook (Hike 36).**